MEN AND FEMINISM IN MODERN LITERATURE

MEN AND FEMINISM IN MODERN LITERATURE

Declan Kiberd

St. Martin's Press   New York

ISBN 0-312-52878-7

Library of Congress Cataloging in Publication Data
Kiberd, Declan.
    Men and feminism in modern literature.
    Bibliography: p.
    Includes index.
    1. Women in literature.   2. Sex role in literature.
3. Men in literature.   4. Feminism in literature.
5. Literature, Modern—20th century—History and
criticism.   6. Literature, Modern—19th century—History and
criticism. I. Title.
PN56.5.W64K48 1985   809'.93353   84-17935
ISBN 0-312-52878-7

To Beth

Contents

Preface   ix

Acknowledgements   xii

1 NEW WOMAN, NEW MAN   1

2 STRINDBERG'S VILLAINS: THE NEW WOMAN   34
   AS PREDATOR

3 IBSEN'S HEROINES: THE NEW WOMAN AS   61
   REBEL

4 HARDY'S SUE: THE NEW WOMAN AS NEUROTIC   85

5 W. B. YEATS: ROBARTES' QUARREL WITH THE   103
   DANCER

6 D. H. LAWRENCE: THE NEW MAN AS PROPHET   136

7 JOYCE'S *ULYSSES*: PAST EVE AND ADAM   168

8 THE MALE RESPONSE TO FEMINISM   204

CONCLUSION   229

Notes and References   230

Index   244

Preface

In all the contemporary literature of women's liberation, it is rare to come upon a volume written by a man, much less a book which sets out to explore the male response to feminism. *The Prisoner of Sex* by Norman Mailer is the one work of this kind to have reached a mass audience, and even it was advertised as an explosive personal reaction rather than a considered intellectual response to the contemporary feminists. More than a decade after its first publication, *The Prisoner of Sex* still impresses as an eloquent cry of protest, but a protest against the inevitable. The New Woman was here to stay, whether Mailer liked it or not, but he was so enraged by her overweening demands that he never confronted the most interesting issue of all – what kind of man will emerge as an answer to the challenge which she poses? That is the question which underlies every chapter in this book. In my own search for answers, I found myself returning to the first wave of feminism between the 1890s and the 1920s, and to the more copious male responses of that time in the writings of Havelock Ellis, Edward Carpenter and others. However, it was in the creative masterpieces written by the leading male artists of that era that I found most of the answers which I was seeking.

Hence the final shape of this book, which looks at the various ways in which writers have described the relationship between a masterful woman and a passive man. The opening chapter is an assessment of pre-modern versions of this relationship, and a summary of contemporary evaluations of its possibilities and limits. This culminates in an outline of the problem bequeathed to the modernist generation – how to create a woman who might be both imperious and admirable, and a man who could be at once passive and exemplary. The boyish girls of Shakespeare's comedies were unfailingly charming, but his womanly males were all either public failures or moral weaklings. By the late nineteenth century, the passive male was a characteristic hero of Arnold and Tennyson, but the manly woman had become a dark destroyer, as documented with such bitter lucidity by Mario Praz in *The Romantic Agony*. The problem facing the next generation was how to reconcile the two types in a relationship of concord and challenge which might point the way to a future sexuality.

This is the task faced by all six authors treated in this study. Chapters 2, 3 and 4 deal with the New Woman in her developing role as predator, rebel and neurotic; while Chapters 5, 6 and 7 present in somewhat greater detail the emergence of the New Man who may well be the answer to which she provided the question. In the process, many secondary themes are tackled, such as the pleasures and perils of androgyny, the problem of narcissism, the danger of cultivating an excessive sense of sexual difference, the vice of specialisation in personal and professional life, and the place of the radical will in the modern world. An attempt is made to relate the literary presentation of these issues to wider cultural developments in the areas of clothing, fashion, advertising, modern psychology and conventional sexual behaviour. The final chapter demonstrates how, after the 1920s, the ideas adumbrated by these modern writers slowly passed into the popular culture, until they were reformulated on a more rigorous basis by the leading feminist theorists of the past twenty years. Not all of the problems posed for these six authors were satisfactorily solved by them, and many major issues are still not finally settled. This closing chapter also offers a personal view of what these questions are, and some tentative suggestions as to where the solutions may lie.

I am greatly indebted to Beth Kiberd, who offered fresh ideas and timely warnings as the work moved forward or ground to a temporary halt. It was she who introduced me to June Singer's magnificent *Androgyny: Towards a New Theory of Sexuality*, a book on which I have drawn most freely and gratefully in virtually every chapter. Also of immense assistance were Elémire Zolla's *The Androgyne: Fusion of the Sexes*, Christopher Lasch's *The Culture of Narcissism*, Germaine Greer's *The Female Eunuch* and Kate Millett's *Sexual Politics*. I have indicated in the text those points for which I am indebted to Carolyn Heilbrun's *Toward Androgyny*, but I have not itemised the occasions on which I am in disagreement with her lively and provocative interpretations of Shakespeare, Defoe, Hawthorne, Lawrence and others. All who explore the question of androgyny in literature must acknowledge the value of this pioneering book, which covered almost 100

Preface

authors, some few of whom are treated in greater detail in my study. Ms Heilbrun concentrated on the self-confident New Woman as Hero, whereas my real interest is in the self-doubting new Man, whose very passivity makes his heroism so problematic.

My other intellectual debts are fully documented in extensive footnotes at the end of this volume. On a more personal level I want to thank Marguerite Kiberd for her incisive but sympathetic criticisms of the book, as it went through its seemingly endless redrafting. For help with details in specific chapters I must also thank Terry Dolan, Johnnie Gratton, Nicholas Grene, Toni O'Brien Johnson and Liam MacGloinn. Dr Paul McCarthy and Dr Ann Moriarty gave lucid answers to my naive and ill-formulated questions on matters of psychiatry and psychology, as well as lending me useful papers and books. Finally, a word of gratitude is due to the Yeats Society in Sligo for inviting me to talk at successive summer schools on the depiction of modern sexuality in the plays of Wilde, the poetry of Yeats and the prose of Joyce.

On the term 'androgyny', Ms Heilbrun's definition cannot be bettered. Pointing to its Greek origin – from *andro* (male) and *gyn* (female) – she defines it as 'a condition under which the characteristics of the sexes, and the human impulses expressed by men and women, are not rigidly assigned'. By the term 'androgynous relationship', as used in this book, I mean one in which men express a female dimension as well as their time-honoured manliness, and in which women find a natural outlet for their male elements as well as their femininity. Such a relationship, in its ideal form, would be a fusion not only of man and woman, but of the man-in-the-woman with the woman-in-the-man.

DECLAN KIBERD

Acknowledgements

The author and publishers are grateful to Bantam Books Inc, New York, and to Arvid Paulson, for permission to quote from *The Father, Comrades* and *The Bond* by August Strindberg, © 1960 by Bantam Books Inc and *Miss Julie* by August Strindberg, © 1960 by Arvid Paulson, all extracts taken from *Seven Plays of August Strindberg*, edited by Arvid Paulson, all rights reserved; to New American Library Inc, New York, and to Rolf Fjelde, for permission to quote from *A Doll's House* and *The Master Builder* by Henrik Ibsen, translations by Rolf Fjelde, © 1965 from *Ibsen: Four Major Plays*, with all rights reserved; to the Macmillan Publishing Company Inc, and to Michael and Anne Yeats, for permission to quote from *Collected Poems* © 1950 and *Collected Plays* © 1952; to Viking Penguin Inc, New York, and the estate of Mrs Frieda Lawrence Ravagli, for permission to quote from *Women in Love* by D. H. Lawrence, renewed 1948, 1950 by Frieda Lawrence; to Random House Inc and Alfred A. Knopf Inc, New York, and to the estate of James Joyce, for permission to quote from *Ulysses* by James Joyce, © 1936, 1937; and to Faber and Faber Publishers, and to Thom Gunn, for permission to reprint 'Carnal Knowledge' from *Fighting Terms*, © Thom Gunn 1962, all rights reserved.

I   New Woman, New Man

> The main difference between men and women is that men are
> lunatics and women are idiots.   Rebecca West

In the subsistence economy to which our ancestors were
condemned, there can have been little time to develop specialised
notions of 'masculine' and 'feminine'. In the ancient mythologies
of the world it was widely believed that, before the fall into
division, the sexes had been one in the creator, who was a perfect
androgyne. 'Male and female created he them *in his own image.*'
The more widespread account of how Eve was merely *built* from
a rib of Adam is simply a later fabrication to explain why women
are now deemed to be inferior; but when *Genesis* was first
formulated, there was no reason to seek doctrinal evidence of
female subservience.[1] It was only after the fall into difference that
man and woman lost this inner harmony and lapsed into conflict.
Their subsequent lovemaking is an attempt to restore a truce, in
which both partners might recover that lost unity; but, as Yeats's
hero Cuchulain observes, the attempt is usually doomed:

> I never have known love but as a kiss
> In the mid-battle, and a difficult truce
> Of oil and water, candles and dark night,
> Hillside and hollow, the hot-footed sun
> And the cold, sliding, slippery-footed moon –
> A brief forgiveness between opposites
> That have been hatreds for three times the age
> Of this long-'stablished ground.[2]

And yet the search goes on. The women's movement is merely
the latest attempt to fulfil the objectives of orgasm, by which a
man and woman could cease to be known as such and instead
become full persons. 'We two, being one, are it', wrote Donne more

1

in hope than in ecstasy in *The Canonisation*, thereby underlining the ultimately religious implications of all attempts to transcend sexuality. She who came to Donne's bed a woman hoped to leave it a person – precisely the aspiration which animates the millions in the women's movement of today. Yet all too often, sexual ecstasy has been achieved only by the total annihilation of the self, or else personal fulfilment has entailed a massive frustration of the sexual instincts. Nevertheless, the dream of absolute fusion in androgynous being never quite died, but went underground, erupting from time to time in the religions and cults of the world.

Wendy Doninger O'Flaherty has shown how those mythologies which see God as an androgyne depict man as a splintered and debased parody of the godhead.[3] This notion of an androgynous creator may well be explained by Melanie Klein's belief that the child in early infancy cannot distinguish between opposites – self and other, good and evil, male and female – and thus evolves the image of a parental androgyne, a combined parent.[4] Classic Freudian theory holds that the individual grows to maturity by choosing one role or the other, beginning as male–female, but embracing one element and splitting away from its opposite. On the other hand, Jungian analysts assert that a person begins life as male or female, but achieves maturity only by locating and merging with one's opposite. So, the man seeks to come to terms with the 'anima' latent within him and the female lover without, just as the woman seeks out her 'animus' and her lover as well. O'Flaherty reports that return to the androgynous state is celebrated as the ultimate fusion of lovers in the Tantric rituals of the East,[5] but it has a counterpart in certain mystical traditions of the West, which hold that Adam will retain his pristine androgyny on the last day, and with it the perfection of Eden.[6]

The classical Greeks had a schematic explanation of human sexuality in all its forms, an explanation which is a summation of the prevailing archetypes. Aristophanes taught that in the earliest phase of creation there were three sexes, male–male, male–female and female–female; but they fell out with the gods and were each split down the middle, so that now each broken half walks the earth seeking its other. This myth not only explained the incidence of homosexuality and lesbianism, but also the anxiety of men and women to regain their lost integrity in the ecstasy of love. Jacob Boehme taught that by joining with woman man seeks to recover not only his androgyny but also his immortality, to make his human form divine.[7] A. J. L. Busst has seen in this the triumph of innocence over evil, since the splitting of persons was originally a punishment for their rebellion against the gods. Such teachings had a profound influence on the Saint-Simonians of France in the nineteenth century, one of whose leaders declared to the state attorney during his trial: 'Notre Dieu n'est pas le votre. *Il* n'est pas seulement bonne comme un pére, *Elle* est aussi tendre comme une mére, car *Il* est et *Elle* est la mére de tous et de toutes.'[8] The speaker was Enfantin, who was to turn up at a meeting of his followers in November 1831 with an empty chair, the sign of his incomplete selfhood.[9]

Enfantin's gesture may seem theatrical and bizarre, but it must be seen as a radical critique of an ancient symbolic tradition surrounding earthly leaders. Through the ages, men and women had often projected onto their rulers that serene fusion of male and female elements which had eluded them in actual life. So Gaelic bards celebrated their chieftains as potentates who combined the power of a man with the sensitivity of a woman; and the slender eyebrows, sloe-black eyes, fair hair and delicate mouth which the poet praised in his patron were precisely those traits which he had already seen and sung in his mistresses and lovers. The ruler had to be an exponent of the multiple self in order to appear a fitting representative of all his people, rich and poor, strong and weak, male and female. Even in the political world of today, the best leaders are those who manage to be aggressive without seeming so. According to Elémire Zolla in her study of the androgyne, the ruler must appear poor as well as rich, suffering as well as strong, so that he inspires not just fear and wonder, but also pity and contempt.[10] The plaints for more cash from the splendid royal families of contemporary Europe merely confirm the point.

Some religions of the East have sought to make this fusion available to all their adherents and not just to the privileged ruler. Taoism taught that each individual should harmonise within himself those forces of *yin* and *yang* which release the breath of life. Every power in nature has evolved its opposite in order to realise itself, so if the moon and winter are *yin*, then the sun and summer are *yang*. When it came to defining the nature of sexuality, however, the ancient Chinese were more subtle, for woman was classified not as pure *yin* but as 'lesser *yin*', and man as 'lesser *yang*'. As Reay Tannahill has observed: 'It was a recognition of the psychological truth that there is an element of active *yang* in even the most passive woman and of negative *yin* in even the most positive man. The associated belief that, in both sexes, the subsidiary element fed and strengthened the principal one was to play a crucial role in the development of Taoist and indeed all Chinese views on sex.'[11]

*   *   *

Anglo-Saxon culture has been less explicit in its recognition of these truths. The Wife of Bath and Saint Juliana might have been hailed as precursors of a more versatile womanhood, but instead were looked upon as bizarre deviations from a sexual norm. It was only with the advent of Shakespeare that a major writer offered a recognition of the male and female elements in all rich personalities. In *Richard II* the king unfit to rule his people paradoxically discovers the androgyny of the full self only when it is too late – *after* he has reverted to the status of ordinary citizen. Confined within his prison cell, the disgraced male rediscovers elements of his absent queen in himself:

> I have been studying how I may compare
> This prison where I live unto the world:
> And for because the world is populous,
> And here is not a creature but myself,
> I cannot do it. Yet I'll hammer it out:
> My brain I'll prove the female to my soul,
> My soul the father, and these two beget
> A generation of still-breeding thoughts;
> And these same thoughts people this little world,
> In humours like the people of this world,
> For no thought is contented.

In Shakespeare's own life, this same shock of recognition is recorded most poignantly by his sonnets:

> Two loves I have of comfort and despair,
> Which like two spirits do suggest me still,
> The better angel is a man right fair,
> The worser spirit a woman coloured ill.
> To win me soon to Hell, my female evil

Tempteth my better angel from my side,
And would corrupt my saint to be a devil,
Wooing his purity with her foul pride.

Shakespeare's love for the handsome Earl of Southampton is
platonic and noble, whereas his obsession with the dark lady is
lustful and corrupt – and he is happy to indulge in such cosy
traditional divisions. However, when at last he encounters his
two lovers in one another's arms he knows that he has not just
learned something new about the world but that he has also
discovered the truth about his inner self. Good and evil are not
so easily distinguished, nor male and female either. Leslie Fiedler
has argued that this recognition had been implicit in the sonnets
from the outset, for the handsome youth had been compared to
Helen, as well as to Adonis, as far back as Sonnet 53.[12] Like the
Gaelic bards of Ireland and Scotland, Shakespeare transferred
the images of female beauty from the mistress of *amour courtois* to
the young nobleman whom he loved and praised. Moreover, the
epicene beauty of the youth seems to find an answering echo in
the poet's own soul, as if he seeks in him the delicate beauty of
a woman *and* the constancy of a man:

A woman's face with Nature's own hand painted
Hast thou, the master-mistress of my passion,
A woman's gentle heart, but not acquainted
With shifting change, as is false woman's fashion,
An eye more bright than theirs, less false in rolling,
Gilding the object whereupon it gazeth,
A man in hue, all hues in his controlling,
Which steals men's eyes, and women's souls amazeth.
And for a woman wert thou first created,
Till Nature, as she wrought thee, fell a-doting,
And by addition me of thee defeated
By adding one thing to my purpose nothing.
    But since she pricked thee out for women's pleasure
    Mine be thy love, and thy love's use their treasure.

In the final distinction between love and its physical embodiment,
Fiedler sees Shakespeare arguing for the superior integrity of his
own passion, which is innocent of lustful desire. Hence the
sharpness of his disappointment to find his noblest love in the

arms of his own lusty whore. Disinterested friendship between males proves just as impossible as a pure love for a women. Even more notable is the way in which a failed friendship between males becomes the basis for a disclosure of the androgyny of the full personality, a point to be developed over three centuries later by Lawrence and Joyce.

Fiedler sees Sonnet 144 as Shakespeare's admission that the seed of corruption was in his friend from the start, in the female element of Southampton's personality, and that 'since there is no pure masculine principle, no male is immune to the evil represented by the female'.[13] But Shakespeare's disclosure that human motives are as mixed as human sexuality does not permit so clearcut an equation of 'evil' and 'female'. His whole art is to question such stereotypes. Those who continue to endorse them in his plays are, like Posthumus in *Cymbeline*, written off as jealous victims of self-defeating emotionalism, prissy men who actually believe all that they read in books:

> Could I find out
> The woman's part in me! For there's no motion
> That tends to vice in man but I affirm
> It is the woman's part. Be it lying, note it
> The woman's; flattering, hers; deceiving, hers;
> Lust and rank thoughts, hers, hers

That is Shakespeare's description of the art of his precursors in Europe, but his own work is a generous celebration of the woman's part in man, and even more notably of the man's part in woman.

In the forest, where all repressed instincts are liberated, Shakespeare's young lovers discern their deepest selves. The pansexuality of the couples in *A Midsummer Night's Dream* as they fall in and out of love with one another at a bewildering pace, is a sign that they are still experimenting with roles in an adolescent fashion. It is also a mark of the adolescent to reject the absolute differentiation of male and female, for this is a period in life when the identity is as yet unresolved and could go either way. Disguised as Ganymede in the forest of Arden, Rosalind discovers and savours the male element in herself, not merely as a trick, but in order that her lover may learn to see that she is a person before she is a woman. Moreover, in her male disguise, she has the opportunity to see Orlando as he really is in the company of other men, and not simply in his assumed role as a gallant theatrically seeking his lady's love. She has already parodied such swaggering performances in her role as Ganymede, so there is nothing left for Orlando but to offer himself, as he is, to another honest person. By way of contrast, the courtship of Phoebe and Silvius is factitious and jagged, precisely because it is a set of clumsy performances, based, in the words of Juliet Dusinberre, on 'the artificial exaggeration of masculine and feminine difference'.[14] Dusinberre wryly adds that Rosalind, always acting the part of Ganymede, presents her real self, while Phoebe, lamentably herself, is always acting.[15] It is interesting, too, that, like an adolescent girl with a crush on an older friend, Phoebe should isolate those feminine qualities in Ganymede as the traits which make him worthy of her love. In the end, it is left to Rosalind to explain the true nature of Phoebe and Silvius as opposed to their romantic self-deception. This is something which Rosalind has known for herself all along.[16] Her intimate awareness of the opposite sex is matched by a corresponding ability to see that there are two sides to every story. So, even as she submits to her lover Orlando, she does so in the knowledge that 'men are April when they woo, December when they wed'; and she knows that such a relationship, if based on true love and bonding, must be able to· survive its own self-questioning. All good marriages, no less than all good artistic conventions, must contain the essential criticism of the morality to which they adhere. Hence T. S. Eliot's praise of the play might be applied with equal justice to Rosalind, for he saw in it the intelligent 'recognition, implicit in the expression of every experience, of other kinds of experience which are possible'.[17]

Rosalind is simply the most striking example of those resourceful and charming heroines for whom Shakespeare can find no better destiny than the love of a passive and featureless man. In *The Two Gentlemen of Verona*, a vibrant girl finally weds herself to a somewhat girlish man, simply because he is honest enough to accept himself for what he is. It is clear that Shakespeare was fascinated by such heroines long before they put on those male garments which are the ultimate symbols of their intellectual daring and emotional versatility. These figures normally appear in the comedies, not because the genre is more trivial than tragedy, but because it is the real medium for the fate of the self in society. In this context, Dusinberre valuably recalls for us

George Meredith's observation, in his *Essay on Comedy*, that the comic poet 'dares to show us men and women coming together to this mutual likeness; he is for saying that when they draw together in social life their minds grow liker; just as the philosopher discerns the similarity of boy and girl, until the girl is marched away to the nursery'.[18]

In *Twelfth Night* this androgynous vision is made flesh in the scene where Viola is mistaken for her identical twin brother Sebastian. The amazed Orsino exclaims:

> One face, one voice, one habit, and two persons!
> A natural perspective, that is and is not.

Viola has disguised herself as Cesario, page to the Orsino whom she loves. She is forced, however, to carry his highflown professions of passion to Olivia, who promptly falls for the attractive page. Only when the missing Sebastian reappears is all set to rights, as Viola wins her man and Olivia falls in love with the new arrival, who tells her:

> So comes it, lady, you have been mistook.
> But nature to her bias drew in that.

Nature, like the bowler who casts his ball with due deference to its bias, has seen to it that Olivia went wrong in order to go right. In her flirtation with Cesario, she was prepared for her true love Sebastian, just as Orsino, having been educated in the nature of real love by Cesario, is thereby prepared to love Viola. Throughout these discussions Viola was hard put to hold back her true identity and deepest feelings, but she did so, and therefore taught Orsino that his fancy for Olivia was scarcely the basis for a lasting commitment. Like Posthumus, Orsino rehashes the bookish protests against the fickleness of woman, but Viola strongly demurs:

> My father had a daughter loved a man,
> As it might be, perhaps, were I a woman,
> I should your lordship. She never told her love,
> But let concealment like a worm i' the bud
> Feed on her damask cheek: she pined in thought
> And with a green and yellow melancholy

She sat like Patience on a monument,
Smiling at grief. Was not this love, indeed?
We men say more, swear more – but indeed
Our shows are more than will; for still we prove
Much in our vows, but little in our love.

In those scenes where Viola woos Olivia on behalf of a man whom she herself adores, we are given the measure of her selfless personality, just as in her response to physical danger we witness the extent of her courage. As C. L. Barber has observed: 'Her constant shifting of tone in response to the situation goes with her manipulation of her role in disguise, so that instead of simply listening to her speak, we watch her conduct her speech, and through it feel her secure sense of proportion and her easy, alert consciousness.'[19] As a disadvantaged woman who must live on her wits, she makes common cause with the clown and becomes a past master of his professional techniques: 'he must observe their mood on whom he jests'. At various stages, she runs the risk of exposure, or even death by duelling: 'Pray God defend me! A little thing would make me tell them how much I lack of man.' But, like Rosalind, she holds back the tears and puts on a brave front. Her boldness inspires a love in Olivia, which will find its resting-place in the peerless Sebastian; just as her male apparel simply serves to set off her deep-seated feminine appeal to Orsino. As Cesario, she combines the finest traits of Viola and Sebastian. Walter King has written that 'Viola and Sebastian, both of whom are Cesario, are emblems of a metaphysical possibilty – that oneness cannot be so easily distinguished from twoness as human beings like to think; and of a psychological reality – that Olivia and Orsino fell in love with given human potentialities far more than with given human bodies.'[20]

Once again, the strong ties of honour that bind man to man are jeopardised and broken against the backdrop of an androgynous love, as Antonio is left to fend for himself in the belief that Sebastian has betrayed him. Sebastian conducts himself with a feminine delicacy, just as Olivia pursues Cesario with a positively masculine aggression. It is no wonder that the clown's song promises her a true love 'that can sing both high and low'. The fact that Cesario is played by Viola, who was herself played by a boy, added to the jest for Shakespeare's original audience, who would have had far less difficulty believing in Cesario's boyhood than in Viola's girlishness. Dusinberre has argued that the fact that boy actors would always look like boys, however effective their apparel and make-up, forced Shakespeare to create a femininity deeper than mere costume and closer to the real nature of woman.[21] The acquired trappings of femininity are replaced by a flesh-and-blood woman of high spirits; and the all-male cast frees Shakespeare to record the racy dialogue of Rosalind and Celia, the dialogue of women as they are in company together rather than as men would believe them to be. Moreover, by his use of the boy-actors, Shakespeare can give added point to his conviction of how little substance there is in the conventional notions of 'masculine' and 'feminine'. Portia can outwit male lawyers at their own game, while Richard II weeps like a woman. More subtly, a woman like Imogen is praised by different men for widely discrepant qualities, forcing Dusinberre to the conclusion that 'femininity is all things to all men – what a man finds feminine defines not the nature of women, but his own nature'.[22] Polonius, looking at a cloud, says it is very like a whale, because Hamlet has told him so; and the same fanciful subjectivity governs most of Shakespeare's men in their dealings with women. Dusinberre marvels at how Imogen is a housewife to one, a gentle singer to another, and a traitor to a third. As Stanislaus Joyce wryly observed, in the end women are always blamed by men for being precisely what men themselves have made them.

It has always seemed charming and arresting when women become boyish as Ganymede and usurp male functions, but the reverse is not always true, even for the open-hearted Shakespeare. Men who become effeminate are often suspect, unless like the hero in *The Two Gentlemen of Verona* they impress their lovers by the honesty with which they accept their own passivity and weakness. Perhaps all this is merely to say that the weak one who seeks power is always admirable, while the strong one who yearns for weakness (like Lear) is not. The woman who can ape the man seems to add an exciting dimension to her personality, but the man who grows passive and womanly seems to subtract an important dimension from his. 'No man can ever be worthy of a woman's love', wrote James Joyce to his wife, and this is certainly true of the effete and over-elegant males who win the hands of Rosalind, Viola and Portia. Dusinberre has gone so far as to suggest that the audience is truly disappointed when Viola settles for Orsino, because her other self is not the man she loves but her brother. She sees the real marriage of the play as the magical reunion of the separated twins, by which 'Shakespeare soothes the mind with an illusion of concord between the masculine and feminine only to dispel the illusion by separating Viola from the second self with whom she has learned to live.' The liberated woman must become a fetish of the pallid male imagination, Orsino's mistress and (most suspiciously) his fancy's queen, after she has thrown away her male clothes. True androgyny has been achieved at the start of Act 5, only to be lost at the very conclusion.

Even Shakespeare's androgyny must pay its respects to social convention and so the high spirits of his heroines cannot survive their return to female clothing. Coming from a skirted lady, the probing comment might seem shrewish, and self-confident demeanour might seem like aggressiveness. For a brief spell, male disguise freed Rosalind and Viola to be more irreverently sparkish with men than they normally dared, but even then their wit was exercised only within the traditional female domain of love. For all their sharp criticisms of romantic posturing, the ultimate joke on Rosalind and Viola is that they themselves are hopelessly in love with forgettable nonentities. Clara Claiborne Park has shown in an essay that they are devotees of a tradition which finds its most spectacular exponent in Kate – the male fantasy of the high-spirited woman who will ideally tame herself.[24]

Yet, for all that, these girls are a great deal more vivacious and forceful than the sighing, ultrafeminine heroines of Shakespeare's tragedies. They attain a personal authenticity unknown to the simpering Ophelia or the suffering Cordelia, just as they achieve an inner harmony impossible to the unbalanced and self-divided Hamlet or Lear. In the great tragedies, Shakespeare seems to have shifted the focus of his investigations from the manly woman to the womanly man. That androgyny which was an enrichment to the comic heroine now becomes a dangerous liability for the tragic male. Hamlet is passive to a fault, not just in politics but in love. He is callous in his treatment of Ophelia, in hopes that he will provoke her to treat him more harshly. His demeanour is more that of the sighing lovelorn woman of tradition than of the aggressive all-conquering man. As Ophelia herself reports:

> He took me by the wrist and held me hard;
> Then goes he to the length of all his arm;
> And, with his other hand thus o'er his brow,

> He falls to such perusal of my face
> As he would draw it. Long stayed he so;
> At last a little shaking of mine arm
> And thrice his head thus waving up and down
> He raised a sigh so piteous and profound
> As it did seem to shatter all his bulk
> And end his being . . . .

The female element in Hamlet is attracted by the boy-actors, whose voices are still unbroken. That same element is defeated by an Ophelia who has been trained to suppress all traces of masculinity in herself. Hamlet's problem is that he is too feminine, 'passion's slave', and so he despises femininity when he finds it exaggerated in Ophelia, whom he would prefer to be more coarse and masculine.[25] At the play, he goads her into a response with his obscene innuendoes, but she merely observes that he is 'keen' in both senses. As a woman she has trained herself to be submissive to elders and gentlemen, so her slender wit can operate only within stark constraints. In performing the role of an obedient and delicate girl, she has colluded with her father in the attempt to deceive Hamlet. So, when he unmasks the deception, he sees in her mincing femininity the key to her falseness:

> I have heard of your paintings too, well enough; God has given you one face, and you make yourselves another: you jig, you amble, and you lisp, and nickname God's creatures, and make your wantonness your ignorance. Go to, I'll no more on 't; it hath made me mad. I say we will have no more marriage. Those that are married already, all but one, shall live; the rest shall keep as they are. To a nunnery, go.

So the androgynous hero, who says that 'man delights me not, nor woman neither', is forced to turn to the players for entertainment. Yet, at the same time, it is the actress in Ophelia, the performer of femininity, who so enrages Hamlet.

Like Viola, like the clown, the woman of Shakespeare's tragedies must live on her wits, by pleasing elders and superior males. Men have made women their dependants and yet, as Marianne Novy notes, they are the first to complain when this leads to the insincere role-playing of which women like Ophelia are so often accused.[26] The reason male actors played women so successfully in Shakespeare's theatre, according to Novy, is that the very precariousness of their profession enabled them to identify with the traditional dependence of women and 'the need to please'. The Hamlet who loves male actors and hates female acting is himself fatally in thrall to the histrionic temperament. As androgynous as any actor, as soft as any woman, as ambitious as any man, he is an exponent of multiple selfhood at a time when he needs to act with a single will. He, too, would like to cut out the woman's part in himself, but that is not so easily done, as even the manly Laertes discovers after his sister's death by drowning:

> Too much of water hast thou, poor Ophelia,
> And therefore I forbid my tears: but yet
> It is our trick; nature her custom holds,
> Let shame say what it will: when these are gone,
> The woman will be out.

Shakespeare's sharp awareness of the hollowness of traditional notions of 'masculinity' and 'femininity' is the basis of his lifelong attempt to define where true manliness and womanhood reside. The Lady Macbeth who is so ashamed of her woman's part that she all but denies her own sexuality is not a resourceful heroine but a monster. She is ashamed of her androgyny and her craving for complete manliness constitutes a parody of the very notion. Instead of honestly confronting the masculine element within herself, she projects it onto her husband and asks him to live out her own repressed masculinity. She steels herself for a deed of murder, asks the spirits to unsex her, and would resolutely repudiate her own motherhood, if that proved necessary to the success of her enterprise. Her husband, by contrast, she berates for his unmanly irresolution and remorse of conscience. She who would pluck the nipple from a sucking babe fears that he is too natural, 'too full o' the milk of human kindness', to be a true man, whom she defines as one who acts on his desires. But Macbeth subtly redefines the concept of manhood:

> I dare do all that may become a man;
> Who dares do more is none.

Dusinberre acutely points out that in denying that masculinity ordains brute power in action, Shakespeare 'undermines the logic which declares women to be weak and ignoble because incapable of fighting'.[27] Moreover, in his portrait of Lady Macbeth, he depicts a woman who cultivates male attributes only at the cost of her female virtues, thereby getting the worst of both worlds, the squeamishness of a woman who fears blood allied to the callous indifference of a man. Through her Shakespeare warns women that liberation will not be found in emulating the brutality and egotism of incomplete men, but rather in a joint attempt by the sexes to discriminate true authority from false power, strength from force, conviction from self-assertion, and sensitivity from squeamishness. Those women who deny the virtues of their own sex are the ultimate slaves to the male principle and so they mistake an intelligent sensitivity in men for a feminine weakness. 'I pray you father, being weak, seem so', says Regan to Lear, despising in him the female element which she has already suppressed in herself. As Lear's dutiless daughters grow more manly, he himself becomes more womanly, a development common in most of Shakespeare's doting old fathers, who seem as emotional and androgynous as babies. Polonius is the most credible old woman Shakespeare ever created, just as Joan is the most martial man.

*   *   *

The slow growth of Shakespeare's prestige in the centuries that followed was not accompanied by any desire to extend his investigations into the androgyny of the person. Contemporary figures such as Donne were a great deal more explicit in their accounts of the fusion of the sexes than those who came after. It was only a mystic like Blake who had the courage to raise the issue again. Believing that God is neither male nor female but One, Blake saw the fall as the moment when the ideal androgyne was degraded into a split hermaphrodite, with all the suffering consequent on that loss of unity. Urizen, the man of war and reason, catches only glimpses of his lost female dimension in dreams; and this sense of incompleteness, according to Elémire Zolla, increases his misery. In losing contact with his female instincts, man has lost half his potential wisdom, his oneness with nature and compassion for all that lives. Without these attributes, his own gifts are no longer a source of strength, but a grave liability – reason untempered by emotion has led to the vices of exploitation and specialisation, slavery to technology, and death in war. In her study of the androgyne, Zolla reminds us that his analysis is even more applicable today than it was almost two centuries ago.[28] 'Sooner murder an infant in its cradle than nurse unacted desires', wrote Blake, especially when the repressed female element in man will otherwise emerge in stunted and unnatural forms. The art of the drag-show arose in an industrial England whose males, terrified of the female principle, sought at once to disarm, degrade, displace but still express it in the leering obscenities of the female impersonator.

The attempts of early male novelists, such as Richardson and Fielding, to depict the personalities of women are more a contribution to that tradition of female impersonation than a conscious return to the androgyny of Shakespeare. Only Defoe seems to have tried to see the women of his time as they were seeing themselves. His Moll Flanders combines a cosy feminine domesticity with an aggressively masculine attitude to cash, a concern for the physical well-being of her males with a profound indifference to her own motherhood. 'The way to be happy through children', she says, 'is to have them taken off one's hands.' This multiplicity of Moll's roles is deemed 'most attractive' by Heilbrun, yet, in the end, such alternations of female compassion and male callousness are too schematic to be psychologically convincing. 'All these contradictions are the consequence of a process to which first-person narrative is peculiarly prone', says Ian Watt, arguing 'that Defoe's identification with Moll Flanders was so complete that, despite a few feminine traits, he created a personality that was, in essence, his own'[29] – the calculating, shrewd and comfortable personality of a middle-class tradesman. Nevertheless, Moll Flanders could be seriously presented by Defoe as one solution to the problem of unemancipated woman. For him the prostitute was a kind of hero who had, economically speaking, become a tradesman, by necessity rather than conviction. Moll only develops her masculine and mercantile dimension after her disappointments in life, and, whenever possible, she reverts to the female role.

Moll competes on a man's terms in a man's world when she must, because Defoe believed not so much in women's innate androgyny as in their need 'to educate themselves for survival in a masculine world'.[30] He did not believe that the world would change, so he urged women to change instead. He endorsed Thomas More's argument that unless women were given equal access to education, they could never be expected to provide spiritual companionship for men, who would be driven to seek from other men the intellectual fulfilment that should be the basis of any lasting marriage. But Defoe never seems to have questioned the superiority of the male principle – he simply asserted his belief that women should have equal access to it.

In the prostitute Roxana, Defoe chose as his exemplar a female militant who successfully usurps all male prerogatives. She feels only contempt for her easy-going brewer husband: 'I had now five children by him; the only work perhaps that fools are good for.' Yet she rejects the overtures of a more impressive Dutchman who loves her sincerely, because she prefers economic self-reliance to legal dependence on a husband: 'I told him that I had, perhaps, differing notions of matrimony from what the receiv'd custom had given us of it . . . that a woman gave herself entirely away from herself in marriage, and capitulated only to be at best but an upper-servant.' Roxana believes that a woman can survive as well without a man as a man may do without a woman, 'and that, if she had a mind to gratifie herself as to sexes, she might entertain a man as a man does a mistress'. Such arguments are given added force by the fact that they are in no way theoretical or self-conscious, but are advanced as Roxana's instinctive response to her own predicament. Virginia Woolf doubted if Roxana or Moll would appeal as patron saints to the advocates of women's rights, but was willing to concede that 'Defoe not only intended them to speak some very modern notions upon the subject, but placed them in circumstances where their peculiar hardships are displayed in such a way as to elicit our sympathy.'[31]

The literature of eighteenth-century England produced, if not a return to Shakespearean androgyny, then at least a 'feminisation of discourse'. It has been shown that, in the previous century, Milton had mitigated his own patriarchal stance with a plea for rational esteem in marriage, while Dryden qualified his aggressive heroics with a deference for tender and compassionate love.[32] This 'domestication of heroism' is seen by Terry Eagleton as an attempt to replace the naked militarism and male hauteur of a predatory aristocracy with the more serviceable bourgeois virtues of sensibility and civility.[33] So, Richardson can make Sir Charles Grandison the hero of his final novel in order to demonstrate that men can be chaste and manly, passive and materially successful. 'What is at stake in *Sir Charles Grandison* is nothing less than the production of a new kind of male subject', says Eagleton, 'for Richardson has grasped the point that the so-called "woman question" is nothing of the kind – that the root of the sexual problem is men.'[34] Grandison thus becomes the first fully *successful* womanly man in English literature. Unlike Hamlet or Macbeth, he is cast not as a warning of what may befall a man who is a slave to emotion, but is proposed as the model for a new kind of manhood. Eagleton insists, however, that the deeper sexual inequality remains unchallenged in Richardson's book, since 'in a patriarchal society it does not *matter* whether men are chaste or not'.[35] The virginity of Grandison, unlike that of Clarissa, has no exchange value, because he is not a commodity on the sex market. But what Eagleton does not add is – all the more credit to him that his passivity and chastity are voluntary rather than compelled!

It has been convincingly demonstrated that the spread of rationalism in the eighteenth century did at least as much as the Richardsonian cult of sentiment to redress the wrongs of women. Katherine Rogers has shown, in her book *Feminism in Eighteenth Century England*, that women were at last allowed a wider choice of marriage partners and were given a good education in order that they might provide intellectual companionship for their husbands. The doctrine of rational love dismissed the stereotype of silliness and helplessness in woman as 'weaknesses unworthy of a rational being'.[36] The proviso scenes of Restoration comedy had already demonstrated the need for mutual fulfilment in marriage, as did the reemergence of the Shakespearean comic convention that it was the self-reliant witty woman, rather than the abject and deferential maiden, who won the heart of the new type of male hero.[37] It was left to Swift, however, to press the implications of rational esteem to limits which uncannily anticipate the doctrines espoused almost two centuries later by the denizens of Bloomsbury. The Dean depicted Lilliput as a state where boys and girls had equal access to efficient schools, with the result that the young ladies 'are as much ashamed of being Cowards and Fools as the Men; and despise all personal ornaments beyond Decency and Cleanliness'.[38]

Rogers has also shown how Swift's friend Stella is praised for 'the Fire that forms a manly Soul', as well as a 'Fund of Wit and

Sense'. Swift concedes that these are qualities which few men can find in women, not because women lack them, but because sentimental men have been trained by a sexist society to look for the wrong things.[39] This is doubtless why Swift was nauseated by Addison's patronising hints for pouting ladies and was driven to the famous complaint: 'Let him fair-sex it to the world's end.' His own advice was quite at variance with Addison's coy messages to the weaker sex, for he declared that 'there is no quality whereby Women endeavour to distinguish themselves from Men, for which they are not just so much the worse'.[40] Having cited such statements as evidence of Swift's progressive stance, Rogers goes on to concede that such wisdom was purchased only for a high price – the intellectual cost of rejecting all traditional female qualities as false and degrading.[41] In the end, Swift's women are celebrated not for a truly androgynous fusion of sexual qualities but, quite bluntly, for being mannish. His programme for rational esteem is more asexual than any doctrine propounded in Bloomsbury in our own century, and it cannot conceal its author's irrational contempt for the female. Women are not to liberate society from its slavery to the male principle, but are urged instead to join the latest band of new recruits. Swift's prescription for Stella is no different from Defoe's remedy for Moll and Roxana – if you can't change the society, then you must alter the self.

A more likely model than these ladies for contemporary feminists may be found in Catherine Earnshaw, the doomed heroine of Emily Brontë's *Wuthering Heights*. Her famous protest, 'I am Heathcliff', expresses not only the ecstasy of a true lover, but the rediscovery of the suppressed male element in the Victorian lady. Constricted by convention, yet outrageously aware of her thwarted gifts, she dreams of releasing them vicariously through the power and will of Heathcliff. She sees this urchin from the slums as the man to challenge a dessicated landlord class. In the image of the Linton children fighting over a luxury poodle that neither brother nor sister really wants, Brontë presents the self-destructive *ennui* of Big House life. Though temporarily fascinated by such redundant opulence, Catherine sides in the end with the proletarian insurgent and repudiates her position as esteemed wife at Edgar Linton's table, instructing Nelly to set a separate place for Heathcliff and herself, 'being of the lower orders'. On the wild crags and moors, as Heilbrun has shown, she rejects all limiting notions of Victorian femininity in her honest horseplay with her lover. A tamer, but no less eloquent, protest is made in the French literature of the time by Madame Bovary, who can only find freedom in acts of transgression, in espousing failure and social ostracism. So she flaunts her illicit lover outside the windows of provincial nosey-parkers, smokes cigarettes out of doors, and arrays herself in men's clothing, all for a single purpose, to sever the bonds of respectability. In her, Flaubert covertly reincarnated his own androgyny – 'Madame Bovary, c'est moi' – to such telling effect that Baudelaire could complain that she was really a man. 'The woman who always wants to be a man', added Baudelaire darkly, 'is a sign of great depravity.'

Even as late as the nineteenth century, the art of creative writing was seen as a male prerogative which women usurped at their peril. So Charlotte Brontë sought to ensure a fair reception for her book by suppressing all trace of its female authorship and publishing it under the pseudonym Currer Bell. In America, Nathaniel Hawthorne faced the reverse problem in his attempt to win an audience weaned on masculine virtues over to a story with the unpromising title 'The Gentle Boy'. So he removed all trace of its male authorship and sought safety, as well as popularity, in anonymity. The business of America was business. At best, the American artist was seen as an idler at odds with the work ethic; at worst, he could appear as a social deviant, an effeminate fellow of unsavoury tendencies. America's greatest novelist in the nineteenth century, Herman Melville, did append his name to a heartfelt critique of the cult of masculinity, but only by opening *Moby Dick* in a style which seemed to capitulate to that cult. The gruff man-to-man tone of the initial sentence – 'Call me Ishmael' – sounds more like a deadpan message delivered by John Wayne astride a horse than a credible introduction to the self-doubting male whom we come to know and admire as the narrator of *Moby Dick*. Melville found his own questioning and sceptical cast of mind a great asset in creating the role of Ishmael, but in his own life it was also his greatest handicap, for the questioning soon became self-questioning and the scepticism was directed finally and most potently against himself. His failure in business was construed by society as an inability to provide for his wife, who turned to her illustrious father for support for Melville's own children. The result was an inevitable sense of shame in the artist and an insecure sense of his own manliness.[42] Sensing that feminine element in his personality which was invaluable to the artist, but disastrous to the American, he sought to conceal it with a fabricated image of masculinity. Hence the blunt opening to *Moby Dick*. Hence, too, the awful sexual puns all through the book, so reminiscent of the worst traditions of locker-room humour. Melville must have felt obliged to present a metaphysical romance in the guise of a salty sea anecdote, in order to win a hearing for it from the American public. But the tough-guy pose is a mere ticket-of-entry to a book which proceeds to demolish the very cult which it seems to espouse. Within a few dozen pages, this gruff sailor Ishmael is sleeping like a bridegroom in the arms of a dark-skinned savage. Here is the real significance of Ishmael's passivity and anxious self-scrutiny, to be explored not only in his love for Queequeg, but also in his humble spectator-like status on the ship. It has often been remarked that in most of his novels Melville chose to write about closed communities of men on ships, as if such contexts afforded him the opportunity of assessing his own timidity against the backdrop of an aggressive all-male world.[43] But the price of that investigation was the intermittent need to exude an aggressive masculinity which must have been profoundly reassuring to Melville's original audience. It would be pleasant to report that Ishmael's uncertainty of tone is coolly assessed by the author in his diagnosis of the plight of the passive male, but it is clear that, more often than not, the inner confusions of the narrator are a reflection of the author's. The androgyny of nineteenth-century artists and characters is, as yet, a disturbing problem rather than a clinical subject.

*   *   *

It was only with the unprecedented spread of the women's movement in the second half of the nineteenth century that writers – as apparently disparate as Hawthorne, Arnold and Wilde – addressed themselves with full rigour to the themes adumbrated by Shakespeare. All of a sudden, artists began to depict relationships between a masterful female and a passive male, as the child–wife Dora Copperfield gave way to the 'divinely tall and most divinely fair' heroines of Tennyson. According to Reay Tannahill, 'Charles Dana Gibson's long-legged autocrats came to epitomise the voluptuous man-eater of the popular imagination.' The Byronic *homme fatale* was supplanted by 'the fatal woman whose power lay in pain, who was the antithesis of the Victorian "angel of the house", and by whom the man who dominated timid, deferential women at home was in turn reduced to abject subjection'.[44] In England, Harriet Martineau acquired such a daunting reputation that F. W. Newman jumped from a window rather than face the ordeal of meeting her. In France, George Sand wore male clothing, smoked cigars and seemed to cast a cruel spell over every timid but gifted man whom she met, Chopin, Lizst and Musset included. She was always the dominant partner in affairs of love, imperiously passionate one moment, pleading frigidity the next, but always in supreme control.

The rise of such *femmes fatales* has been explained in psychological terms – in the belief that their masculine element appealed to the latent homosexuality in passive males. The masterful woman allowed a man to indulge in illicit passion without his having to commit a public violation of the sexual code. The cruelty of such a woman enacted the punishment which a fastidious male might feel was necessary to purge his sin against his own masculinity. In the words of Isabelle de Courtivron: 'Symbolising both sides of this inescapable pattern, she was seen as both the catalyst and the consequence: hence her power.'[45] Courtivron cites the findings of contemporary psychologists to explain the abiding fascination of the 'Sand image'. The feeling of maleness is now believed to be less strong in males than that of femaleness in women. Hence, feminisation of the male, the wish to adopt feminine attributes, is much more threatening to a man than is masculisation to a woman, and 'is therefore more likely to undergo severe punishment from the ego'.[46] For such a man, the New Woman was at once a delicious occasion of sin and an even more enthralling exponent of retribution, the punishment itself merely compounding the sense of excited transgression. The prototype may be found in a French novel like Gautier's *Mademoiselle de Maupin*, but Nathaniel Hawthorne's *The Scarlet Letter* offers the most subtle of all variations on the theme.

In this tale the proud heroine, Hester Prynne, refuses to name and shame the Reverend Arthur Dimmesdale before the puritan community as the father of her illegitimate child. Her daily proximity to the clergyman is her greatest thrill, for it allows her to repeat the sin in her own mind. Looking deep into the eyes of the hypocrite who is the father he challenges her to name, she responds 'Never' and prays that it might be given to her to endure his agony as well. That Dimmesdale construes this as a declaration of love is clear from his whisper: 'Wondrous strength and generosity of a woman's heart. She will not speak.' Hawthorne knows how a repressed sexuality will express itself in alternative ways, as in the powerful attraction exercised by the clergyman over the ladies of his flock. The spectacle of a strong man (as they think him) indulging in a generalised outburst of self-recrimination is irresistible to maidens who are 'victims of a passion so imbued with religious sentiment that they imagined it to be all religion'. Small wonder, then, that a masterly woman should feel a compulsion to ease the pain of this self-lacerating male; or that Dimmesdale should resort to a perverse, self-directed sexuality, flogging himself with a bloody scourge, heightening the illicit pleasure even as he fancied himself to be expiating his own guilt.[47] D. H. Lawrence remarked that 'the blue-eyed darling Nathaniel knew disagreeable things in his inner soul', 'but he was careful to send them out in disguise'.[48] Hester's fierce resolve to wear the scarlet letter is a similar act of self-degradation which, by its very nature, must have further inflamed the strange imagination of her lover. It is not surprising that the more subtle puritan divines wonder if she is taking as much pleasure in the spectacle of her self-humiliation as she did in the original sin. She knows her man and his kinks. Lawrence caught this perverse logic at its most simple when he wrote: 'The greatest triumph an American woman can have is the triumph of seducing a man – especially if he is pure. And he gets the greatest thrill of all in falling.'[49]

That is, of course, why Dimmesdale needs to scourge himself, for, like Hester, he daily repeats the thrill of the sin in his own mind. At the outset, one of the shrewder divines had argued against the sadistic punishment of the letter by assuring Dimmesdale that 'the shame lay in the commission of the sin, and not in the showing of it forth'. *That* is a crucial indictment of what follows, when the entire community, including Dimmesdale, becomes obsessed not with the passionate deed in the forest, but with the orgies of self-recrimination to which it gives rise. In this tale, the only crime is punishment, for, as Lawrence said, 'the birth of the sin – not doing it, but knowing about it – the sin was the self-watching, the self-consciousness'.[50] It is this self-watching which unsexes Dimmesdale and prevents him from lying again with the woman he loves. He loves her in his weakling way, but he is far more in love with his own remorse. It is left to the feminist Hester, living on the fringes of society by the edge of the forest, to work out a more honest code, as she ponders the riddle of sexuality and the prospects for the self-sufficient woman:

> Then, the very nature of the opposite sex, or its hereditary habit which has become like nature, is to be essentially modified, before woman can be allowed to assume a fair and suitable position. Finally, all other difficulties being obviated, woman cannot take advantage of these preliminary reforms, until she herself shall have undergone a still mightier change; in which, perhaps, the etherial essence, wherein she has her truest life, will be found to have evaporated.

Behind the coy circumlocution, the implication is that the price of sexual freedom may be femininity itself – the fear that the New Woman may be just a predator and the New Man a nervous wreck.

In the end, Dimmesdale confesses in public and dies in a blaze of self-abnegation which is scarcely distinguishable from male vanity. Moreover, he repudiates Hester and rejects the notion that they might meet again in heaven. In such a manner does the powerful instinct for self-laceration overwhelm the tenuous capacity for love in a timid male who, in the words of Frederick Crews, 'is not saved but doomed by his moral sensitivity, which amounts to squeamishness rather than virtue'.[51] As for Hester, her real error may have been to conceive a magnificent love for an entirely unworthy object. There are times when she seems to be enacting the traditional role of the male seducer who has to overpower the fastidious moral reservations of an old-fashioned heroine; while Dimmesdale resembles a genteel but coy maiden, toying beautifully with scruples, intermittently astounded, unnerved and flattered by such energetic devotion.[52] There is a sense in which Hawthorne is finally as embarrassed as Dimmesdale by the dynamic charm of Hester Prynne, with the result that the author is forced to deflect the radical implications of her feminism at the end. His heroine lives out her days in New England, helping those women who have been wronged by their men: 'Hester comforted and counselled them as best she could. She assured them, too, of her firm belief that, at some brighter period, when the world should have grown ripe for it, a new truth would be revealed, in order to establish the whole relation between men and women on a surer ground of mutual happiness.' Despite the benefit of more than two centuries of hindsight, Hawthorne never reveals how this 'new truth' might come to pass. In that sense, the glib ending of the novel does not reflect the complexity of its exposition; and the feelings of frustration and discontent, which led Hester to fall in love with an emotional bankrupt, are as unappeased at the end as they were at the beginning.

Passive to a fault, Hawthorne himself knew all the anxieties of the self-doubting male. Oliver Wendell Holmes found that conversing with him 'was almost like love-making, and his shy, beautiful soul had to be wooed from its bashful pudency like an unschooled maiden'.[53] James Russell Lowell wrote of him in *A Fable for Critics*:

> When Nature was shaping him, clay was not granted
> For making so full-sized a man as she wanted,
> So, to fill out her model, a little she spared
> From some finer-grained stuff for a woman prepared.[54]

Hence Hawthorne's fascination with the strong-willed woman whose power fills him with both longing and envy; and his painful awareness that only in the past was such power wedded to tenderness of the emotions. Hester Prynne is, by definition, an historical figure and her modern counterparts, such as Zenobia in *The Blithedale Romance*, are mere curiosities, living in experimental communities, but not in middle America. Zenobia is an amazon in a nation of dessicated wives and spinsters. It is as a magnificent exception to the decline of the American woman that Hawthorne (through the words of his hero Coverdale) celebrates her: 'we seldom meet with women nowadays, and in this country, who impress us as being women at all, – their sex fades away, and goes for nothing.' The model for Zenobia was the radical feminist, Margaret Fuller, whom the cowed author seems to have avoided in life, even as he sought to repossess her for his art.

One fact above all others needs to be noted of this literary period. From being an image of emotional versatility in the comedies of Shakespeare, the New Woman has now become at best a source of suffering and at worst a dire destroyer – and this in a period when the sensitive man is most often presented as a wronged but admirable fellow. The boyish girl of Shakespeare has been superseded by the mannish woman of the Victorians. Matthew Arnold in 'A Farewell' could attribute the collapse of his relationship with Marguerite to his want of masculine hardness and self-confidence. He found that women increasingly seek in their lovers 'stern strength and promise of control', only to be surprised by the disclosure of a superior power in themselves. Earlier than most, he bitterly noted the paradox whereby the woman who insists most forcefully on independence often secretly despises the man who concedes it. She has usurped but not destroyed the male prerogative, and has yet to learn that the man who refuses to exploit and dominate is not on that account less virile. In his poem, Arnold sees no solution on earth, but looks forward to an achieved androgyny in heaven, when we

> Shall see ourselves, and learn at last
> Our true affinities of soul.

In the next life, if not in this, hopes Arnold, women will not mistake 'hardness' for 'force'.

Arnold's poem is fairly typical of Victorian works in which the male androgyne sees himself as a hero, while the female with androgynous tendencies is dismissed as a near villain. It would be tempting to attribute this trend to the fact that literature in the nineteenth century was still mainly written by men, to extol their own species and put the female in her place. It would even be possible to assert that since men are less assured in their maleness than women in their femaleness, it is statistically predictable that many sensitive men will share Arnold's experience of rejection at the hands of a woman in search of a more conventional lover. But the problem seems to arise from an even deeper level of human experience. In all the mythologies of the world, writes Wendy Doninger O'Flaherty, 'male androgynes by far outnumber female androgynes and are generally regarded as positive, while female androgynes are generally negative'.[55] This dual interpretation seems to epitomise a universal unsureness about the value of androgyny itself, ranging from the Navajo Indians, who cast hermaphrodites in the role of tribal leaders, to the East African Pokot tribe, who kill them all at birth.

There is, of course, no such thing as a pure androgyne – there are merely men and women possessed of widely varying combinations of masculine and feminine elements in their personalities. Since absolute androgyny is a myth, its meaning is open to a wide range of interpretations. A. J. L. Busst has documented the fluctuations in the image throughout the nineteenth century in France. For revolutionaries like Enfantin, it epitomised the yearning for social equality and the emancipation of women;[56] but, after the mid-century, it came increasingly to stand for 'intellectual depravity', 'self-sufficient onanism' and 'the confusion of good and evil in an age deprived of values'.[57] This was particularly true of such female androgynes as Mademoiselle de Maupin, whose ambivalent sexuality allowed the hero d'Albert to act out his homoerotic impulses in an atmosphere of cultivated depravity. Ostensibly, the hero's aspirations are noble, to love the boy-Madeleine as a person, beyond mere sexuality; but the tone of the narrative makes it clear that the latent motivation is a homosexual thrill-seeking. The high-minded dream of Enfantin has been corrupted by a knowing masochism.[58] The search for a glorious transcendence has become a dreary and programmatic attempt to multiply sensations.

'The possibilities of love exhaust themselves', says Gerald Crich of such sexual thrill-seeking in *Women in Love*; 'then you die.' This is to concede that the logical consummation of the pornographic imagination is death. Here the death may ultimately be found in the demise of the androgyne as a symbol, that fatal decline which Mircea Eliade has found in the writers of the French decadence:

> As in all the great spiritual crises of Europe, here once again we meet *the degradation of the symbol*. When the mind is no longer capable of perceiving the metaphysical significance of a symbol, it is understood at levels which become increasingly coarse . . . The androgyne is understood by decadent writers simply as a hermaphrodite in whom both sexes exist anatomically and physiologically. They are concerned not with a wholeness resulting from the fusion of the sexes, but with a superabundance of erotic possibilities.[59]

Yet, in order to multiply these erotic possibilities, the male had to submit to the power of a sadistic woman. Since guilt and its consequent pain were an integral part of the pleasures offered by the romantic agony, it is no great surprise that the female androgyne should so often have been depicted as a monster. But such a *femme fatale* is not so much a symbol of degradation as a degradation of the symbol. She appeals to the covert homosexuality of males who have refused to come directly to terms with the woman in themselves, whereas the true androgyne displays a willingness to acknowledge all aspects of the self, conscious and unconscious.

* * *

'The most courageous man among us is terrified of himself', wrote Oscar Wilde. His Lady Windermere asserts that 'there is the same world for all of us, and good and evil, sin and innocence, go through it hand in hand. To shut one's eyes to half of life that one may live securely is as though one blinded oneself that one might walk with more safety in a land of pit and precipice.' Wilde is the first major modern writer to reject the romantic antithesis of good and evil and to take as his subject the knowledge of good-and-evil.[60] In *The Importance of Being Earnest* his heroine Cecily rejects the notion of an antithesis between herself and others, because she has already recognised the antithesis within herself. So, though doomed to tedious isolation under the grim, all-female regime of Miss Prism, she expresses the male element in herself by conducting an imaginary love affair and sending letters to a lover who exists only in her own head. Just before meeting the 'wicked uncle' who will in fact become that lover in her real life, she exclaims: 'I have never met any really wicked person before. I feel rather frightened. I am so afraid he will look just like everyone else.' The moral uncertainty which surrounds the androgyne in nineteenth-century literature becomes the major theme of Wilde's most important play, which is an attack on all black-and-white interpretations of experience.

In his social comedies, Wilde – a peerless advocate of women's rights – rejected the *femme fatale*, with whose image he was still to flirt in *Salomé*, and instead announced the advent of a new breed of androgynes here on earth. It is unfortunate that his theatrical performance of homosexuality should have obscured his far more revolutionary teaching on the androgyny of the full person. Homosexuality is an interpersonal relationship between two persons, which Wilde sought repeatedly in his life. Androgyny is an intrapsychic harmonisation of male and female elements within the self,[61] whose fate in modern society is the underlying subject of Wilde's art. The man who believed that a truth in art is that whose opposite is also true was quick to point out that every good man has an element of the woman in him. 'All women become like their mothers. That is their tragedy. No man does. That's his', observes Algernon in *The Importance of Being Earnest* – and the apparent sexism of the first half of that jibe is retrieved by the sharp feminist intelligence of the conclusion. It is an intelligence which is bound to appeal to Gwendolen, who salutes the emergence of a new sexuality:

> Outside the family circle, papa, I am glad to say, is entirely unknown. I think that is quite as it should be. The home seems to me to be the proper sphere for a man. And certainly once a man begins to neglect his domestic duties he becomes painfully effeminate, does he not? And I don't like that. It makes men so very attractive . . .

In *The Importance of Being Earnest*, what seems like an opposite turns out to be a double, as Algy becomes Bunbury and Jack becomes Earnest. Many critics fall into the trap of seeing in the play an obvious contrast between the cynicism of the town-dwellers and the tedious rectitude of the rural characters. That is not, however, how things work in practice, for characters like Chasuble and Prism contain the seeds of corruption from the start and Cecily has her most interesting, i.e. evil, inspirations in a garden. So every apparent dichotomy dichotomises in an art of endless inversion. Thus, the women in the play read heavy works of German philosophy and attend university courses, while the men lounge elegantly on sofas and eat cucumber sandwiches. Far from listening to the men in a time-honoured discussion of the finer points of female physique, we find the girls coolly assessing the physical appeal of the men. When Algernon proposes to Cecily, it is *she* who runs her fingers through *his* hair and sternly asks: 'I hope your hair curls naturally, does it?'; and the answer is 'Yes, darling, with a little help from others.' When Algernon rushes out, Cecily's instant response is 'What an impetuous boy he is! I like his hair so much.'

It would be facile to see this cult of inversion as Wilde's private little joke about his own homosexuality, for it is much more radical than that. At the root of his paradoxes is a scorn for the absolute Victorian distinction between male and female, which he sought to combat in his critical writings no less than in his art. So, in the *Pall Mall Gazette* of April 1888, he ironically welcomed M. Elmer Caro's *Life of George Sand* as 'the biography of a very great man from the pen of a very ladylike writer'. He went on to berate Caro for being 'too feminine to appreciate the grandeur of that large womanly nature, too much of a dilettante to realise the masculine force of that strong and ardent mind'.[62] Wilde's distinction of what is 'feminine' from what is truly 'womanly' is an example of the radical intelligence at work. As an Irishman at Oxford, he had doubtless heard endless disquisitions on the feminine or childish temperament of the Celts. The implications of that equation for Victorian conservatives were clear. Either as woman or as child the Irishman was incapable of self-government, unlike the manly Anglo-Saxon. At the root of many an Englishman's suspicion of the Irish was an unease about the woman or the child who lurked deep within himself. The flaunted effeminacy of Wilde, along with his espousal of the inner world of the child in his stories, may well constitute a sly comment on these hidden fears. The master of paradox is interested finally in the moment of modernism when the dualism is dissolved and the apparent polarities are shown to be identical. The exponent of antithesis employs this favourite device to question the manic Victorian urge to antithesis, which caused people to make absolute divisions not just between male and female, but also between black and white, native and foreign, English and Irish. Wilde saw that by this mechanism the English male could attribute to the Irish all those traits of poetry, emotion and soft charm which a stern Victorain code had led him to suppress in himself. But the dramatist saw that the two races are a lot more alike than they pretend, for he knew from experience that the Irish are as often cold, polite and calculating, as the English are sentimental, emotional and violent. In the same way, Wilde saw Victorian males demand that their women epitomise all those traits of softness, domesticity and fidelity which a harsh business world had led them to deny in themselves, but in his most famous play, he proved that such an antithesis does not work in practice. In *The Importance of Being Earnest*, it is the women who are businesslike and make cynical calculations about the financial attractiveness of a marriage proposal, while it is the men who are sentimental, breathless and impractical.

It is ironic, in this context, that the greatest mocker of the

Victorian urge to antithesis should ultimately have become its most spectacular victim, a casualty of the regime which fostered an excessive sense of difference between men and women. It was precisely because of the crazy policy of putting boys and girls in separate nurseries from the earliest age that the numbers of homosexuals and lesbians increased so greatly in the age of Victoria. Young men, denied a relationship with girls of their own age, were forced to reincarnate in themselves the missing female presence, and those youths with a stronger-than-average female dimension were often compelled by their schoolmates to impersonate the absent women. These trends could develop only in secret or illicit practices, because in public the Victorian was all-male. For his part, Wilde often confessed himself ashamed of his own homosexuality, which was the inexorable result of an educational system which denied those feminine components which form an aspect of every integrated personality. If the Victorians had not indulged this pretence of an absolute difference between men and women, the incidence of homosexuality and lesbianism might not have been so high. The findings of Kinsey and his modern researchers suggest that there is rarely such a being as an 'absolute homosexual' and that it makes better sense to speak of homosexually-oriented persons.[63] Kinsey posits instead a seven-point scale of human sexuality, ranging from o (absolute heterosexuality) to 6 (absolute homosexuality). He suggests that most men who have homosexual experiences appear on the scale between points i and 4, while continuing to enjoy heterosexual activities. His comments on homosexuality are very similar to Wilde's remarks on sexuality, as yet another dichotomy dichotomises:

> Males do not represent two discrete populations, heterosexual and homosexual. The world is not to be divided into sheep and goats. Not all things are black nor all things white, for nature rarely deals with discrete categories. Only the human mind invents categories and tries to force facts into separated pigeon-holes. The living world is a continuum in each and every one of its aspects. The sooner we learn this concerning human sexual behaviour, the sooner we shall reach a sound understanding of the realities of sex.[64]

In all likelihood, Wilde would have fallen by nature on some early point of Kinsey's scale, yet such were the constraints of his age that he seems to have been compelled to take up a position much closer to 5 or 6. This is a fate still cruelly reserved for many people who, finding no acceptance for the intermediate sexuality which they embody, choose instead to end the intolerable ambiguity of their plight by impersonating an absolute homosexuality which they do not feel. Hence the clichéd gestures of the 'camp' performer. In a similar fashion, Melville was forced in parts of *Moby Dick* to impersonate an absolute masculinity at odds with his true nature. Even today, that old Victorian antithesis persists in devious and distressing forms. Kinsey's research is not only an indictment of the intolerance of our ancestors, but a proof that the nineteenth century is still alive and well in the middle of the twentieth.

'Every step towards identity of habits between men and women', thundered Mrs Lynn Linton in *Nineteenth Century* in 1891, 'is a step downwards in refinement and delicacy – wherein lies the essential core of civilisation.'[65] Such sneers at women bold enough to wear sailor suits in public had no little effect on a generation which liked to remind its children that Joan of Arc had been burned at the stake for – among other crimes against nature – wearing male clothing. Samuel Butler once retailed an anecdote which may well explain the hysteria that is latent in such outbursts as Mrs Linton's:

A little boy and a little girl were looking at a picture of Adam and Eve.
'Which is Adam and which is Eve?' said one.
'I do not know', said the other, 'but I could tell if they had their clothes on.'[66]

This would have raised the heart of Wilde who knew that it is only shallow people who do not judge by appearances and who tirelessly repeated that people are at their most naked when they put their clothes on.

A recent historian of clothing has remarked that if a Martian had visited Victorian England and seen the clothes worn by the men and women there, he could have been forgiven for thinking that each sex belonged to a different species.[67] In the varied history of fashion over the past four centuries, it was only in the Victorian age that men presented themselves with no trace of the feminine. The Elizabethan gallant was admired for his shapely legs, starched ruff and ear-rings; the Restoration rake for his ribbons, muff and scent; the Romantics for their nipped-in waists, exotic perfumes and hour-glass shapes. (Lord Byron once confessed to wearing a corset, as did many men of his day, though one shudders to think what Lady Caroline Lamb would have said, if she found out.) Such details indicate that the androgyny of the male and female has rarely been fully suppressed and suggest that extreme homosexuality is more prevalent in those eras when men are not allowed to express a feminine dimension in direct and outgoing ways. Of course, one must also beware of reading too much symbolism into the language of costume. The outraged parents of today worry themselves sick about the psychological deformities of young couples who exchange clothing as if to prove that men and women are in all things alike; but they might be consoled to note on closer observation that their son's tee-shirt, as modelled by his latest girl-friend, is also a pointed reminder of the abiding biological difference.

These recent developments would have appealed greatly to Wilde. He had seen in his mother a woman who could edit journals and mount political campaigns as well as any man; and it was from her that he inherited a lifelong commitment to feminism. 'Why should there be one law for men and another for women?' asks Jack of Miss Prism, at the close of a play which has argued that there should be no rigid laws for either. In most of Wilde's plays, a similar question is asked. In *Lady Windermere's Fan*, Lord Darlington wonders if there should be identical laws for men and for women, and Lady Windermere replies 'Certainly.' If the double standard is right for men, then it is right for women; if it is wrong for women, then it is also wrong for men.

Along with Shakespeare, Wilde was one of those writers whose work justifies Virginia Woolf's famous observation that 'it is one of the tokens of the fully developed mind that it does not think specially or separately of sex'. Woolf found in Shakespeare a truth which the reawakened feminist movement was revealing to large numbers of radicals and artists, that 'it is fatal to be a man or woman pure and simple; one must be woman-manly or man-womanly'.[68] The resistance of men to that doctrine was even more dogged than the rearguard action against the suffragettes. The rights to vote and to work on an equal footing had long been conceded by men, who continued to deny the more far-reaching implications of the new androgyny. Women might become honorary men, as Defoe had predicted, but few men were prepared to become honorary women. Only a handful of radicals and artists – among them the six authors treated in the chapters of this book – had the courage for that. At the root of the defiant masculinity of the majority lay a fear of feminisation and of lost power. Like those tribes which do not allow male hunters to marry or mingle with women, men experienced the fear that the species itself was in decline. 'The strong woman should remain a symbol', said Balzac, 'she frightens when seen in reality.' For every man who was roused by the challenge of the masterful new woman, there were a dozen who were frightened into postures ranging from impotence to rage. Virginia Woolf's declaration in *A Room of One's Own* (1928) became a prophecy of the future, as well as an account of the past: 'the history of men's opposition to women's emancipation is more interesting perhaps than the story of that emancipation itself'.[69] It is with that male response to feminism – as reported and represented by six major male writers – that this work will now deal. That response will range from the dire despair of August Strindberg, through the qualified optimism of Ibsen and Hardy, to the fearless exploration of new manhood – and new womanhood – in the work of Yeats, Lawrence and Joyce. It is a story of growing hope and imagination, in the face of disillusion and defeat. In order to appreciate the achievements of the later writers, it is first necessary to consider the immensity of the problems which they faced. There could be no bleaker account of the impasse in which the New Woman and the passive man found themselves at the end of the nineteenth century than that given in the plays of Strindberg.

2 Strindberg's Villains: The New Woman as Predator

> God created Adam lord of all living creatures, but Eve spoiled
> it all.   Martin Luther

It is unfair to write Strindberg off as an arrant misogynist. He
was the first modern writer to make androgyny *the* central issue
in his accounts of sexual relations. Honest enough to admit the
female element in himself, he was sufficiently traditionalist to be
unnerved by the implications of that concession. His rage with
the feminists of his era is based not so much on his need to
humiliate women as on his compulsion to take massive revenge
on the woman in himself. The real reason for feminist distrust of
Strindberg is not his misogyny, which is melodramatic and stagey,
but the realisation that the first major artist to apply the radical
theories of androgyny was reduced to blind hatred, instead of
being elevated to wisdom.

Strindberg believes that male and female are at constant war,
not half so mortally in society as in the self. The self so divided
is doomed to become neither male nor female, but a 'characterless
character', devoid of the strenuous will which alone makes life a
triumph. Yet that fragmentation of the personality, which spells
the defeat of the forceful person, is the guarantee of his triumph
as an artist. The ferocious subjectivity of Strindberg does not mar
his dramatic tact, for he learns to see the world at varying times
through the eyes of each of his major characters, male and female,
aristocrat and serf. Like Keats, he knows that the poet is the most
unpoetical of God's creatures, having no identity of his own, but
rather a capacity to enter into the thoughts and feelings of others.
As an artist, Strindberg could celebrate this blessed state: 'I live
multifariously the lives of all the people I describe. I am happy
with the happy, evil with the evil, good with the good . . . All

34

opinions are mine, and I confess all creeds. I live in all ages, and my own self has ceased to exist. This is a state that brings indescribable happiness.'[1] Strindberg knew that the surest way to strengthen the intellect is to make up one's mind about nothing, but to let it be, in Keats's phrase, a thoroughfare for all thoughts. 'The moment I make up my mind to fight for this or that I feel tied', said Strindberg, 'and then I no longer grow.'[2] Yet it is this artistic capacity to see all points of view which finally reduced the man to moral and sexual paralysis. The master of the multiple self learns too late that he has no self that he can call his own. All he has is a set of gestures and performances, which do not constitute a full personality. In desperation, he seeks in the masterful woman the strong will which he deems to be lacking in himself and he hopes that such a woman will complete him as a man. But he is jealous of the very strength he courts in woman, for her mastery threatens not so much to complete as to shatter his self-composure. The man with no self has no self to give, and so his love is doomed from the start. Yet he persists and marries three women, an aristocrat, a journalist and an actress. In each case, his intellect tells him that he must love this woman as a comrade, while his emotions cause him to dread the very freedoms which the radical intellect bestows. He begins as a critic of traditional marriage, but ends as the scourge of his feminist comrades. His plays are studies in a failed androgyny, accounts of characterless characters who reincarnate in themselves his own tenuous, if multiple, self. Seeking versatility and a comprehensive wisdom, his protagonists shatter into fragments which pointlessly and painfully collide.

The Father provides a lucid example of the Strindbergian stalemate. Its central figure, the Captain, is given no name because he has no fixed identity, unlike his wife Laura and daughter Bertha. He believes himself to have been an unwanted child, born without a will of his own. 'Then, when you and I became one', he tells Laura, 'I felt myself strengthened by your will, and so I allowed you to be the master in the house. I – who was used to giving the commands to my troopers – I now became the one to take orders, and I grew to be part of you – looked up to you as to a superior intelligence.' Now, however, he feels himself a white slave rather than a husband, for he has discovered that women are nature's aristocrats and men nature's slaves. He believes, with some justification, that his wife is plotting to educate their daughter into the belief that male and female are opposed to each other in all respects. Rejecting such hateful motives, he holds that the differences between the sexes are the basis for complementarity rather than rivalry, and that these differences are not as great as they seem. Strindberg conspires in this valuation, if only by the frequency with which he inverts traditional sexual roles in the belief that they are interchangeable. So the Captain complains to his doctor that convention denies men the right to express the full range of their emotions. Men are not allowed self-analysis in the language of feeling, lest it seem like a failure of stoicism; but, for the Captain, grace under pressure is a poor substitute for true self-expression. Within minutes, his charge is vindicated when his wife mocks his flowing tears. In a sly paraphrase of Shylock, he repeats his point: 'Yes – I am crying, even though I am a man. But has a man not eyes? Has a man not hands, limbs, likes, dislikes, passions . . . ? If you prick us, do we not bleed – if you tickle us, do we not burst into laughter? If you poison us, do we not die? Then why should not a man complain, a soldier cry? Because it is not manly? Why is it not manly?' Such subtleties are lost on the wife, who sees in her husband the pathos of a dependent child rather than the honesty of an emotionally versatile man. His defect reinforces her defect, his jealousy and paranoia merely flatter her lust for dominance and power. She hates him only on those rare occasions when he is a man; otherwise, she despises his more usual weakness. He compares her feelings to racial hatred and helplessly concludes 'we two are not alike, are we?', a statement in direct contravention of his professed conviction.

This portrayal of human inconsistency in the irrational zone of sexual relations is one of Strindberg's great legacies. Succeeding writers such as Lawrence would henceforth be unafraid to create characters who blatantly contradicted themselves within the scope of a single work. To the modernist, consistency became the mark of the second-rate mind, which fails to appreciate just how often the seeming opposite is really a secret double. In the world of Strindberg, traits and emotions seem far stronger than the tenuous selves to which they are attached; and often an attribute can pass from one man to another in the course of a short scene. At the start of *The Father* the Pastor recalls how Laura, as a child, would lie prostrate until she got what she wanted – at which point she gave it back. Later in the same scene, however, Laura makes an identical complaint against her husband – that he wants his way in everything, but as soon as he gets his wish, he drops the matter and pleads with her to decide. The doctor gravely announces that the Captain's will is impaired, with the likelihood that his mind and soul will disintegrate. At the root of this scene is Strindberg's conviction, based on his own experience, that as soon as a man admits the female elements in himself, he becomes weak, will-less and vacillating – just as, in a later play, Miss Julie, the manly woman, will despair of her capacity to do anything and will be forced to ask her servant to order her like a dog. In both characters, male and female elements are stalemated in a war of attrition, mutually self-cancelling rather than jointly enriching. Miss Julie has to cajole a servant into helping her stage-manage her own suicide, but at least she has the aristocratic courage for that. Such bleak dignity is denied Strindberg's men, to whom it is given to long for suicide but never to find the inner resources to commit it.

And yet it is Strindberg's men who bleat on endlessly about their honour. Like Ibsen's Helmer, the Captain insists that a man cannot live without honour, and he receives much the same reply as Helmer did from his wife: 'But a woman can.' The Captain explains this by arguing that the wife always has her children to live for, whereas no man can ever be certain that his child is truly his own. If a man were wholly honest, therefore, he would speak of 'my wife's children', a point endorsed by James Joyce many years later.[3] It is this alienation from the procreative powers of woman which leaves Strindberg's men riven with self-doubt, jealousy and, above all, a crippling sense of their own marginality. His captains and lawyers are emotionally marooned, unsure of the love of their wives. Having ceded all power to his wife, the Captain is foolish enough to enter combat with a stronger antagonist, who cannot look at a man without feeling herself his natural superior. Determinist enough to believe the old male lie that might is right, the husband can only await his inevitable downfall in sadness and foreboding. While he waits, he turns for comfort to his child, only to find in her the same terrors and doubts which led him to seek out her company.

In the eyes of a parent, each child is an androgynous being, a blend of both fatherly and motherly attributes. The Captain, disbelieving in the hereafter, finds in his daughter the only embodiment of his idea of a life after death. He looks into her eyes in search of his soul, only to find his wife's soul as well. So, the inner conflict between male and female which paralysed the Captain's will is reincarnated in his child. Already, Bertha's own sense of selfhood has grown fragile, as each parent seeks to make her wholly his or her own. 'I don't want that!', she protests, 'I want to be myself.' It could be the epitaph for her father, who never even achieved that rudimentary sense of identity. He has sought a partner but found a rival because, as he had suspected all along, he and his wife were too similar for their own good. Her androgynous nature is a great deal more covert in its manifestations than his, but all the more deep-seated for that. What made the Captain so attractive to her in the first place was his yielding nature, which seemed the ideal complement to her aggressive personality. Now, however, that shared androgyny which made the relationship possible is preventing its fulfilment. She can love the Captain as if he were a child, but each time he approaches her as a manly lover, she feels disgusted and ashamed. The mother-turned-mistress is not a role she cherishes, and so she hates him 'when you are a man'. (The fact that she can equally mock him for unmanly tears is just one of the many interesting inconsistencies in her personality.) Although he noticed her distaste for his sexual overtures, he mistakenly put this down to her contempt for his uncertain manhood; and so he exacerbated the problem by making himself seem even more virile than he really wished to be. In seeking to make himself more attractive, he becomes only more odious to his wife. If he had had the courage to be himself, all would have been well, but because he insisted on impersonating a traditional hero, he incurred her wrath and his own sexual failure. There is nobody more unattractive than the man who cannot accept himself.

Strindberg's implications could hardly be clearer. Passivity in the male is not to be suppressed as a mark of weakness. It may rather be seen as the attribute of a rich personality which has the strength to expose all its aspects, its doubts as well as its assertions. Only the truly strong have the courage to confess their weaknesses and this is a principle which the Captain understands but fails to apply in his own marriage. The uncertain male is only weak, says Strindberg, when he lacks the courage to express his hesitations. In similar fashion, the self-assertive woman is not all-powerful, because her very power creates new problems which must produce, even in the most confident women, a state of confusion and doubt. Hence the contradictions within a woman as forceful as Laura. Her tragedy is finally her husband's – that her level of androgyny is even closer to equilibrium than his, but she lacks the courage to admit this and to tell him what she really wants, until it is too late.

In casting his uncertain male hero as a military leader and theorist, Strindberg sought to emphasise the nature of a character who could be sturdily masculine in his professional life, even as he sought to express his feminine attributes in the life of the emotions. Despite this, a whole generation of feminist critics has fastened on the Captain's stridency, as if it arose from the crass certitude of a chauvinist bigot, rather than the uncertainty of a self-tormented soul. Germaine Greer sees the Captain (and, by implication, Strindberg) as a traditional psychologist who arbitrarily assumes that women have been subjected to conditioning which is improper to their biological function of breeding children and tidying houses. 'The unsuspecting woman seeks aid from psychiatry because she's unhappy, and psychology persuades her to seek the cause in herself', complains Greer, adding the bleak afterthought that 'the person is easier to change than the status quo'.[4] But, if anything, the recent experience of feminists proves just the reverse – that it is comparatively easy to change laws and statutes, but far more difficult to prepare oneself for the full psychological implications of these changes. Even a woman as liberated as Bertha has not fully confronted her androgynous nature, and in this respect she lags far behind her husband, who may be a misogynist, but is certainly *not* a traditional psychologist. If he were that, he would scarcely have gone in search of a lifelong relationship with a masterful woman. His nostalgia for a time when one married a wife and enjoyed sensual love is seen by Greer as a failure to admit that marriage is at root a business partnership. Such a taunt is ignoble. The Captain never asked his wife to be what she was not and, if anybody was foolish enough to try changing the self rather than the situation, it was he, in the pathetic attempt to seem more manly. In that sense, at least, his plight is that of the very women whose rights Germaine Greer seeks to defend, for he spent his nights trying to negotiate the painful discrepancies between his true nature and the manly person that society wanted him to be. If his wife at times speaks coldly of their marriage as an affair of calculation and self-interest, that may be seen as the new woman's self-protective refusal to expose herself through excessive emotion. She makes it perfectly clear that she loved him when they married and that she believes in the emotions which should attend that contract. In seeking to reduce marriage to a business deal and the play to an anti-feminist tract, Germaine Greer is in grave danger of shrugging off the mantle of Emily Pankhurst for that of Jane Austen.

*   *   *

Strindberg's mastery of the art of inversion is demonstrated even more triumphantly in *Miss Julie*, a play whose plot hinges not only on the discrepancies between the sexes, but also on the differences between the classes. This bleak drama tells of how an aristocratic young lady seeks to seduce a manservant of her father in a short, sharp, pointless relationship which culminates in her suicide. In this case, it is the woman and not the man who will die rather than lose honour. The manservant, being of the lower orders, can survive and prosper untrammelled by the self-destructive aristocratic notions of 'face' and 'reputation'. It is Strindberg's implication that he is the truer aristocrat, who uses brain and muscle to survive, and that Julie, like Hedda Gabler, is the last of a decadent aristocratic line, which somehow or other finds the saving grace to abolish itself. The shrewd and the resourceful will inherit the earth from those whom they supplant; and in his preface to the play the author claims to uphold this Darwinian belief. Yet his drama is a great deal more subtle, in its insistence on how much both classes have in common, if only their pretensions to other ways of living. While Jean the servant affects a taste for wine, Miss Julie prefers the workingman's beer. While Jean insists fastidiously on heated plates for dinner, Miss Julie dances with gamekeepers and doubtless follows her mother's example in wearing dirty cuffs. Moreover, the play has not progressed far before each character is caught in some glaring contradiction on the question of the classes. At one stage, Jean can plead the cause of the lower orders and, at another moment, dissociate himself from the riff-raff at the dance. Miss Julie can disown her aristocratic background, while at the same time issuing peremptory orders. The ultimate effect of all this is to throw into question the notions of rank and degree. If humans are at once so pretentious and so interchangeable, then a class-based society is a farce. The differences between the classes may be erased in due time, if we are to judge by the relations between Miss Julie and Jean; but the sexual differences between men and women are shown by Strindberg to be tragically irreconcilable.[5]

By making his heroine an aristocrat, the playwright is testing the hint, thrown out in *The Father*, that women rather than men are nature's aristocrats. But it is not long till he comes to a more complex conclusion. Miss Julie may be the social aristocrat on this particular stage, but Jean is undoubtedly the sexual aristocrat, 'because of his male strength, his more acutely developed senses, and his capacity for taking the initiative' (Preface).[6] So the scales at the start are finely balanced, as the traditional constraints on women are mitigated by Miss Julie's rank. In this sense, the plot is an outright reversal of the norms of classic melodrama, where the tyrannical overlord exercised his *droit de seigneur* over a luckless maidservant whom he left in the lurch. All through the nineteenth century, the maidservant had been the major sexual opportunity of a closed and prurient society. 'Economic control seemed to guarantee erotic control', writes Mary Ellmann, 'and for the sadistic, exceptional rights of discipline lay in the relationship of employer and employee.'[7] Indeed, she cites an event from Strindberg's own youth, when a maidservant uncovered his body as he slept, for which crime he was entitled to whip her. 'Both to their own diversions', comments the acid lady critic, but one can appreciate just how fascinating to a mind like Strindberg's was the prospect of inverting the sexual identities of the protagonists in this particular situation.

Miss Julie is introduced as a predatory version of the New Woman, a man-hater who makes her fiancé jump like a dog, while she flails his back with a whip. It is not clear whether he or she breaks off the engagement but, given such exotic behaviour, it is not hard to guess. Soon her interest is aroused by the manservant Jean. She invokes her rights as an employer in order to compel him to keep her company, but with due decorum he insists that he was not hired to be her playmate, that he is above that. Already, however, their personalities are beginning to merge. Whereas Jean had earlier pronounced Miss Julie too haughty in some respects, and too abject in others, *now* he tells her that *he* is proud in some ways, if not in others. That may, of course, be just a ploy to whet her interest. At any rate, one of the fascinations of the play is the way in which the initiative ebbs and flows, now to Julie, now to Jean. Character develops in a jagged fashion in the work of this playwright, whose greatest gift is to hint constantly at levels of meaning below the surface of things. It is never fully clear whether Jean is exciting his mistress by passive provocation, or whether she is actively seducing him. Strindberg may not even know himself, but may simply be anxious to show how, in the decisive moments of their lives, people often act under the sway of forces which are not fully clear to them at the time. At all events, one moment Miss Julie is teasing the reluctant Jean into a mild flirtation, and the next she is cravenly begging this servant, who has violated her honour, to take her away from her father's house. She tries to clothe her erotic adventure in the idiom of romantic love, but Jean cruelly reminds her that she has only done what many others have done before her. At heart, she knows that his power over her was the spell which the strong will always cast over the weak, the man on the rise over the woman on the wane. Yet inconsistencies remain. She professes to have divested herself of aristocratic pretensions, yet cannot bear the prospect of public outrage at her loss of honour to an underling. He professes to be a democrat, yet anticipates with relish the prospect of Swiss citizens prostrating themselves before his porter's uniform. He protests that men are all the same at root, yet finds it hurtful to learn that the aristocratic glamour of Miss Julie is so insubstantial. He talks as if he already felt himself above her, yet he will quake before the return of her father at the end. In the meantime, he dreams of escape with Miss Julie in an alliance based not on a self-deluding love, but on a shrewd sense of mutual material self-interest. While she toys with this proposal, Miss Julie recounts the details of a life that has turned her at once into a ruined aristocrat and a New Woman.

Her tale might be that of the Captain's daughter in *The Father*, for in this case, too, the androgyny of the child is less a source of hope than an outcome of revenge. Strindberg does not see in it the promise of an integrated personality, but the signs of a bitter battle between husband and wife. For Miss Julie came into the world, unwanted by her frustrated mother, who created a manly daughter in order to revenge herself on her hated husband, and to free the child from the necessity of repeating her own error of dependence on a man. In addition to her conventional training, Miss Julie was made to wear boy's clothes, perform boy's chores with horses, and given a harsh training, in order to demonstrate the mother's thesis that a woman is as good as any man. In retrospect, it is clear that the androgyny of Miss Julie appeals to her mother not only as a source of revenge, but also as a mode of consolation. The lonely woman, estranged from her husband, liberates the hidden male in her daughter in order to console herself for the lack of a man in her deepest emotional life. She recreates in her daughter the male companion she cannot find in her husband; and, while she defrauds her husband in business and betrays him in life, she teaches her daughter to vow eternal enmity to the sex. Her *coup de grâce* is to run the family estate as a kind of inverts' colony, where men perform domestic chores and women undertake the heavy labouring, with the result that it falls into ruin.

Miss Julie lives out the implications of this devastating programme of female revenge. She becomes engaged to the county prosecutor, with the purpose of whipping him into submission. Bored with this diversion, she gives her body to the servant Jean and plays on his bad conscience in an attempt to lure him into marriage. She reminds him of what a man owes to a woman of whom he has taken advantage, but his only reply is to toss her a coin and to make a thoroughly Strindbergian complaint against the law which provides no punishment for the woman who seduces a man. In this, at least, he exposes the radical inconsistency of Miss Julie, who claims all the freedoms of a man, while continuing to assume all the traditional privileges of a woman. Moreover, in contrasting the sexual attitudes of the aristocracy with those of their servants, he exposes the greatest flaw of all in Miss Julie, the fact that, like all those with the leisure to make of love a complex art, she is nothing less than preposterous in the expectations which she invests in her own sexuality. She commits the error of seeking in sex the enlightenment which men once expected only from the deepest experience of religion. Jean rebukes her for it:

> Miss Julie – I know you must be suffering – but I can't understand you . . . . We have no such strange notions as you have – we don't hate as you do! To us love is nothing but playfulness – we play when our work is done. We haven't the whole day and the whole night for it like you! I think you must be sick . . .

This cuts to the heart of Strindberg's critique of modern sexuality. He knows that with the massive opportunities for leisure among all classes, what was once a merely aristocratic affectation has now become the besetting vice of nations. The element of play has rapidly been lost in sexual relationships, which are now conducted with a solemn self-analytical intensity once the preserve of mere aristocrats. The substance of Jean's complaint is that people like Miss Julie now approach lovemaking with a puritanical solemnity. The art of love has grown so morbidly self-conscious, as Christopher Lasch has drily observed, that it is now a surprise to encounter a manual in which the epithet 'sexual' is divorced from the noun 'performance'.[8] 'Froken Julie, c'est moi.'

It was not always so. In medieval times, sex was a boisterous game which provoked even children to riotous mirth; and this attitude lasted down to the seventeenth century.[9] Only then was playful sex converted into serious discourse. Thereafter, according to Michel Foucault, the flesh was deemed the source of all evil and the moment of transgression was located not in the act of sex, but in the stirrings of desire.[10] The search for 'occasions of sin' in dreams and actual situations gave rise to a self-conscious discourse, which resulted in the displacement and intensification of desire itself. Whereas the ancient *ars erotica* involved the search for pleasure for its own sake in a secret lore shared only by master and disciple, the modern science of sex must measure pleasure in relation to the law of the permitted and the forbidden, in a confessional rhetoric which exposes all secret discoveries in the self of public scrutiny. Foucault holds that a *scientia sexualis* usurped the *ars erotica* and men who had feared that they could imagine no new pleasure surprised themselves with their pleasure in the knowledge of pleasure.[11] After the seventeenth century, such knowledge became the preserve of the upper class, but for a long period the lower classes escaped the dubious privilege of a self-monitored sexuality. As Jean hints to Miss Julie, those whose task is to fill a day with work are not expected to cultivate theories of pleasure or to degrade sexuality into a science.

Although workers were shamelessly repressed in economic and political affairs, their sexuality went unrestricted by rulers forever anxious for cannon-fodder. For centuries, these leaders were concerned only with the sexual health and primogeniture of the aristocracy, whose lives were constantly hedged with rules. Only when the workers discovered the wonders of birth control, says

Foucault, did the upper classes initiate a crusade for the conversion of the masses to true morality. With the emergence of the bourgeoisie, the old aristocratic obsession with blood lineage was replaced by the modern concern for heredity. Families were no longer symbolised by heraldic crests but by hereditary ailments, like the syphilis inherited by the son in Ibsen's *Ghosts* or the decayed teeth of artistic sons in the burgher families of Thomas Mann. Miss Julie perfectly epitomises this bankruptcy of the aristocratic ideal as it faces the exactions of the bourgeois world. She is the last of her line. Her coat of arms will be broken against her coffin, for she has been destroyed by a mere family ailment. From her parents she has inherited thinned blood and an over-fastidious sexuality. Already, as she borrows ideas and sentences from her servant, she exudes that longing for death which is at the root of all plagiarism. Her personality is one that has lived through the consequences of its own extinction before it has even begun to exist. Yet she retains at least one trait of the old aristocracy to which Jean could never hope to aspire, the capacity for excruciating self-analysis. 'Stop thinking, stop thinking', yells Jean, as she goes out to die rather than lose honour. But she cannot. In this, too, Miss Julie inverts the norms of her sex, to which it was not given to engage in protracted self-analysis of sexual options. By convention and tradition, women did not elaborately plot proposals but simply offered a direct response to an overture. Denied the time for extended self-appraisal (which was the privilege of the male lover), their position in that respect resembled that of the lower orders. Jean implies this in stating that the class difference between himself and Miss Julie is 'the same difference – as – between man and woman'.

It is Miss Julie's tragedy to bear the burden of an overwhelming guilt, yet never to have an assured sense of the self which sinned. Her plight repeats that of Arthur Dimmesdale in *The Scarlet Letter*. He, too, has done no wrong, but is tortured by shame and guilt, precisely because the convicting intelligence is so much stronger than the offending instinct. Miss Julie's sexual impulses are weak and uncertain, but it is her hyperactive mind which finally divests her of any sense of self. Instead, her tortured self-analyses disintegrate her own personality into a series of impersonations learned from others – self-contempt acquired from a father who taught her to distrust women; hatred of men imbued from a fanatical mother; aristocratic pride learned from both; egalitarian principles learned from her fiancé. Such attributes do not coalesce to form a definite personality which is greater than the sum of its parts. Instead, each quality manages to cancel another out, leaving Miss Julie prey to an inauthenticity which is all the more painful because she has just enough intelligence to know how little she really has. Unlike Kristin, she cannot offload her moral scruples onto a comforting but mindless Christianity. As Strindberg wrote elsewhere: 'an individual who does not think for himself has – because of this very fact – a vigorous belief in himself.'[12] Miss Julie, on the other hand, has the courage to accept responsibility for a self which she is doomed never to know.

In the end, she kills herself because she has no self to kill. Her plight is that of the ventriloquist's dummy, held accountable for the vices of its master. If there is something histrionic and stagey about her actions and inactions, that is only because the naturalist who has abolished God is left feeling like an actor of bit parts. The dummy remains after the master ventriloquist has gone, marooned onstage without a script or the possibility of action. Miss Julie's plight is that of a broken aristocracy, but also, by inference, that of all modern democrats who must share in the civilised disabilities of the aristocracy, if they want to live in a world where every man is a king. In the world of the sovereign self, no self has any final sovereignty. Mass democracy is simply the freedom of the masses to conform to a culture of mediocrity, where the admired images will be chosen by the vulgar rather than the fastidious. 'Oh, I am so tired', says Miss Julie, 'I have no strength to do anything – not even to feel repentant – or to get away from here – or to stay here – to live – or to die! . . . Help me, please! Order me to do something – and I'll obey like a dog.' The last words of this doomed aristrocrat become the themesong of democratic man, who may inherit the earth, but not the ability to rule it. The old repressive régime has built a replica of itself in the head of the porter who, once he has donned his servingman's coat, lacks the willpower to give orders to his master's daughter. Conditioning is everything, the self a puny *tabula rasa* which simply records the inexorable traces of that social conditioning. The lower orders would gladly cut their own throats at the request of their masters, but left to their own devices, they are as incapable of purposeful action as Miss Julie. She has enough of the serf in her to find the prospect of an honourable suicide painful and so, in the end, her death, like her life, must be performed as an act rather than executed as an action. Jean must deploy his histrionic abilities, perfected at the theatre, in order to impersonate the aristocratic voice that nerves the serf-like Julie for her self-destruction. In the Strindbergian world, all acts are gratuitous, motivation is a farce, and anyone who wishes to do must first learn not to think. The world of the play is filled with interpretations, yet nothing is certain for these people, who feel oppressed rather than enlightened by the sheer volume of information available.

The notion of character proposed in the famous preface to *Miss Julie* is immensely rich in promise, but the play demonstrates how the multiple self poses far more problems than it solves. Rejecting the one-dimensional puppets of traditional drama, who are dominated by a single motive such as Harpagon's miserliness or a single phrase such as 'Barkis is willin' ', Strindberg proposes a more complex character who is the exponent of a whole series of underlying motives. So Miss Julie's catastrophic fling with Jean may be attributed to her father's stunted upbringing of her, the prejudices ingrained by her mother, her recent break with her fiancé, her monthly period, the festive occasion of a midsummer dance, and so on. No longer can the spectator isolate the single motive most flattering to his personal prejudice or intellectual judgement. The ultimate effect of these diverse explanations is to suggest the patent inadequacy of anyone to account for the actions of a character as impulse-ridden as Miss Julie. Along with Strindberg's recognition of the multiplicity of her possible motives goes the even more radical suggestion that such a woman need have no particular reason for committing a momentous action. The dramatist thus discriminates the notion of 'character' from that of 'temperament', which once denoted the domination of a particular humour in the constitution of a personality.

Strindberg rescues the word 'character' from its distortion by a middle class which learned to equate it with steadfast virtue. A man was popularly held to have character when he had become an automaton, fixed in a single specialist role without potential for growth, whereas the man who was still developing and changing was held to be fickle and 'lacking in character'. The bourgeoisie loved made men and despised men in the making, for they were impossible to pin down. Hence the middle-class obsession with the need to choose a career, to define a specialist sense of self by means of a vocation.[13] How many great novels from *Mansfield Park* to *Middlemarch* present young men hesitating fatally on the brink of such a decision. In the former novel Edmund Bertram is admired for his forthright choice of the Church as surely as Will Ladislaw is distrusted for his endless vacillation in the latter. Ladislaw is something of an artist, always remaking himself, but that dynamic irresolution which enriches the artist's personality spells the ruination of the bourgeois in his life. Hence the puritan opposition to the theatricals and play-acting proposed in *Mansfield Park*; and hence, also, the dominance of the middle-class notion of character in theatres anxious to pass muster with a suspicious bourgeoisie.

Unfortunately, Strindberg's redefined version of 'character' is scarcely as liberating as it seems. The multiple self is just a series of impersonations and the freedom to cultivate a protean personality turns out to be the freedom to be like everybody else. So Kristin lives by the clichés of her pastor's Sunday sermon: Miss Julie purloins ideas and phrases from her servant Jean, who in turn learns how to ape his betters by studying performances in his local theatre. Each person has a frighteningly tenuous sense of selfhood, and each turns for inspiration to others who are secretly even more unsure than he. The modern personality, in craving for anonymity, resembles the chameleon who takes on the protective coloration of his surroundings. Such a person dons many differing guises with the humble intention of fading into various crowds, the sporting, the formal, the elegantly casual, etc. Most people dress to conform with the world rather than to stand out from it. Consequently, the multiple self which they cultivate is not exhibitionist, but the reverse – although these timid souls would never suspect it, they resemble nothing so much as the gangsters of nineteenth-century Paris who sought shelter in the mob. They can 'multiply variety in a wildernerss of mirrors', but, like Strindberg's characters, they know that each performance is but a pale imitation of a pale imitation.

In that respect, the new methods of characterisation in *Miss Julie* uncannily anticipate the mass-men of the following age. The exponent of all selves turns out to be a man without qualities. If, like those of the lower orders, he is forced to fix on a specialist sense of self in a definite career, this merely heightens the problem. All actions other than those which fall within the strict confines of his professional duty seem bogus and are performed without conviction – the accountant who hammers a crooked nail into a wall performs his deed with the same dismissive shrug that Jean reserves for his impersonations of aristocratic manners. Worse still, the specialist skill itself soon becomes an 'act', precisely because it is repeated so often. The abstracted and detached way in which Kristin performs her tasks as cook (which provoked such derision in Strindberg's early critics) is a perfect illustration of the modern character whose work engages only a fragment of the personality. A person is now praised for being 'professional' when he performs an assignment with cool impersonality, when the deeper elements of his personality are withheld for the duration of the assignment. So, Strindberg gives a bleaker and more complex meaning to the phrase 'lacking in character' which is, paradoxically, a function of the multiple self. He sees, more than half a century before Beckett, how repetition will be the characterising feature of the modern person. The telephonist who relays a simple message for the twenty-seventh time in a morning necessarily begins to monitor and despise his own patter as a mere performance, exacted by an increasingly specialist world.

*   *   *

In the preface to *Miss Julie* may be found the following analysis. It was written *after* the play was completed and applies more justly to another play published in the same year, 1888, under the ironic title *Comrades*:

> Miss Julie is a modern character. Not that the half-woman, the man-hater, has not existed since time immemorial but because she has now been discovered, has trod into the open and begun to create a stir. The half-woman of today is a type who pushes herself forward; today she is selling herself for power, decorations, aggrandisement, diplomas, as she did formerly for money; and the type is indicative of degeneration. It is not a wholesome type and it is not enduring, but unfortunately it can reproduce and transplant its misery into another generation. And degenerate men seem instinctively to choose their mates from among such women; and so they multiply and bring into the world progeny of indeterminate sex, to whom life becomes a torture. Fortunately, however, they come to an end, either from being unable to face and withstand life, or from the irresistible rebellion of their

suppressed desires, or because their hope of coming up to men has been thwarted. It is a tragic type, revealing the spectacle of a desperate struggle against nature . . .[14]

This vituperative passage is written with a deeply personal rage and the self-laceration implicit in the phrase 'degenerate men' leaves nothing to the imagination. The man who accused his aristocratic wife, Siri von Essen, of putting her acting career and lesbian love-affairs ahead of their marriage lurks far more transparently behind these lines than behind the play which they purport to explain. In dealing with Strindberg's notorious misogyny, it is well to recall that he describes it as 'the reverse side of my fearful attraction to the other sex',[15] an attraction which always found its focus in some spirited, self-sufficient woman. If Strindberg can be convicted of strident antifeminism, that is only because he found such masterful women of boundless interest and could fall in love with no other kind. He reserved his scorn for the mindless Kristins of this world, but to the feminists of his day he paid the subtle tribute of an anger without parallel in the history of drama. He once planned to visit Ibsen in Rome in the spring of 1884, saying that he wanted to see the angriest man in Europe before he died, but he cancelled the trip and looked into a mirror instead.

Strindberg's is not the rage of an antifeminist bigot, but the anger of a frustrated radical. *Comrades* is a study of applied feminism by a man who endorsed the ideal of 'a woman who could earn her living, someone he could look upon as an equal and who would be a companion for life, and not a mere housekeeper'.[16] Four years earlier, in a story entitled 'An Attempt at Reform', Strindberg had used these words to describe such a free-spirited marriage, but this ideal is shattered by the birth of a child which marks the end of the woman's career. Yet Strindberg never fell into the trite belief that a woman's biology is her destiny. At the root of all his rage with human biology is the conviction that there should not be one law for men and another for women.

Comrades begins on that feminist premise and proceeds to demonstrate just how few men and women truly accept it. Axel and Bertha are artists who live together as comrades in the belief that friendship is finer and more lasting than love. Axel's friends are outraged by his bland acceptance of Bertha's right to work unchaperoned in a room with a nude male model. He counters with an exposure of their hypocrisy, pointing out that they see nothing amiss in a man working in similar circumstances with a woman. Yet, before the end of the act, Axel is compelled to admit to a similar hypocrisy in himself. Despite his radicalism, he still finds it more repulsive to see a drunken woman than a drunken man. This minor confusion is as nothing compared with the massive hypocrisy of Bertha, who pretends to be a comrade but is really a competitor. She invokes all the traditional privileges of the genteel stay-at-home wife, while at the same time claiming the rights of an emancipated woman. So Axel has to pay for her painting lessons and professional expenses, put his own artistic reputation at risk by endorsing her dubious claims to hang in galleries, and support her in the old chivalric way. This he does, even to the point of submitting his own superior paintings under her name and enduring public humiliation when he submits her shoddy work under his own. In return, he receives not gratitude and love, but cold contempt. Bertha hears the news that 'his' picture has been rejected by the Salon without a flicker of emotion, other than the immediate response 'How about me?' While his first thought is always of her, Bertha's is always of herself. When he accepts the rejection of his painting and decides to become a draftsman instead, she replies: 'You won't have to. As soon as I begin to sell, I can take care of myself.' But not of him. She is no comrade, merely a woman seeking self-sufficiency.

It is Axel rather than Bertha who emerges as the real radical in this play. Bertha is still traditional enough to see divorce as a blot on a man's honour and it is this conventional morality which allows her to insist on the old-fashioned deference due to a wife. Her friend Abel exposes the purely theoretical nature of her feminism by asking Bertha 'Why should a man have any special respect for a woman when they are supposed to be equals?' Bertha persists, however, for her real desire is to use all strategies available to a woman to humiliate her husband and she knows that the old code of manners offers far more opportunities in this regard than the new. This woman, who rolls her own cigarettes, wants all the privileges of the female along with the powers of the male. She has fallen into the common error of mistaking liberation for the right to imitate the traditional callousness of men. Axel has enough of the woman in him to find this aspiration derivative and boring. 'If you women want to do something, do something which we men have not done before!' It is scarcely the statement of a man enamoured with the achievement of his fellows; and he is remarkably free of the male vanity which, despite her protestations, is the key to Bertha's personality. Her exhilaration at finding a man so free of traditional prejudices is such that she cannot resist converting the freedoms he gives into an opportunity for revenge. The disabilities endured by women are so crippling that it is hard for them to accept the good faith of the rare male who tries to remove them. So Bertha goes to work on her spouse, fastening upon the female element in his personality, which seemed so rich and promising, and turning it into an occasion for his degradation. She, rather than Miss Julie, is Strindberg's most comprehensive study of the half-woman man-hater. At the root of her hatred of her husband's tactful consideration is her hatred of the woman in herself. She wants to be a man and so she turns the feminine element in her husband's personality into a revolting caricature of degraded womanhood. At heart, she really believes in the necessary subjugation of women. Her attitude is identical to that of the heroine of Strindberg's short story called 'The Stronger One', who turns her husband into a laughing-stock: 'But what was ludicrous about it was not that he did chores that are ordinarily performed by women; it was the fact that he alone did them. Had they both done these tasks, neither of them would have appeared ridiculous.'[17]

So, in *Comrades*, the manly woman Bertha sets about the systematic degradation of her womanly man. Their androgyny is a painful humiliation rather than a liberation, as the myth of complementary lovers is shattered by the fact of their rivalry. 'The struggle for position has come between us', says Axel, 'from now on we can never be friends again.' The man who was first to concede that men and women are a great deal more alike than convention admits is also the first to discover that this does not spell the end of their troubles. The equalisation of the sexes may simply cause each to reincarnate in the self the most odious qualities of the other. Bertha assumes the aggression and harshness of the male, but not his sense of honour and principle; Axel takes on the passivity and weakness of the woman, but not her sensitivity and charm. The feminists profess a belief in androgyny, but secretly despise the man weak enough to take them at their word. The emancipated lady-friend Abel feels obliged to put Axel wise:

Abel: Do you call yourself a man? You who are toiling for a woman and go about dressed like a woman –

Axel: I – dressed like a woman?

Abel: You have a bang and go barenecked, while she wears a high collar and has her hair cut like a boy. Watch out, Axel! Soon she will take your pants from you!

Axel: What silly nonsense!

Yet he is sufficiently distraught by his uncertain manhood to make a virtual proposition to the mannish Abel in this very scene. In part, his imagination is challenged by her apparent immunity to romantic feeling; and no doubt his feminine susceptibilities are roused by a woman with 'the mentality of a man'. But, in the main, his proposition seems an attempt to prove something to himself. In this respect, he acts on behalf of his author. Many great dramatic scenes are found to recapitulate some decisive moment in a writer's life, but only rarely do they anticipate the crisis which Strindberg was to describe in a letter to his third wife in 1901: 'The day after we were wed, you declared that I was not a man. A week later you were eager to let the world know that you were not yet the wife of August Strindberg, and that your sisters considered you "unmarried". Was that kind? And was it wise?'[18]

Abel is by far the most interesting character in *Comrades*, if only because her character is a much more self-conscious and honest blend of female convention and feminist conviction than Bertha's. She cheerfully admits that her lack of feeling is the key to her success, which will always be denied the sentimental Axel. She has contempt for the effeminate men like Axel who are attracted to her sturdy personality, and she admits that if she met a masterful man, then she would love him. Her native intelligence makes her sceptical of all devotees of -isms, for 'anything stupid or inane can grow into a movement'. She is fully alert to the hypocrisy of Bertha, yet surprisingly willing to collude with it. After Axel has been uncharacteristically dominant in conversation with Bertha, Abel comments with some sarcasm: 'How cocky your lord and master was.' This suggests that she is as two-faced as Bertha, *for* male dominance in theory but *against* it in practice. She suggests that Bertha could best humiliate her husband by ensuring that his rejected painting is returned during a party planned at his house on the following day. So she conspires to degrade the very man with whom she has just spoken in strictest confidence. Yet she is fair-minded enough to believe that Bertha should have shared the proceeds of a sale with her comrade, rather than secretly keeping all the money for herself. Because the old-fashioned law stipulates that a wife owes no earnings to her husband, she hypocritically counsels Bertha to take advantage of that technicality, 'if for no other reason than to make an example of him'. Neither woman admits that Axel's anger with his wife (for not telling of her sale) is that of a thwarted comrade rather than a greedy husband. In the event, both women find unacceptable the notion that the same law should apply to men and to women. So, while Bertha spreads false rumours about Axel, he makes it clear that he will never make public reference to the financial and artistic help which he gave her.

Axel's degradation continues. While Bertha publicly compels him to don the costume of a Spanish lady for his own party, she privately asks the maid if he has ever made indiscreet overtures to her. But he was always the perfect gentleman. Now, however, his wife's refusal to share the proceeds of her sale has convinced him that she married him not for love, but for material self-interest. He feels unclean in his marriage and wants no more of it:

> It now looks to me as if I had fallen into the hands of an adventuress who tried to entice my money away from me in a hotel-room; and I almost feel as if I had been living in sin after being married to you! (He gets up.) As you stand there with your back turned to me and I see the back of your head with your cropped hair, I feel as if – well, it's just as if – ugh! – as if you were Judith and had given your body to me so that you could have my head. There – there is the costume I was to wear in order that you might debase me! Yes, for you know it would be debasing to wear those thick folds that were meant to hide in order to entice – this corseted bodice with its low neck that was intended to show off what I had to offer . . . Oh no! Here is the payment for your love! I am casting off the chains. (He throws down his wedding ring.)

He forbears from striking her, but only, he says, because she is morally irresponsible, and so, instead, he forces her to her knees. It is at this point that Bertha's real beliefs become clear. Rather

han vilify her husband for resorting to brute force, she announces
hat she is now passionately in love with this masterful stranger
who has suddenly emerged. It is the feminine principle which she
secretly hates, but she can love this fascinating new tyrant who
has thrown his Spanish costume away. For his part, Axel cannot
forsake his radicalism so easily. 'To be good is to be stupid – so
let us be mean to each other', he says parodically, 'is that what
you mean?' Unfortunately, it is, for she can love an oppressor
more easily than a weakling. She will even share his love with
another woman, so long as he says he loves her; but the truth is
that she no longer attracts him and he has found another.
Henceforth, it will also be a man's privilege to say no, if only
because he has the human capacity to be propositioned and
seduced.

'Think of a woman offering herself to a man and being refused!'
pleads Bertha, asking her husband to indulge once again that
very empathy with women which she secretly despises. But he
has already suppressed the female element in his personality. In
exposing herself to the risk of refusal, the desperate wife is
unwittingly usurping the traditional male role and this is something which the coarsened Axel can no longer allow. 'Think how
we men must feel pleading for the privilege of giving what you
women so easily accept without having to give anything in return.
If you can understand this – then you can talk about how it feels
to be refused!' There speaks the voice of Strindberg, who saw the
capacity to give love as an essentially male attribute, whereas it
was the woman's prerogative to be loved. In one of Strindberg's
stories, a young bachelor asks when will he ever hear a poem in
praise of men by a woman.

Axel's conclusions are devastating. Like the characters in
Bergman's *Scenes from a Marriage*, he declares that his only hope
of reconstituting the relationship would be for the partners to
meet by chance under a streetlamp at some future time. The
constraints of a formalised marriage, however liberated the
underlying principles of the contract, act to suffocate all the
deepest emotions. In the meantime, it is men rather than women
who need emancipation, says Axel, whom a friend named Carl
congratulates on seeming suddenly more masculine. He is still
sensitive enough to wonder how the wife of Carl can tolerate her
overweening husband, but of course Carl never thought to ask
her that: 'But judging by what I saw, she found it quite as it

should be. If a woman gets a *real* man, one can make human beings even of women!' This could be the moment when *Comrade* collapses into antifeminist wish-fulfilment on Strindberg's part, but this does not happen. Axel remains, in one sense, true to his egalitarian principles. He is sickened by his old-fashioned triumph and rejects the congratulations of Abel, who voices her admiration for a man who can leave his wife's wrists black and blue. Bertha loves him now that he has shown the strength to put her in her place, but he cannot love so abject a woman, any more than she could love a supine man. Abel was right when she prophesied that as long as there are two sexes, just as surely will there be fire.

The real problem for Abel, Axel and Bertha – and ultimately for Strindberg – lies in the fact that artists seem to constitute a third sex. The notorious inability of artists to form lasting marriages may arise not so much from egomania as androgyny. Every artist must incarnate within himself many features of the opposite sex, if his art is to have amplitude and resonance, yet to do that is to jeopardise forever the chances of fulfilment in a complementary relationship between man and wife. The making of the artist are the ruination of the man. The compromise worked out by Axel at the end is a shoddy betrayal of his principles. He opts for the viability of the double-standard, of meeting 'comrades' at the cafe and going home to a wife. The experiment of having a wife who is also a comrade has dismally failed, so Axel pays off Bertha in cash. In a rage, she asks if a woman should allow herself to be treated in this way, but his retort is a sly parody of her feminist rhetoric: 'You once asked me to forget that you were a woman. Very well – I forget it!' It is a cruel jibe, because it hurts him too. It represents the betrayal of a noble experiment in androgyny, which promised to raise their relationship to a high spiritual plane, beyond sexuality itself, only to fizzle out in the atrophy of desire.

Axel concludes that the experiment was misguided – that it is the *heightening* of sexual difference which excites desire, just as it is the erosion of that difference which kills off passion. When each sex is divested of its aura in the eyes of the other, then disaster follows. The self-disgust with which he speaks to Abel at the close indicates the victory in his own personality of the bourgeois over the artist. He wonders if all artists are bastard hybrids, 'a cross between man and woman', and asks if Abel sought to estrange him from Bertha in order to have him for herself. She denies this, admitting that the ability to love has atrophied in herself. Stalled in an indeterminate state, halfway between a man and a woman, she sees herself as, at best, a voyeur watching the struggles of others, at worst, a defective, a misfit. Even if she did desire Axel, he could not now return her love, since her mannish clothes are a source of distress to his new-found conventionalism. 'And why do you get youself up in a manner to make one think of the penal code when one sees you?' he asks with the sarcasm of a male chauvinist, not seeing that the failure of imagination is as much his own. He denies that he was ever attracted to her, but this is blatant self-deception. 'To me you were merely an interesting and amusing comrade who happened to be dressed as a woman. You never gave me the impression of belonging to the other sex; and love, you see, can and should exist only between individuals of opposite sexes.' It was, in fact, these very attributes which drew him to her side in his hour of need, but now that he has suppressed the woman in himself, he can only be unnerved by the man in her. To her retort that he is speaking only of sexual love, he asks if there is any other kind. It is a measure of the defeat which has overtaken him. He may bowl along to the cafe with his mistress, but it is made abundantly clear that his new sexual composure is purchased at the cost of his integrity as an artist. He may never paint another good picture.

The tragedy of Axel is that of Strindberg. Having failed in his attempt to assert the androgynous personality in all its positive aspects, he opted instead to suppress the female in himself and to assert the strenuous masculine will. At times, his defiance could be ludicrous, as when he resigned from the theosophists on hearing that the movement had been founded by a woman. But, as Robert Brustein has pointed out, his defiant masculinity is more an impersonation than an actuality,[19] for in his art the playwright continued to embrace the feminine principle. It is indeed ironic that Nietzsche, from whom Strindberg derived this cult of masculine will, should have been privately embraced in notes and diaries by Strindberg as the 'husband', from whom the dramatist received 'a tremendous outpouring of seed'. Nietzsche preached that sexual love necessarily produces spiritual hate and resentment against the person upon whom one comes to depend. The result is that 'procreation depends on the duality of the sexes, involving perpetual strife with only periodically intervening reconciliations'. At the heart of this perverse, if radical, philosophy is a very Victorian contempt for the body and its functions. Man is seen as the prisoner of his physical lusts, which are seen as a bait set by the gods to ensure the continuance of life. Strindberg gave this theory a weird twist of his own when he asserted that where sensual pleasure is sought by a couple, their lovemaking will not be blessed by the conception of children – a proposition which, if it were true, would long since have solved most of mankind's problems. Interestingly, Yeats held to the contrary view that we beget and bear children because of the incompleteness of our love – a much more likely proposition.

It was his distrust of the body which caused Strindberg to flirt with notions of androgyny and ultimately to confuse androgyny with asexuality. He implies, again and again, that his most radical and successful couples are innocent of sexual relations. Axel and Bertha have separate rooms at opposite ends of the house, more like brother and sister than man and wife. The couple in 'An Attempt at Reform' are described in a similar arrangement:

> It was a chaste, beautiful marriage. The two lived in three rooms in Passy. He had a room of his own at one end of the flat and she had hers at the other end; and the room in the middle served as their studio. They were not to share the same bed – that would be nothing short of obscenity, an indecent beastliness which had not the slightest counterpart in nature and which only led to excesses and mischief. And, of all things – think of it! – having to undress in the same room! Phew! No, each one to his own room . . .[20]

It is only when they have sexual relations and, in consequence, children, that this idyll is broken and the troubles begin.

Perhaps the most valid of Strindberg's theories is that androgyny increases with the years. Physical observation will confirm that aged men often come to resemble their female counterparts. More than one newspaper copysetter confused pictures of Golda Meir and Lyndon Baines Johnson in the 1960s and everybody has his own favourite examples. Here in Dublin where I write, a well-known IRA leader has often been mistaken for a middle-aged woman and, indeed, has broken out of jail on more than one occasion by exploiting the resemblance. Everybody notices how like one another the faces of husbands and wives become with the passing years. These are merely the physical manifestations of a deeper psychological truth, which Strindberg places at the centre of his play *The Bond*, written in 1892, after his divorce from Siri von Essen and the humiliating trial which accompanied it. *The Bond* is a study of the effects of such a trial on a middle-aged couple. Strindberg depicts the increasing hatred of the wife for a husband who thinks he can explain its source: 'And why? – why this abominable hate? Perhaps I lost sight of the fact that you are nearing your forties and that something masculine is beginning to take root in you. Perhaps it is this touch of the male that I have felt in your kisses, in your embraces, that I find so repulsive.' Of course, the male element was rooted in the Baroness from birth – her greatest sorrow was not to have been born a man – but the process of ageing serves to emphasise this aspect of her personality, which is common to virtually all the women mentioned in the play. The Constable's wife believes that, if there was any justice in the world, men would have to bear children too, while the Sheriff's wife feeds her imagination with newspaper reports of bricklaying women and husband-beaters. The fundamental situation is a repeat of Strindberg's earlier plots. The frustrated Baroness revenges herself on her husband by raising her boy as one of her own sex with dolls, dresses and girlish long hair, while her daughters have close-cropped hair and are sent to work in the fields. At an earlier period in the marriage, there had been some happiness, but only when the Baron dominated his wife and excited her imagination with his infidelities. Then she was 'the most female of women I have ever known', deeply infatuated by 'the male in me'; but, since then, the man in her has emerged to the disgust of her husband. It is the same boring old story of a couple caught in the dance of death, doomed to a meaningless cycle of sensual love and spiritual hate, until death mercifully supervenes. As always, androgyny is exploited by a frustrated partner in thoroughly negative circumstances, as a revenge on an unsatisfactory spouse or as a stalking-horse for one's own asexuality. Never is it seen as a positive challenge to discover the rich potential in the self. At best, as in *The Dance of Death*, it can produce only the ghastly truce of a tired old couple waiting for the end.

There is no doubt that Strindberg loaded the moral dice against women in his plays, which monotonously treat men as paragons of principle and women as creatures of instability. In the event, he gave crude expression to the oldest misogynistic clichés on the planet, but not before he had terrified himself by confronting the full implications of the female within. As a young man, he took the assertions of radical feminists at face value and tried to apply them in his own life. When they failed him, he tried again, and again, just in case he had not given them a fair trial. It is for this, as much as for his eventual misogyny, that today's feminists fear and despise him – for seeking out New Women as comrades and wives, for assessing their claims with full seriousness, for giving them intellectual assent, for trying to live them out, and for proving them – to his own satisfaction – to be thoroughly wanting. It is too naive to call him a woman-hater and leave it at that. He is the most gifted casualty of the feminist movement.

3 Ibsen's Heroines:
The New Woman As Rebel

Whatever women do they must do twice as well as men to be
thought half as good. Luckily, this is not difficult.

Charlotte Whitton

'All good women are manly and all good men are womanly',
wrote George Bernard Shaw in *The Quintessence of Ibsenism*; and
characters such as St Joan and Major Barbara bear out his claim
that a woman could be both brave and tender. Moreover, in
Arms and the Man, the chocolate soldier Bluntschli has the courage
to admit that all good military men reject the notion of heroism
just as they fear the prospect of death. 'Though I am only a
woman', says the play's heroine Raina, 'I think I am at heart as
brave as you', a proposition to which he readily assents. Bluntschli
cannot, however, bring himself to admire the 'noble attitude' and
'thrilling voice' adopted by Raina in her heroic moods, and curtly
tells her that she is lying. Her impulse is to accuse him of slander,
but instead she asks 'How did you find me out?' Freed from her
role as the wilting but patriotic heroine, she realises that he is the
first man to speak to her without pretence, person to person
rather than man to woman. The rest of the play chronicles their
further deflation of sexual heroics. Sergius, the hero home from
his triumph in battle, says that he is never sorry for what he does;
but Laika, the servant girl, replies: 'I wish I could believe a man
could be as unlike a woman as that. I wonder are you really a
brave man.' By the end of the drama, Sergius is exposed as just
another fallible youth, while the chocolate soldier triumphs
because of his modest refusal to pose. 'What a man!' exclaims
Sergius in tribute, adding a final question 'Is he a man?'
     All would have been well if Shaw could have left his delicate
suggestion at that, but, being Shaw, he had to push the insight

to the extremes of paradox. 'The secret of the extraordinary knowledge of women which I show in my plays' turned out to be very simple after all – 'I have always assumed that a woman is a person exactly like myself, and that is how the trick is done.'[1] All too often, this was true. His Vivie Warren (in *Mrs Warren's Profession*) is not so much a New Woman as a man in drag, breaking men's bones with her handshake and chortling over cigars and detective novels. Such a caricature was a godsend to the antifeminists, whose cause Shaw scorned but unwittingly served. It played right into the hands of Ibsen's detractors in London, one of whom offered the following description of the Norwegian's admirers in a magazine entitled *Truth*: 'The sexless, the unwomanly woman, the unsexed females, the whole army of unprepossessing cranks in petticoats . . . Effeminate men and male women . . . They all of them – men and women alike – know that they are doing not only a nasty but an illegal thing.'[2] In such a fashion, the leader-writers of England distilled the quintessence of Ibsenism.

The real Ibsen was very different, as we know from Michael Meyer's biography. Those who knew him remarked on his 'uncommon toughness' in the face of early poverty at Grimstaad. He grew up in a world where the strict separation of boys and girls was still in the future. At Grimstaad, the apprentice apothecary tobogganed down the hill with young girls, according to Marthe Erikson, who added: 'there wasn't such a difference between girls and boys then'. Along with this robustness, there was also a deeply passive element in Ibsen's personality, which manifested itself in his aversion to schoolboy fights and, later, in his timidity before the self-assured and playful women to whom he was invariably attracted. His first love, Rikke Holst, found him so slow to make a romantic overture that she resorted to the desperate strategy of throwing a posy of flowers in his face. Although they exchanged rings, he fled the relationship when confronted by her angry father. He was eventually to marry an even more spirited radical, the unwomanly[3] and self-reliant[4] Suzannah Thoresen, who mocked his personal timidity even as she protected his subversive genius.

Freud's theory that feminine men attract masculine women is borne out by the marriage of the Ibsens. 'She was the character, he was the genius', their son recalled. 'Genius is always part-feminine' commented Shaw (a partner in a somewhat similar marriage), who once held that the artist has the temperament of an old maid. This may help to explain why the aged Ibsen carried a mirror in his hat and used it, to the consternation of Queen Victoria's grand-daughter, 'like a woman when combing his hair'.[5] The dramatist was fully aware of this dimension to his personality and said that 'women have something in common with the true artist . . . something that is a good substitute for worldly understanding'.[6] Only 'something', only 'part-feminine', for the true artist is an androgynous blend of intellect and intuition, system and instinct. Joyce seemed to think so and his short essay on Ibsen is an analysis of the Norwegian's androgynous genius and a prophecy of his own:

> Ibsen's knowledge of humanity is nowhere more obvious than in his portrayal of women. He amazes one by his painful introspection; he seems to know them better than they know themselves. Indeed, if one may say so of an eminently virile man, there is a curious admixture of the woman in his nature. His marvellous accuracy, his faint traces of femininity, his delicacy of swift touch, are perhaps attributable to that admixture. But that he knows women is an incontrovertible fact. He appears to have sounded them to almost unfathomable depths.[7]

At those depths, Ibsen found that all men and women, and not just artists, are androgynous, with a capacity to incorporate into their personalities elements once thought peculiar to the opposite sex. It is this psychological realism which Joyce found in the Norwegian's depiction of 'men and women as we meet them in the real world, not as we apprehend them in the world of faery'.[8]

Ibsen's account of the sufferings of couples who reject the stereotypes of masculinity and femininity, only to face more daunting social and personal problems in their attempt at an honest sexuality, seemed to Joyce *the* central issue of the age. The radical critique of bourgeois marriage in *A Doll's House* was a challenge to its own generation, just as *The Master Builder* offered glimpses of an uncertain future.

*　　*　　*

'You are totally unaware of the spirit which prompted him', said Joyce to a friend in defence of Ibsen. 'The purpose of *A Doll's*

House for instance is to further the emancipation of the woman, which is the most important revolution of our time because it concerns the most important relationship possible – thaι between the man and the woman.'[9] Joyce may well have been paraphrasing Ibsen's own complaint to Georg Brandes that he was bored by external political revolutions: 'what is really wanted is a revolution in the spirit of man'.[10] There were times when Ibsen feared that feminists were so obsessed with 'externals' that they misread *A Doll's House* as a play about a woman who slammed a door. It is also a play about the plight of the man who is left behind and it is on his tragedy that the curtain finally falls. The man who was to die uttering the immortal word 'Nevertheless' was not the sort to settle for one side of any story. Although he poured scorn on the opponents of feminism – and especially on those women who failed to assert their rights – he reserved the deepest suspicion for his own uncritical disciples who failed to accept the entire logic of his argument. Near the end of his career, he reprimanded the extremists of the Norwegian Society for Women's Rights: 'I am not even quite sure what women's rights really are. To me it has been a question of human rights . . . Of course, it is incidentally desirable to solve the problem of women.'[11]

Twenty years earlier, in his 'Notes for a Modern Tragedy', Ibsen was in no doubt as to what constituted 'the problem of women':

> There are two kinds of moral laws, two kinds of conscience, one for men and one, quite different, for women. They don't understand each other; but in practical life, woman is judged by masculine law, as though she weren't a woman but a man.
>
> The wife in the play ends by having no idea what is right and what is wrong; natural feelings on the one hand and belief in authority on the other lead to utter destruction.
>
> A woman cannot be herself in modern society. It is an exclusively male society, with laws made by men and with prosecutors and judges who assess feminine conduct from a masculine standpoint.[12]

As an artist, Ibsen's aim was to reverse the process of a law which, in the words of Krogstad, does not investigate motives – and to examine just those motives from the female standpoint. He realised that men and women are a lot less alike than the law pretends, and a lot more alike than the culture admits. The challenge was to make the law as androgynous in its world-view as art, so that it recognises *all* the faculties of the human mind, the 'natural feelings' of the female allied to the male belief in 'authority'. The man who lives only by authority, like the woman who lives purely on feelings, can never be whole. Hence the two-dimensional character of Helmer is not a flaw in Ibsen's dramatic technique, but part of the play's psychological point. Helmer has projected all the emotional aspects of his personality onto Nora, the doll-wife, who in turn projects all her own childishness onto her 'doll-babies' that 'dogs never bite'. At the end, it is her fear that she will perpetuate those values if she does not leave: 'But our home's been nothing but a playpen . . . I thought it was fun when you played with me, just as they thought it fun when I played with them. That's been our marriage, Torvald.' Helmer's hypocrisy is manifest. He treats his wife like a juvenile and then complains when she acts like a child, making noise or scoffing macaroons.

The free woman who walks out in the finish is latent in Nora from the outset, in her private commitment to the male values of work as well as to the female code of self-sacrifice. Faced with the financial stringencies of the previous Christmas, she locked herself in a room making decorations. To Helmer's complaint that it was the dullest time he ever lived through, Nora brightly responds that it wasn't at all dull for her. In those late December nights, she had a rare sense of self-sufficiency and learned the joy of 'being' rather than 'having'. The greatest threat which Nora now faces is Helmer's new-found affluence which will deny her the few remaining opportunities for being and instead compel her to become the full-time female fetish of his possessive dreams. The macaroons will ruin her white teeth and rotten teeth will not excite him. 'You wanted so much to please us all', drools Helmer, who has trained Nora in the art of self-censorship, so much so that she is surprised by her repeated candour in the presence of Mrs Linde ('thoughtless me, to sit here chattering away' or 'I'm talking of nothing but my own affairs'). Family life has surely threatened her selfhood, just as it jeopardised the life of her husband, who overworked to the point of serious illness in order to support the couple in their early days. In his permanent obsession with letter-writing, bank business and work, Helmer is as much a victim of a specialist code as his wife. Every major play by Ibsen foretells the death of the family as an institution based on a false specialism of roles, man for work, woman for the home. Torvald's role sits a little more easily on him, but the strain is beginning to show. He extols domesticity, but cannot bear the noise of children, rather like Strindberg who sang the praises of infants, provided the nappies were kept well out of his sight.

That Nora is not the doll she impersonates is clear from the beginning. It is the suppressed adult in her who complains that everything seems so ridiculous, so inane. She may be ignorant of her disadvantages under the law and have to be told that a wife cannot borrow without her husband's consent, but she is all too well aware of the discrepancy between her assigned role and her real contribution in the home. She has kept the secret of how she borrowed money on false pretences to save Torvald's life, because she understands the fiction on which the family is based. 'Besides, Torvald – with all his masculine pride – how painfully humiliating for him if he ever found out he was in debt to me.' She jokes of deliverance from her debt by an admirer of her beauty, but in the end it will be necessary for her complete freedom that she walk out to an uncertain future without even that consolation. She is fully conscious of her role as child-wife, enacting for a prosaic husband all the playfulness he has learned to suppress in himself. Her secret may well have the coercive power of this manipulation in years to come when she is no longer attractive – 'Don't laugh! I only mean when he loves me less than now, when he stops enjoying my dancing and dressing up and reciting for him. Then it might be wise to have something in reserve.' She knows just how precarious is an institution which is based more on a youthful figure than on a spiritual affinity. The fact that all the other marriages mentioned at the start are hollow mockeries is scarcely encouraging. So already, even in her attempts to save her own marriage and defray the awful debt by extra work as a copyist, Nora is half-consciously preparing for the moment of self-support. 'But still it was wonderful fun, sitting and working like that, earning money. It was almost like being a man.' The masculine element is beginning to emerge not only in Nora's desire to say 'to hell and be damned' but also in Mrs Linde's successful usurpation of her former lover in his post at the bank. It is brutally appropriate that the undoing of Krogstad should be achieved by Nora's skilful playing on Helmer's vanity as a male – 'she's terribly eager to come under a capable man's supervision'. Helmer's supposition that Mrs Linde is a widow speaks volumes for his conviction that no husbanded woman *works* and his assumption that she will now evacuate a room unbearable for anyone but mothers suggests a cosy assurance that motherhood and work are strangely incompatible. Most damning, however, is the fact that he leaves at once, showing no interest in Mrs Linde as the friend of his wife, much less as a future employee of his. When later in the play he calls the woman a 'deadly bore' – this woman with whom he has never bothered to converse – something permanent has been implied about his own moral emptiness. People who say such things are usually the greatest bores of all, exponents of a tedious insecurity which hides itself behind a mask of aggressive complacency.

One of the great achievements of this play is to suggest an underlying similarity between the plight of Nora as a woman and that of her blackmailer Krogstad as a criminal. He, too, uses his obligations to his own family as a licence for threats and deceit, just as Mrs Linde invoked her family as a justification of her cruelty to him. In such a context, Nora's final abandonment of the family as an institution may not be as shocking as it is sometimes made to seem. Her warning to Krogstad seems to hint at an identity in their predicaments: 'When one has a subordinate position, Mr Krogstad, one really ought to be careful.' This equation is underlined by Helmer's admonition that such a guilt-ridden one must always wear a mask, even before his own children. Nora's lifeless admission to Krogstad that she, too, lacked the courage for suicide suggests the kind of candour in their relationship which in her marriage itself would be as yet unthinkable.

At this early stage, as Ronald Gray and John Northam have argued, Nora has no vision of society as a whole. At the start, she told Helmer that if she died in debt, she would care little for the strangers to whom the money was owing. 'Just like a woman', he responded, but her reply showed a more fundamental, non-legalistic intelligence: 'If anything so awful happened, then it just wouldn't matter if I had debts or not.' Now in Act 2 she still shows scant regard for the rights of strangers, when she wonders if Helmer could dismiss some clerk other than Krogstad. In this case, 'natural feelings' win out over 'authority', but in the case of her children, such is the force of 'authority' over 'natural feelings' that Nora loses faith in her own fitness to be a mother. All around her is the evidence of corruption by inheritance – in Rank's mortal disease, in her own amoral attitude to society – with the result that Nora cannot bear the thought of infecting her children. Mrs Linde stresses the positive elegance and charm in Nora's inheritance from her dead father, but the evidence is all against her. There is nothing left for Nora but to revert to the role of doll-fetish, amazing Helmer by rebellious irony ('But wasn't I good to give into you?'), or teasing Rank with the stockings which she snaps in his longing face. Such a scene proves that Nora is a doll only by curtailing her sensitivity to the feelings of others – that all too often manipulativeness is mistaken for femininity. It is at this unlikely moment, however, that Nora achieves an heroic self-sufficiency and rejects the easy option of having Rank solve her financial problems. She has manipulated him shamelessly, because that is her time-honoured role; but now, shocked at her own success in putting him into her power, a more honest woman emerges in Nora and steadfastly refuses to press her advantage home. She is angry at Rank not for loving her, but for telling of his love. When he asks if she knew all along, her reply works on many levels: 'how can I tell what I know or don't know?' Elizabeth Hardwick has pointed out how in Ibsen's plays it is normally the wife who welcomes a third party (either male or female) into the home, as if to promise the alleviation of boredom and a clarifying exchange of views. Nora's explanation is uncanny enough to convince Rank: 'there are some people that one loves most and other people that one would almost prefer being with'. As a child, she loved Papa but preferred the talk of the kitchen, on the principle, perhaps, that our servants do our real living for us.

Act 2 ends with Nora waiting for the miracle which will occur when her husband decides to take all the blame of her bad debt on himself. According to her idealistic plan, he will do this only to discover that she has already beaten him to it and taken her own life. The idea of an impossibly noble self-sacrifice seems to dominate every major character in the play. When Mrs Linde proposes marriage to the disillusioned Krogstad in the final act, with the explanation that there's no joy for a woman in working for herself, he suspects 'some hysterical female urge to go out and make a noble sacrifice'. But she has already made one sacrifice too many in sacrificing him. The woman who sold herself once, for the sake of a dying mother, won't (she assures him) do it again. Her homely realism, which admits its own selfishness, contrasts refreshingly with the rather unreal sacrifices preached, but not practised, by the others. Everybody, of course, has made sacrifices for the family, because those with nothing to live for are unspeakably empty. Rand is one such and he tries to retrieve his life by offering some great proof of his friendship for Nora. Even Helmer has delusions of melodramatic self-sacrifice, wishing to find himself in some terrible danger, so that he could risk his life for the sake of his wife. It is part of Nora's weakness that, far from seeing through such rhetoric, she should embrace it as her own. It is her last and greatest illusion of all, that Helmer will take on the guilt and shame. He would need to love her to do that, but all he loves are his reasons for loving her. The 'helpless' doll whom he loved is a fetish of his own creation, who now trembles as she dances the tarantella. The masterful woman who sought to influence his decisions at the bank or who rebuked him for pettiness is another proposition altogether and he bludgeons her into submission by a burst of anger and recrimination. Somewhere hidden in Nora was a real woman who for a while lived vicariously through her husband and found it 'amusing that we – that Torvald has so much power now over those people'. But now, as she dances the tarantella, the real priorities of Nora and her husband are laid bare, for in the mythologies of the world, the tarantella is a dance of androgynes, after which women behave like men.

Torvald has dressed Nora in a fishergirl's costume to gratify his fantasies, but also to display her beauty as his prized possession. He does not love her for herself, but for the sake of his own aggrandisement. Her performance of the tarantella was a little 'too naturalistic', but this is forgivable in one who 'made a success'. It was naturalistic because Nora was truly doing the dance of death, expressing at once her colossal vitality and the imminence of her chosen doom. Helmer is as unaware of this as he is of the forecasting irony of his next complaint about Nora's strange reluctance to leave the dance: 'An exit should always be effective, Mrs Linde, but that's what I can't get Nora to grasp.' He talks of Nora in the third person, as if she were a demented child with no mind of her own, and his relationship with her is the clearest indication that his life is conducted on modes of 'having' rather than 'being'. Flushed by champagne – which

Nora, with uncharacteristic bitchiness, says makes him 'so enter-
taining' – he spouts about 'the beauty that's mine, mine alone,
completely and utterly'. Mrs Linde's belief that Nora would have
been wiser to tell her husband everything is now put to the test
and found wanting. The same lady's decision to precipitate the
catastrophe by not recalling Krogstad's letter is vindicated,
however, in her own words: 'these two have to come to an
understanding; all those lies and evasions can't go on'.

Helmer's explosion into recrimination, just after his prayer for
the chance to sacrifice himself for Nora, is the deflation of her
final illusion. There will be no miracle. With callous pragmatism
he points out that her suicide would solve nothing. The only
thing for it is to put up a brave front of domestic harmony,
despite the fact that Nora will no longer be allowed to bring up
the children. The theory of inherited guilt has its consummation
in Helmer's conviction that he is justly punished for overlooking
the irregularities of Nora's father, whose asocial values are now
reincarnated in his daughter. It is presumably at this point that
Nora realises that her dream of a noble suicide is entirely
inadequate to the occasion. As John Northam has written: 'One
doesn't die for an illusion, once it is recognised as such'[13] and an
illusion is what Helmer's love has turned out to be. A deeper
question remains, however, about her own attitude to him. If
Helmer were to shoulder the blame, the consequences for his
entire family would be far more disastrous than if Nora were
merely to plead inexperience. Such an act would be impractical
as well as counterproductive. Moreover, it would offer just the
kind of male protectiveness which Nora has found so nauseating
in his performances. As Ronald Gray has written: 'She blames
him now for not thinking of undertaking precisely the kind of
knightly rescue of a damsel in distress which would assert his
male superiority all over again.'[14] The myth of the 'helpless
creature' is the one illusion which remains to be dismantled.

It is this very myth which Helmer hastily tries to reactivate,
as soon as he learns that Krogstad has decided to show mercy.
He reverts to it in his attempts to woo Nora back from the brink:
'I wouldn't be a man if this feminine helplessness didn't make
you twice as attractive to me.' In the past, one of his favourite
games was to smile at Nora across a crowded room, imagine that
she was his bride-to-be and woo her all over again. Now, in a
pretentious metaphor of forgiveness, he relaunches this fantasy:

'It's as if she belongs to him in two ways now; in a sense he's given her fresh into the world again and she's become his wife and child again.' Unfortunately for him, Nora by now has changed out of her fishergirl's costume and into her regular clothes, as if to suggest her rejection of her role as a fetish of the male imagination. It is the adult in her who now takes command and regrets that she has lived by doing tricks for him, without a serious discussion between them over eight whole years. The fault is not entirely his, of course, for in withholding her secret, Nora has shown a deep distrust of Helmer from the start. In playing the coquette so obligingly, and for so long, she has merely fed his foolish fantasies. It is he, rather than she, who is finally revealed as the perpetual child, unable to change or grow. It is he, and not she, who is the logical heir to her guilty father – and the guilt is not a technicality of business malpractice, but the immoral refusal to take a young woman seriously:

Nora: When I lived at home with Papa, he told me all his opinions, so I had the same ones too; or if they were different I hid them . . . Then I came into your house . . .

Helmer: How can you speak of our marriage like that?

Helmer knew well that the woman he married had no sense of social responsibility, but he liked things that way, married to 'a wife and child'. It is this scenario which he tries to recreate in the closing scene: 'I'll be conscience and will to you both.' He does not try to educate her, preferring to find her ignorance charming. Rightly can Nora complain that her father and husband are to blame that nothing has come of her.

Lacking an education, Nora now advances a rational rather than a superstitious explanation of her rejection of her children. She cannot presume to teach them until she has first educated herself. Perhaps her departure is made easier by the knowledge that she is not giving up all that much, for in her stratum of fashionable society, elegant ladies were not only denied by their husbands the right to a job but were also denied by professional nannies the dignity of motherhood. If our servants are going to do our living for us, they are likely to make better mothers as well. Like many other Ibsen heroines, Nora grew up without a mother, but she leaves her children to her own nanny with the remark that they are in better hands than hers. The usurpation of the traditional female role of housekeeper and mother is admitted in Nora's assertion that the maids know how to keep up the house better than she does.

These remarks are all uttered with a staccato lucidity which gives the lie to those critics who feel that Nora is confused in this scene. She herself says that she never felt more clear-headed in her life. If anything, it is Helmer who grows confused, as his surface confidence evaporates and he tries to assimilate what is about to happen. Nora's first lesson is for him more than for herself:

Helmer: To part . . . I can't imagine it.

Nora: All the more reason why it has to be.

True education is about imagining future virtues, which will be admirable precisely because we cannot now conceive them.[15] In a play where the word 'past' is interchangeable with the word 'guilt', the idea of an uncertain future has a liberating force, as much because it is uncertain as because it is the future. 'Every epoch not only dreams the next', wrote Walter Benjamin, 'but while dreaming impels it towards wakefulness.' The pull from a dead past is epitomised for Nora not just by the truisms of the majority, but also by what is written in books. In an era when the grim determinism of inheritance kills the notion of personal freedom and choice, a book-ridden culture is an unwitting agent of the oppression. This applies as much to Helmer as to Nora, for even before she embarks on her education, she completes his:

Helmer: But there's no one who gives up honour for love.

Nora: Millions of women have done just that.

But what if the culture and laws of the future were truly an androgynous blend of male honour and female love, to such a point that it became foolish to equate the one virtue exclusively with either sex? Then the living together of a couple would be a real marriage of minds, fulfilled in the very scope of their attributes. It is on this note of qualified optimism about the future of marriage that the play ends, a play which has already seen one good marriage contracted on the pragmatic understanding that is purged of all sentimental illusion. Ibsen has turned his suspicious gaze onto the institution of marriage, but has not yet given up all hope for its redemption.

Strindberg denounced *A Doll's House* for its assault on the male and wrote off Ibsen as an 'ignorant woman's writer' who had nothing to teach him. He insisted that Nora is a compulsive liar as well as a flirt, whereas Helmer is too honest a lawyer to plead for a shady client. This is untrue – Helmer's deal with Nora's father involved a technical dishonesty – and in the world of the emotions, it is he rather than she who lives a lie. Nothing daunted, Strindberg asserted that 'woman is in general by nature mean and instinctively dishonest, though we ruttish cocks have not been able to see it'. Nevertheless, he conceded that *A Doll's House* revealed marriage to be 'a far from divine institution', with the result that divorce between ill-sorted couples was increasingly considered justifiable.

In subsequent plays, such as *Rosmersholm* and *Hedda Gabler*, Ibsen developed this basic formula of an unequal encounter between a masterful woman and a timid, conscience-stricken man. In *Hedda Gabler*, the proud girl who galloped on horseback, like a conquering soldier with a plume in her hat, must now make a betraying peace with a scholar who is the pallid product of an all-female regime of ailing godmothers and doting aunts. Tesman is as effeminate as Hedda is manly, and hence he is doubly attractive to the woman who can mould him as putty in her strong hands. In the end, however, that very pliability which made him so attractive is found to be obnoxious and debilitating. At the heart of her contempt for her 'specialist' husband is Hedda's conviction that he achieves a limited competence only by killing off the greater part of his human potential. She would prefer to be baffled and complex than to achieve that dubious lucidity; and she must be the first heroine in modern drama whose speech is at once so powerful and so fragmented. At the close, she prefers to commit suicide than to simplify herself so obscenely, and even in her last action we sense that whole elements of her fractured personality are withheld from the deed. Joyce's description of the classic Ibsen heroine fits perfectly: 'the very aloofness from passion, which is not separable from her, forbids classification. She interests us strangely, magnetically, because of her inner power of character.'[16]

Gifted with multiple talents, but denied a vocation in which these might be fulfilled, the heroines of Ibsen are forced to live vicariously through some chosen man. Power over another offers the only hope of significance. John Stuart Mill in *The Subjection of Women* has written that 'where liberty cannot be hoped for, and power can, power becomes the grand object of human desire.'[17] Hence Nora Helmer's fantasy of ruling an entire bank through her husband, or Hedda's uncharacteristically candid outburst: 'For once in my life I want to have power over a human being.' Yet the control which she achieves over Tesman is self-defeating. She marries a pliable weakling only to discover that his weakness robs his pliability of all its attraction.

*   *   *

Even today, there is a kind of woman who gets all she wants, simply by assuming it to be her right. Men find the assumption disarming. Isabel Archer was one such, for a while, and *The Master Builder* contains two, Kaja Fosli and Hilda Wangel. Both share Ibsen's conviction that one only has to wish something powerfully to make it come true. Kaja Fosli walked into the Master Builder's office one day, fell in love with him, and asked at once where her job in his office would be and whether she would start the very next morning. By contrast, *her* lover Ragnar Brovik is forced to wait years for their promised marriage, because the Builder is afraid that Brovik's talent will soon eclipse his own and obliterate his master. So Solness feigns devotion to Kaja, strokes her hair and flirts with her, in order to keep her, and, therefore, his best worker Ragnar, with the enterprise. Ragnar's plight is that of the woman of untapped potential in Ibsen's earlier plays – because he is modern and efficient, he is denied an outlet for his abilities. Meanwhile, it is unclear whether Solness really admires Kaja or simply her usefulness to his career. Darkly, he tells his prim wife that the girl is a comfort, 'especially when one is so used to doing without'. To his doctor he explains that there is 'a kind of beneficial self-torment in letting Aline do me an injustice', if only because the undeserved punishment helps to expiate his marital sins of omission. From the outset, he has neglected his wife in fanatic pursuit of his career and now he feels that this may have cost him his sanity. Once again, Ibsen has written a tragedy of specialisation, this time with an autobiographical dimension, for it seems to reflect his own marriage, where conjugal tenderness was too often sacrificed to his art. His definition of a tragic love was not two sweethearts failing to get each other, but rather two true lovers marrying for life, only to discover a psychological incompatibility which prevents them from being happy together.

No sooner has the Master Builder voiced his fear of madness and of losing out to youth, than the wild Hilda Wangel walks through his door. She is tough, self-assured and instantly familiar, exuding the gamin charm of a New Woman from the mountains dressed in hiking clothes and a sailor's blouse, the only clothes in her possession. 'I almost think you don't recognise me', she remarks with provocative intimacy and at once this forward girl starts touring his quarters and fingering his possessions. She has come partly because Mrs Solness invited her, 'even though she didn't really have to', but mainly in order to force the builder to keep the promise made to her as a little girl in Lysanger that he would turn her into a princess. In that day ten years ago, he had kissed her after crowning the steeple of the church he had built there and she watched him breathlessly, with music ringing in her ears, amazed that he did not fall or grow dizzy. 'What makes you so sure I wasn't?', he asks; but the New Woman, by refusing even to contemplate such a thing, restores his youthful confidence in himself. She represents the youth which he needs, but of which he is afraid and so he welcomes her heartily, despite the absurdity of her expectations and the extremity of her demands. To his suggestion that she visit the city shops and fit herself in style, she responds with amused contempt for such feminine frippery. This prompts Solness to utter the classic male response to the self-sufficient lady: 'I can't make out whether you mean what you say – or whether you're just having some fun.' The New Woman, a mistress of irony, greets each situation with a new performance, all her utterances encased in the parodic parentheses perfected by Hedda. Soon we shall see Hilda behave very differently in relation to the builder's wife, but for now her role is that of temptress. Ibsen claimed to have based her on Emilie Bardach, 'the demonic little wrecker' with whom he became infatuated for a time in Vienna – she cheerfully told him that her goal was not a respectable marriage but to seduce other women's husbands.[18]

As is often the case in Ibsen's plays, the house of the Solnesses is never a home. Worse still, the childless wife feels absolutely nothing about the spectacular new house which her husband is building for them. She is glad enough to find a use for the nursery by lodging Hilda there, but her welcome is less a matter of enthusiasm than of duty. It is this same obsession with 'duty' which cost her her own infants years ago, when she insisted on feeding them with her own bad milk, after she had lost strength because of the fire which destroyed her parents' home. Yet it was this fire which gave Solness his break as a young man, for his successful erection of a new house brought in a flood of commissions in the area. Now Mrs Solness blames herself in front of her husband: 'Yes, you know I had my duties on both sides – both to you and to the babies . . . ' She, too, is a victim of the specialist code, which leaves her a purely private life, as surely as it condemns her husband to a purely professional existence. Moreover, even within her private world, she specialises in such virtues as 'duty', but only at the expense of others such as kindness. Like many people of her time, she becomes obsessed with a single moral virtue and practises it to the exclusion of others, to such an extreme that it becomes immoral, as when she 'kills' her infants with bad milk. Ibsen himself believed that all virtue is relative and that those who claim a monopoly of wisdom have most surely lost it. His plays are an attack on all forms of moral absolutism and, as F.W. Kaufmann says, 'by pointing out the incompatibility of the specific demands of a code, Ibsen indicates another problem, namely that every choice involves the rejection of other possibilities of perhaps equal moral importance'.[19] This is precisely the point made by Hilda in rejecting 'duty', a 'mean ugly word' when used by Mrs Solness as a reason for helping the girl to find her way about the city. 'She should have said she'd do it because she liked me a lot.' In fact, Hilda would prefer to walk into the town unaccompanied and is excited by Mrs Solness's warning that people might stare at her rugged mountain clothes. What seemed at first like insolent brashness appears now as a girlish spontaneity in the face of Aline Solness's frozen duty. Hilda elevates the claims of nature over those of culture in her dismissal of books, to which she says she cannot relate anymore. Ibsen admires this, for he told the feminist Helene Raff that 'only when one is free of the mass of inherited opinions which school and church hand down can one become outwardly and inwardly strong like you'. Like Gide's immoralist, Hilda takes a stance beyond culture, in the knowledge that authentic being is achieved only when the veneer of acquired knowledge is sloughed off. In *Fruits of the Earth* Gide observed that 'every choice is frightening when you think about it: frightening a freedom no longer guarded by duty'. But not half so frightening as Mrs Solness's myopic commitment to duty for its own sake, even when that commitment flies in the face of higher moral virtues. Her numb acceptance of seductive rivals and her husband's neglect in the name of 'duty' proves to be ultimately meaningless, with the result that at the close of the play her duty to entertain some ladies seems more pressing than the impulse to save her husband from his mortal folly. Her concept of duty proves as counterproductive as her husband's conviction that it is his obligation to build homes for others.

In devoting himself to that ideal, Solness had to give up a home of his own and the prospect of children: 'And not just my own happiness. With others', too. You understand Hilda! That's the price my name as an artist has cost me – and others.' Ibsen, who often described the playwright as an architect, is here probing the cost of his own career and the word 'artist' is deliberately substituted. The costs to Aline Solness have been huge, for her life-work as a mother was ended by that fire, which the builder now guiltily believes he could have averted. He had spotted the crack in the chimney which led to the conflagration, but had remained silent, knowing that the chance to rebuild the house would be the basis of his professional success. So now he is crushed by a vague but enormous guilt in the face of his unfulfilled wife. Her bitterness seems to him more a divine reproach than a human irritation: 'But her life-work had to be cut down, crushed, broken to bits, so that mine could win through to – to some kind of great victory.' The traditional notion of marriage as a haven from a heartless world of work, in which the troubled Solness might find consolation, will no longer hold good. In his wife's unhappy face, Solness reads the costs of his own triumph. Those who marry, as Chekhov said, must prepare to be lonely, because conjugal relations have themselves been corrupted by the capitalist modes of specialisation. 'Man for work, woman for the home' is a recipe for joint frustration. As Leo Lowenthal has so acutely observed:

When Ibsen's characters speak of love they often tremble – a phenomenon which proves on examination to be historical and social in its origins. The division of the individual into a professional self and a private self frightens the wife lest her beloved turn out to be someone vastly different from the man she knows; he may even be different from the man he thinks he is. The man who binds himself for life to a woman – to a member of the sex which, in Ibsen's day, society still confined to an existence within conventional marriage – may also expect disappointment. An order of life in which husbands and wives are specialised beings intensifies the anxiety that in any case goes with love.[20]

Solness *does* tremble as he counts the cost to Aline, but there is an even more painful price at which he hardly dares to hint, the cost to himself. The specialism which is the path to success in a capitalist society is an act of violence to the self, as Hedda Gabler had sensed. It produces disoriented beings who repress far more of their personalities than they express. Because of this, Aline Solness focuses in her mind on the loss of her dolls in the fire at her parents' house, since she cannot directly confront the awful thought of her lost children. For much the same reason, her husband has had to suppress all personal instincts of tenderness and love, sublimating them in the guise of a more public service to the community in general. This explains his inner torment, as he experiences paroxysms of guilt, verging on madness. He is a protagonist in the struggle, described by Ibsen, 'which all serious-minded human beings have to wage with themselves to bring their lives into harmony with their convictions. For the different spiritual functions do not develop evenly and abreast of each other in any one human being . . . hence the conflict within the individual.'[21] In conversation with Hilda, Solness skirts this fearful thought, after she has suggested that he alone should have the right to build:

Solness: Here, in my solitude and silence – endlessly – I've been brooding on that same idea.

Hilda: Well, it seems only natural to me.

Solness: (looks rather sharply at her) And I'm sure you've already noticed it.

Hilda: No, not a bit.

Solness: But before – when you said you thought I was – unbalanced, there was one thing –

Hilda: Oh, I was thinking of something quite different.

Solness: What do you mean, different?

Hilda: Never you mind, Mr Solness.

Hilda is thrilled by the idea that Solness may have willed the
catastrophe which led to his success, and that she too might be
one of those chosen, ruthless people who can make her wishes a
reality. She is a believer in the strenuous will, like her creator
who said that 'what is healthy is the happiness one acquires
through the will'.[22] Ibsen was always amused by people who were
disappointed by their failure to achieve what they wanted,
believing that they had simply longed for something rather than
willed it. Hilda, too, seems to endorse the idea that those who
restrain desire do so only because theirs is weak enough to be
restrained. She is somewhat disappointed by the weakness of her
chosen man, who fears youth and heights and who rules pettily
over his skeleton staff. Most of all, she despises his instinctive
desire to be accused, his 'fragile' and 'over-refined conscience', so
different from her own robust compulsion to emulate the women
of the Vikings. 'Those women make perfect sense to me', chortles
this new barbarian, whom Solness likens to a bird of prey. 'And
why not a bird of prey?', asks Hilda. 'Why shouldn't I go hunting
as well? Take the spoil I'm after? If I can once set my claws in
it and have my own way?' Thus she imports into the world of
personal relationships that same code of exploitation which she
found so offensive in the world of business.

Ibsen once defended Hilda by commenting that her love for
Solness was morally more elevating than his wife's dutiful respect,
for Hilda at least impels the builder to give Ragnar his professional
freedom, a duty never even sensed as such by Aline.[23] But now
it is that same competitive code to which Hilda appeals in
justifying the theft of another woman's husband. 'Have you never
really loved anyone?' asks Solness in amazement, for he at least
loved his wife when they married and the memory must make
Hilda's proposal seem faintly shocking. 'Anyone else, you mean',
responds the little monster, and one is left wondering if she refers
to herself or to Solness. Even more callous is her refusal to listen
to Solness's doubts about the advisability of climbing to the apex
of his latest building. His wife knows that he can't even bear to
stand on a balcony and concludes that he is deranged. But the
ferocious lady from the mountains seems as crazy as he and drives

him on with the taunt that 'my master builder dares not – and
can not climb as high as he builds'. It is Ibsen's most radical
questioning of his own role as an artist. He who, in play after
play, had denounced the life-lie of those who lived through others
at one remove is now compelled to admit that this allegation
applies most aptly to his prudent and fearful self. He, too, had
never climbed as high as he built. The real Emilie Bardach was
not quite as imperious as Hilda – 'she didn't get me', boasted the
dramatist, 'but I got her for my art'.[24]

In the next scene the focus is switched to Mrs Solness, within
whose conventional personality lurks a militant feminist struggling
to escape. Encouraged by the bright girl at her side to be more
forthcoming than usual, she announces that it is her duty to
submit to her husband, 'but it isn't always so easy, forcing your
thoughts to obey'. In this conversation, Hilda gives to Mrs Solness
that quick instinctive sympathy which she had earlier lavished
on the Broviks. The fact that she is now in open-hearted exchange
with the woman whose husband she plans to steal does not seem
to bother her. With amazing directness, she tells the wife of how
her husband spoke of the tragedy of the lost children. Mrs Solness
complains that with *her* he seldom speaks so openly of the past,
a complaint Ibsen often made against his own wife. The poignancy
of this 'silent marriage' is hinted in the way Aline always leaves
as soon as he appears on the scene; but Hilda, momentarily seeing
the world through the wife's eyes, tells him a sharp truth – 'the
moment you come, you *make* her go'. She herself now begins to
experience the disadvantages of a fragile conscience which cannot
bear to hurt someone it *knows*. She tries to suppress such scruples
with the kind of remark which was the source of the builder's
success: 'O, its just so senseless, really . . . Not daring to take hold
of one's happiness. Of one's own life. Just because someone you
know is there, standing in the way.' This doctrine which elevates
the strong and repudiates the weak is endorsed in the course of
a scene which reads like a prophecy of the death of the family.
Hilda's own father in the mountains provided no warm home
but a 'cage'. 'Who knows if there'll be any use for such homes in
the future?', muses Solness of all the buildings he has erected.
The man who began by building churches later turned to
providing homes for people, as if his career were a search for a
viable code of ethics which would survive the death of Christianity.
George Eliot, faced with the same problem in terms of God,

Immortality and Duty, concluded that the first was inconceivable, the second unbelievable, but Duty was absolute. After the strident declamations of Aline Solness, her husband is not so sure and, little by little, his new friend teases him free of the sanctions of the past.

Hilda offers him the vision of a new sexuality, to be found on the highest pinnacle of his latest tower. Her thrill in the phallic image is as intensely sexual as her joyful dream of falling through the air with her legs pulled tight against her body. 'Why not? I'll stand right up there and look down on the others – the ones who build churches. And homes for mothers and fathers and droves of children. And you must come up and look down on them too.' Solness is fascinated by the proposal, but more than a little frightened. He recalls that momentous day in Lysanger when he resolved to build no more churches to the glory of the Almighty. From the pinnacle at Lysanger, he had issued his challenge to God: 'From this day on, I'll be a free creator – free in my own realm as you are in yours.' It is the voice of the nineteenth-century writer, from Flaubert to Joyce, asserting that henceforth the artist will be his own god. And the punishment which follows this misuse of art is terrible – the knowledge that humanism has not the power to sustain itself, that homes for humans on their own are not worth a pin, that 'it all comes to nothing'. For, all the time, the mills of the Almighty keep on grinding. The idea of an aesthetic which masquerades as morality, of a purely humanist art devoid of religious content, is an aberration for which Solness, no less than Hilda, is condemned finally to die. The artist-as-specialist is the signatory of his own death warrant; and the death to which Hilda hysterically goads him is, in Muriel Bradbrook's words, 'an inevitable, almost incidental consequence of the Life-in-Death which preceded'.[25] That dying began the moment Solness submitted to the specialist code, for it was then that he lost his chance of becoming himself. In suppressing nine-tenths of his personality for professional acclaim, Solness has destroyed himself.

The efficient division of labour, which was at once the nine-teenth century's proudest boast and greatest shame, presented man with a new problem – the need, defined by Robert Musil, for an institution which would take on the burden of correlating all disciplines. With the decline of religion, only art promised for a brief span, in the golden decades of modernism, to undertake this task. In the event, the burden proved too great and the new scepticism which had exposed the fictions of religion and the relativism of science in due course undermined· the moral foundations of art, which declined into playful self-parody and lost its high seriousness. The only solution which men like Beckett and Nabokov could find to the alienation of the artist was the completion of his alienation into a sealed and specialist world of his own. All this is foretold in *The Master Builder* by a playwright who had himself come to the same desperate conclusion.

Yet, like most prophets, Ibsen dreamed of a future in which a fragmented man would achieve a real integration of public and private self, of reason and emotion, of male and female. It is indeed possible to see in Hilda Wangel not a New Woman but an embodiment of all those instincts and emotions which Solness has learned to deny in himself. Her easy rapport with Mrs Solness, her carelessness about her own reputation, her infectious sense of fun, all seem to emanate from an *anima* buried deep within the builder's personality. Much that seemed strange in the play makes sudden sense if viewed in this light – Hilda's brazen familiarity on arrival at the office ('I almost think you don't recognise me'); her deft circumvention of his plot to employ her in the office, which she anticipates almost before it is fully formed; her intuition of the real cause of the Solness's silent marriage ('the moment you come, you *make* her go'); and her easy appropriation of the public code of the capitalist to the personal life. When Solness asks if Hilda has ever really loved anyone, that becomes an agonised question which he is putting to himself. Her earlier life is now to be seen as a constricted existence within the 'cage' of his incomplete personality. Her madness, in cultivating extreme situations and feelings, is finally revealed to be indistinguishable from his own. When he anxiously asked her what she meant by 'unbalanced', it is all too obvious why she did not reply. Dr Herdal and his wife rightly suspect that Solness may have crossed the threshold of insanity.

Solness himself is willing to believe as much. Convinced as he is of the power of the wish, he is willing to concede that Hilda may be just another of the 'helpers and servers' whom he has summoned. 'But they never come by themselves', he muses, 'one has to call on them, incessantly – within oneself, I mean.' So the promise to the girl may be seen as a vow made by Solness to himself that one day he will break out of the narrow rut of his professional career. His difficulty in recalling the golden day at Lysanger is a mark of the depth of his self-repression, but it is even more significant that his wife cannot recall any of the events which Hilda so vividly describes, most importantly, his climb to the pinnacle. If Hilda eventually goes insane, as he falls to death, it is because we are witnessing the final cleavage of his shattered personality.

In his famous essay defining the *anima*, Carl Jung describes how 'every man carries within him the eternal image of woman, not the image of this or that particular woman, but a definite feminine image'. For Solness, Hilda is such an image and what Jung has to say perfectly describes the dramatic situation: 'Since this image is unconscious, it is always unconsciously projected upon the person of the beloved and is one of the chief reasons for passionate attraction and aversion.'[26] Jung then describes the type of woman who seems by nature to attract the *anima* projection: 'The so-called sphinx-like character is an indispensable part of their equipment, also an equivocalness, an intriguing elusiveness – not an indefinite blur that offers nothing, but an indefiniteness that seems full of promises, like the speaking silence of the Mona Lisa.' That could be a thumbnail sketch of Hilda, the girl whom Solness could never fathom, who seemed half in jest – half in earnest all the time. 'A woman of this kind is both old and young, mother and daughter, of more than doubtful chastity, childlike, and yet endowed with a naive cunning that is extremely disarming to men.'[27] It is that same cunning, both knowing and childlike, which disarms Solness. According to Jung, a man can create for himself a *femme inspiratrice* by his *anima* projection, 'but more often it turns out to be an illusion with destructive consequences'.[28] It is significant that the Solness whom Ibsen describes as 'a middle-aged man, strong and forceful' has reached a point of crisis in mid-life, with his fear of being overtaken by the young. Jung says in the essay that

> Middle life is the moment of greatest unfolding, when a man still gives himself to his work with his whole strength and his whole will. But in this very moment evening is born, and the second half of life begins. Passion now changes her face and is called duty.[29]

That last sentence might have been a sly joke against Aline

Solness. Jung concludes that at this midpoint in life, 'the critical survey of himself and his fate enables a man to recognise his peculiarities. But these insights do not come to him easily; they are gained only through the severest shocks.' Such a shock would be Solness's recognition of his own incompleteness, as he sets about attaining the unity which is lacking. Jung appends to his account an analysis of the wife's dilemma in the face of this crisis: 'For the contained this is only a confirmation of the insecurity she has always felt so painfully; she discovers that in the rooms which apparently belonged to her there dwell other, unwished-for guests.'[30] And so Hilda Wangel moves into the nursery, even as the crestfallen wife is driven further in upon herself. Her best hope is that, in time, her husband will admit that his longing for unity was a mere fantasy, but this the Master Builder will never concede.

It seems doubtful that Ibsen would have admitted it either. In the character of Hilda Wangel, he depicted an ageing man attempting to come to terms with the female within himself. That Ibsen had already done so is clear in the compulsive portraits of modern women in his greatest plays. He offered no ready answers to the challenge of androgyny, beyond the increasing conviction that living in culture was at best a tedious, and at worst a terrifying process. His ideal for womanhood is only glimpsed, never explained. His dream was of someone who might combine the emotional delicacy of a woman with the intellectual clarity of a man. But it was his strength to question and transcend even these stereotypes and write of people in whom such qualities were inextricably but unevenly mingled. The man who always began with the individual demonstrated that the ideal androgyny would be as much a social as a personal discovery. 'Modern society is not a human society', he wrote once in a moment of anger, 'it is only a society of males.'[31]

4 Hardy's Sue:
The New Woman as Neurotic

> Marriage makes an end of many short follies, being one long
> stupidity.   Friedrich Nietzsche

The New Woman who came to prominence in English literature
during the heyday of the feminist movement in the 1890s had
made a first tentative appearance over a century earlier in the
fiction of Daniel Defoe. Among the many disguises resorted to by
the prostitute Moll Flanders was the male masquerade, engaged
in for the titillation of some of her more perverse customers. That
disguise also had a symbolic value for the reader, who, as has
already been shown, found many of the traditional elements of
male psychology in the heroine – an aggressive attitude to other
people, a competitive and exploitative social personality, a
mobility from place to place, an acquisitive attitude to cash, and
above all, an unfeeling approach to the life of the emotions. In
short, the prostitute was the most rudimentary manifestation of
the New Woman who had a definitely masculine side to her
personality. This sense of a covert masculinity was, of course,
enhanced for the reader by the knowledge that the author was
the male Daniel Defoe. So strong was this awareness in more
recent readers still that the classic women of eighteenth-century
fiction have come to seem more like crude female impersonators,
hapless puppets under the control of often prurient men. So,
Pamela's obsession with her own underclothing is seen less as a
credible piece of female psychology than as a clear indication of
a characteristic fetish of her creator Samuel Richardson – a fetish
which gave rise to D. H. Lawrence's allegation that the author
had achieved nothing more than 'calico pornography'. It is
certainly true that these early fictional women appraise their own
bodies and clothes with the practised eye of the male; but whether

this is a crude form of wish-fulfilment on the part of their authors, or an honest account of female psychology in a predominantly masculine culture, is an open question. With the benefit of hindsight, many critics might endorse the latter explanation. The masculine element in a Moll or a Roxana may be no flaw at all, but a mark of the novelist's deep insight into the male who has over the past two centuries been emerging as an important, if subordinate, factor in the female personality.

A further refinement on the socially mobile, acquisitive and assertive woman was offered by Jane Austen in the least likely of her books, the grimly moralistic *Mansfield Park*. In the character of Mary Crawford, she depicted a woman of little moral restraint, whose mobility from place to place contrasted with the fixed serenity of Mansfield Park, and whose commitment was to the speculative values of the cash nexus rather than the traditional pieties of the land. She conceives a grand passion for the young Edmund Bertram, but hints very strongly that the limited financial rewards of life as a rural clergyman are unfitting for a man of his potential and, by implication, for a woman of her restless ambition. After much vacillation, Edmund finally rejects her and opts instead for the unspectacular reliability of Fanny Price. In the novel, Mary Crawford speaks all the bright sparkling lines which in earlier works were the preserve of such witty heroines as Elizabeth Bennett. Yet, finally, it seems as if June Austen were willing to forsake wit and endorse the sobrieties of rural piety. The scene in which Edmund spurns the seductive charms of Mary Crawford is seen as his – and Austen's – endorsement of the puritan ethic. Certainly, that is how he recalls the situation some time later for Fanny:

> . . . She tried to speak carelessly; but she was not so careless as she wanted to appear. I only said in reply that from my heart I wished her well . . . and immediately left the room. I had gone a few steps, Fanny, when I heard the door open behind me. 'Mr. Bertram', said she, with a smile – but it was a smile ill-suited to the conversation that had passed, a saucy playful smile, seeming to invite, in order to subdue me; at least, it appeared so to me. I resisted; it was the impulse of the moment to resist and still walked on. I have since – sometimes – for a moment – regretted that I did not go back; but I know I was right.

Nobody can ever know if he was; but it does seem that he is less than charitable, less than imaginative, in the construction which he puts on Mary Crawford's smile, which is even more puzzling and enigmatic than he thinks. Edmund merely sees it as the come-hither smile of the amoral amoreuse, the seductive ploy of a degenerate vamp – and there is much evidence in the book to suggest that Mary is both wanton and seductive. But, at this particular moment, her inviting smile is the last, desperate ploy of a woman who is deeply in love. Already she has tried to woo him away from the dreary routines of the rural vicar, in part because she is modern and fast, but also because she senses that such routines will violate Edmund's human potential. The side of him that remains haunted by her smile is the side which he will now have to repress as the husband of Fanny Price, a woman who may love him, but who can never respond like Mary to his vitality as well as his self-control. When Mary fails to win him as a husband, she is strong enough to offer her love as an entirely free gift, outside the sanctions of marital control. It is a measure of his own repression that causes Edmund to misconstrue this love as lust, just as it is a mark of his own fear of the masterful New Woman who will live on her own terms or none. It is that hint of mastery in her smile, even more than its saucy lewdness, which unnerves him, 'seeming to invite, in order to subdue me'. In this phrase, the timid male's response to the New Woman is to describe his experience in the clichés which were normally used to chronicle the acquiescent woman's seduction by a masterful man. It is but the first of many such cases in the literature of the nineteenth century.

Mary is a type of the restless woman who, having abandoned the absolute codes of the past, must judge each situation on its merits, without reference to fixed moral principles. She is an exponent of situation ethics, 'a lady of situations' rather than a woman of stern morality. The result is that every situation casts her in a different role, demanding a different performance; and she becomes, like the prostitute with endless disguises, a mistress of the multiple self. She is (to use Yeats's valuable distinction) a personality rather than a character, and all her statements have an element of social performance about them. She *presents* rather than expresses herself, and, as Lionel Trilling has argued in a brilliant essay, she is guilty not of hypocrisy but of insincerity: 'Mary Crawford's intention is not to deceive the world but to comfort herself; she impersonates the woman she thinks she ought to be.'[1] She is the sort of person who savours the sensitive intelligence of her own performance – if she were alive in the 1980s, she would look soulfully into camera one and tell ten million viewers that 'I'm a very private sort of person.' A tenuous and uncertain being, she never learns to articulate her own unique character and is forced to settle instead for speaking in a range of borrowed styles. The live media of today are rich in such 'personalities', who seek in the adulation of the mass audience the reassurance that they are giving the right performance. At one fleeting moment of insight, Edmund accurately captures this condition of inauthenticity at the heart of Mary's performance. He denies to Fanny that the woman is callous or cruel, and goes on:

> . . . I do not consider her as meaning to wound my feelings. The evil lies yet deeper; in her total ignorance, unsuspiciousness of there being such feelings, in a perversion of mind which made it natural to her to treat the subject as she did. She was speaking only as she had been used to hear others speak, as she imagined everybody else would speak.

The New Woman is finally elusive and cannot be pinned down. Though Mary Crawford smiles her way out of the novel with Edmund's moral denunciations ringing in her ears, one cannot help feeling that Austen abandons her with regret – but also with the conviction that the future very definitely belongs to the Mary Crawfords. By the end of the century, Mary Crawford will find her logical consummation in the figure of Hilda Wangel, the self-confident woman who can sympathise with the troubles of a builder's wife and then go out to seduce the builder – with no sense of moral inconsistency or hypocrisy. Hilda's sense of self is unstable, easily dissolved by the empathy she feels for each person in a given situation.

The ultimate development of this personality is to be found in Hardy's *Jude the Obscure*, where Sue Bridehead repeatedly fails to achieve definition. As she escapes into the arms of Phillotson, she is always looking longingly over her shoulder at the abandoned Jude, and vice versa. Her very irresolution is spellbinding in the challenge it poses to a man – the challenge that he may be able to supply the missing element which would make a puzzle into a personality and make a personality into a character. This is obviously what Jude is thinking when he considers Sue and wonders if a woman is a thinking unit or a fraction always wanting its integer. Of course, such a woman in all her vibrating irresolution is also fascinating because she is flirting with the possibility of disintegration.

Jude the Obscure is the perfect novel to describe such a personality, for, as Irving Howe has observed, it is one of the earliest modernist novels in the sense that it is based less on a developing plot than on a succession of situations.[2] A developing plot would imply that there was some logic in sexual relations; but the personality of Sue Bridehead does not develop or grow in such a purposeful way. It is at once static and impulse-ridden, and it finds its definition in exemplary situations rather than in the slow unfolding of a plot.

Probably the most memorable of these situations is the moment when Sue, having waded across the river in her escape from the Training College, sits shivering in Jude's best suit in his sitting-room, an image of the New Woman, at once precarious and magnificent in the finest robes of a man. Jude leaves the room to give her time to change into these new clothes; and when he returns 'sitting in his only arm-chair he saw a slim and fragile being, masquerading as himself on a Sunday, so pathetic in her defencelessness that his heart felt big with the sense of it'. As she sits there, sleeping off her weariness, he stands with his back to the fire and 'saw in her almost a divinity'. He is in love, but what he is worshipping at is the shrine of the New Woman, who has enough of the man in her to seize the initiative in their subsequent relationship. The joke about the woman who wears the trousers will assume a new and tragic dimension. For the moment, however, all is tenderness in what may be the most poignant scene in the book.

Feminists would, of course, say that the charm of the scene for a man is based on its covert appeal to male concepts of superiority. After all, they could point to the fact that the woman's magnificence is based on the fact that she is dressed in clothes *borrowed* from a man; and they might point to the male vanity implicit in Jude's patronising a fragile girl 'masquerading as himself'. But that is not the real appeal of the situation at all. Hardy has absolutely no interest in the masterful female who seeks to usurp the force and power of the male, in the woman who sees sex less as an exploration of variousness than as a mode of revenge. He saw that such a one has surrendered most abjectly to the bankrupt notion of masculine superiority. For him, as for Jude, Sue is never more feminine than when she shivers in the inappropriateness of a man's Sunday suit. It is as if the very masculinity of her clothes has served only to add lustre to her vibrant femininity by contrast – a discovery made only decades later by the dress designers of Paris and London who realised that a woman could look more striking in a trouser-suit than in a ballroom gown. Such a discovery recalls the era of Restoration Comedy when, for the first time, female actresses – many of them prostitutes – appeared on the London stage in roles which required them sometimes to adopt the disguise of men. It was a favourite trick of Restoration dramatists, as of Shakespeare, to have a Rosalind play a Ganymede, because the tight-fitting blouse and hip-hugging trousers of the male allowed these elegant ladies to show off far more of the female form than the billowing dresses and voluminous skirts of the day could ever reveal. For similar reasons, it is foolish of conservative critics to lament the current unisex fashions as a retreat into a dull unimaginative sexlessness. If anything, they are the reverse – the longer hair of males and the tight-fitting trousers of females betoken a return to an even more explicit sexuality.

So Hardy attires Sue in a man's suit because he is anxious to define the precise quality of her femininity, its precarious charm along with its charming precariousness; but also because her clothing represents her rejection of the clichés of sexual stereotyping. Hardy moves beyond the old notion of the passive female in order to capture the actual androgyny of the modern sexual protagonist. So, the 'plot' of *Jude of Obscure* has often been described as a deliberate reversal of the conventions of the Victorian novel. In the typical melodrama (and, indeed, in *Tess of the D'Urbervilles*), the rascally male deflowers a chaste girl, as Alec violates Tess; she is then abandoned to her awful fate; by the end, she has died amid scenes of terrible corruption.[3] In this novel, on the contrary, it is Jude who is seduced by the manipulative Arabella; it is he who is abandoned by her; it is he who turns to her again for a comfort never found in Sue; and it is he who dies at the end, while the reckless female libertine is already making eyes at another man. This nicely illustrates a point first made by Elizabeth Hardwick – that there are two New

Women in this book, not just one. Although Arabella conforms externally as far as she can to the conventions of her time, she conforms only to manipulate those conventions to her own material advantage, for, in her heart, she cares as little for the sanctity of marriage and the welfare of children as Sue. She, too, is restless, acquisitive, mobile, and never satisfied for long. Hardwick may be right in saying that Arabella is really as abstract about life as Sue, as sceptical and as non-conforming,[4] the only difference being that Arabella is more willing to make some concession to the ways of the world and always insistent on gratifying the impulses of the body. At all events, it is she who initiates the courtship, she who bleeds the pig, she who reconstitutes the marriage; whereas Jude meekly submits with the kind of resignation normally reserved for the heroine of a more conventional tale. There seems to be a strong element of the female sensibility in Jude, just as there is an element of the male in Arabella, and, even more subtly, in Sue.

Being more subtle a part of Sue, this male dimension is more attractive in her, not least because it presupposes a certain social risk. This she hints at in conversation with Jude, while she sits shivering in his suit:

> My life has been entirely shaped by what people call a peculiarity in me. I have no fear of men, as such, nor of their books. I have mixed with them – one or two of them particularly – almost as one of their own sex. I mean I have not felt about them as most women are taught to feel – to be on their guard against attacks on their virtue – for no average man will molest a woman unless she invites him . . . and if you never invite with a word or a look, he never comes.

It is this which leads up to her account of life with the young intellectual who died, and to her boast that 'I have remained as I began.' Jude wonders if she is a cold, sexless woman, but Sue denies this. So far from being sexless, she is, in fact, androgynous; and that is what Jude feels, though it is left to Hardy to put it into words: 'Jude felt much depressed; she seemed to get further and further away from him with her strange ways and curious unconsciousness of gender.' He feels that she is treating him cruelly, but cannot explain why – in some strange way, her very helplessness seems to make her far stronger than he. The cruelty may lie in her awareness that the more she denies her own sexuality, the more she puts on male attitudes as well as male clothes, the more overt does her sexual charm become for him, even as it thereby denies the possibility of its own realisation. It is the teasing routine of the Third Reich cabaret show, the woman dressed in male clothing and wielding a psychic whip. Her helplessness is manifest; but deeper still is the awareness that only a woman of massive independence of mind would dare to expose herself to such risk. So, she never seems stronger than when she appears most weak.

On this level, Sue becomes a belated English version of Joan of Arc, who shed female clothing and paid for this transgression with her life. Deuteronomy had taught that all who put on the garments of the opposite sex were an 'abomination unto the Lord thy God'; but Joan not only failed to relent, but steadfastly refused to give any explanation for her behaviour, such as the preservation of her chastity among men. Marina Warner explains this obstinacy:

> Through her transvestism, she abrogated the destiny of womankind. She could thereby transcend her sex; she could set herself apart and usurp the privileges of the male and his claims to superiority. At the same time, by never pretending to be other than a woman and a maid, she was not only usurping a man's function but shaking off the trammels of his sex altogether to occupy a different, third order, neither male nor female, but unearthly, like the angels whose company she loved.[5]

According to Warner, Joan's transvestism unsexed her, but did not confer manhood, leaving her instead an ideal androgyne:

> There is no mode of being particular to the third sex, or to androgyny. But as the rejection of femininity is associated with positive action, it assumes the garb of virtue, in the classical sense, *virtus* . . . so she borrowed the apparel of men, who held a monopoly on virtue, on reason and courage, while eschewing the weakness of women, who were allotted to the negative pole, where virtue meant weakness and humility and nature meant carnality.[6]

So, Joan saw herself not as male, 'but as not-female', a kind of man who, in cutting her hair, renounces and transcends sexuality, on the Pauline principle that after baptism 'there is neither male nor female, for ye are all one in Christ Jesus' (Galatians: 3:28).[7] Warner concedes that such transcendence can never be absolute, because the imitation of Christ is still the imitation of a male and men remain the touchstone. 'Ironically', she concludes, 'Joan's life, probably one of the most heroic a woman has ever lived, is a tribute to the male principle.'[8]

Warner's analysis of Joan offers some fascinating parallels and some important contrasts with D. H. Lawrence's famous essay on Sue Bridehead, whom he saw as 'not the virgin type, but the witch type, which has no sex'. Lawrence sees Sue as one 'born with the vital female atrophied in her', one who is 'almost male'. 'Her *will* was male', he says, 'It was wrong for Jude to take her physically, it was a violation of her.'[9] Like the heroines of Ibsen and Strindberg, who secretly worship the male principle while despising males, Sue is seen by Lawrence as one who commits a cardinal error:

> She wished to identify herself utterly with the male principle. That which was female in her she wished to consume within the male force, to consume it in the fire of understanding, of giving utterance. Whereas an ordinary woman knows that she *contains* all understanding, that she is the unutterable which man must forever continue to try to utter, Sue felt that all must be uttered, must be given to the male, that, in truth, only Male existed.[10]

In this state, Sue exerts a powerful attraction over Jude, who is in flight from the female, after his catastrophic marriage to the sensuous Arabella. That slight residual element of the female in Sue is roused by Jude's manliness and wants even kisses to quicken itself, but nothing more, for, says Lawrence, 'she could only *live* in the mind'. What she wanted was a man who would feed her with his male vitality, with kisses and talk, *without* seeking a corresponding female return from her. 'She made no mistake in marrying Phillotson', observes Lawrence wryly.[11] Jude is destroyed by his very versatility, by his need for the female within, by his refusal to worship always and only the male principle. Sue is developed to the very extreme and so she scarcely lives in the body at all. 'Being of the feminine gender, she is yet no woman at all, nor male; she is almost neuter. He is nearer the balance, nearer the centre, nearer the wholeness.'[12]

If Sue Bridehead is a diluted latter-day version of Joan of Arc, the ultimate illustration of the prototype may be found in the female clothing of our own century. Marlene Dietrich donned the elegant pinstripes of the male to project 'sophistication, power and dangerous eroticism';[13] but most men did not take kindly to the fashion, for which no less a woman than Greta Garbo was hooted off a stage. Although the jeans and jerseys worn by men and women in the 1960s and 1970s were 'a gesture toward sexual equality', the Annie Hall look of the late 1970s revealed the true conservatism at the root of the prototype. In the words of Alison Lurie:

> The Annie Hall style is a double message. It announces that its wearer is a good sport, a pal: not mysteriously and delicately female, but an easy-going, ready-for-anything tomboy type, almost like one of the guys. She will not demand to be protected from the rain or make a fuss about having to stand up at a football game . . . At the same time, however, these clothes convey an ironic antifeminist message. Because they are worn several sizes too large, they suggest a child dressed up in her daddy's or older brother's things for fun and imply 'I'm only playing' . . .[14]

In suggesting that she is only masquerading as a man, the girl projects not an air of authority, but 'a look of helpless cuteness'.

In the end, it is this same conservative streak which comes to dominate in Sue Bridehead. Though she issues her conscious appeal as a radical, on a subconscious level her behaviour has a powerful attraction for the traditionalist mind, a mind such as Jude's when he falls in love with her. For one thing, her offer of a disinterested friendship, beyond the reach of mere sexuality, is based on an aversion to the human body.[15] For another, she is a somewhat selective feminist, in that she rejects only those aspects of the moral tradition which no longer suit her, but she is still willing to exploit other features of the traditional code. All through the nineteenth century, men had put women on a pedestal of purity – women were, by definition, holier, purer and more refined than men. The reasoning behind the ploy was obvious. If women were refined and sensitive, then their delicacy must not be corrupted or lost in confrontations with the workaday world. The woman's place was in the home, as an angel of the house, preserving the values of civilisation. Traditionalists argued that because she was refined, she was excused the sweaty burden of labour; but feminists began to assert that because she was acquiescent, woman was denied the right to work and vote in public affairs. The feminists were right – superior in theory, the woman was deemed inferior in practice. What is interesting, however, is the selective nature of the argument as advanced by most feminists. Although they rejected the notion of the woman's place being in the home, they never rejected the theory of woman's superior refinement and sensitivity. On the contrary, they seized gratefully on the idea and used it as an argument for female independence, and ultimately, in very extreme cases, for female dominance over men. In the 'Bloomsbury years', this movement reached its flowering in a spectacular range of non-sexual friendships between androgynous women and passive men, the assumption being that the woman, by her fastidiousness and grace, might civilise and ennoble her comrade.

Sue Bridehead is the living precursor of that tradition, casting herself in the role of feminist civiliser: 'But I did want and long to ennoble some man to high aims; and when I saw you, and knew you wanted to be my comrade, I thought that man might be you' – she tells Jude. Of course, it is in part the woman in Jude who is responding to the man in Sue, the woman who by tradition longs to have the world explained to her by a resourceful and caring man. It is that male element in Sue which causes Jude to feel that she is so much stronger than he, just as it is precisely because he has a feminine dimension that he can respond so vibrantly to that challenge. But never totally, for their levels of androgyny differ to a marked degree, to the point where a sexual harmonisation is impossible. There is only a hint of the female in Jude; but the male in Sue has already become forceful – if not completely dominant, then at least strong enough to reduce and virtually negate her female sex drive. Jude's psychology is traditional enough for him to anticipate a satisfactory climax to their relationship in the bridal bed; but Sue is seeking a consummation beyond mere sexuality. It is this aspiration which finally confuses and destroys Jude. He can sympathise with it; he can try hard to understand it; but he can never finally condone it:

He looked away, for that epicene tenderness of hers was too harrowing. Was it that which had broken the heart of the poor leader-writer; and was he to be the next one? . . . But Sue was so dear! . . . If he could only get over the sense of her sex, as she seemed to be able to do so easily of his, what a comrade she would make! . . .

There follows a beautiful touch by Hardy, prefiguring so much of their subsequent relationship: 'Her chair being a far more comfortable one than his, she still slept on inside his coat, looking warm as a new bun and boyish as Ganymede.'

This is not to suggest that the male element dominates the female in Sue to such a degree as to make her a lesbian; but it is powerful enough to smother her sexual instincts.[16] If Sue were a lesbian, she might in most respects be more emotionally fulfilled – and consequently more attractive as a person. But she is simply over-fastidious and over-bred, the logical development of one of the strands in the New Womanhood which will result in the evasive androgyny espoused by Virginia Woolf. Although Hardy seems to have been in near total sympathy with women and the women's movement, he chose *Jude the Obscure* as the book in which to shout stop to a tendency which was going too far. It is a crucial aspect of living in culture that each sex should cultivate a sensitive awareness of the needs and aspirations of the other; and one of the great achievements of modern life has been to sharpen this awareness, so that any man can learn of the respective merits of various tampons by taking an escalator on the London underground, and any woman need only watch a television film to know in detail the conversational topics of a footballers' locker-room. The varieties of sexual difference have been demystified, almost to the point where the culture itself is androgynous, as women wear dungarees and work as engineers, while men increasingly push prams and change nappies. These in themselves are progressive and overdue trends, but they carry with them the danger that sex itself will become a victim of the new androgyny, which would be better dubbed the new asexuality – to the very point where there will be no children created for men to wheel around in prams, because sexual difference will have been so diminished as to jeopardise the survival of the species. Already, researchers tell us that autoeroticism (once the pleasant preserve of the adolescent) is now the most common form of sexual gratification between couples in their twenties, married and unmarried, to such a degree that the spectacle of a woman masturbating is seen by an onlooking male as a source of excitement rather than a reproach to his adequacy.[17]

It was the long-term implication of such non-creative asexuality which Hardy had in mind when he depicted Sue's rejection of her own motherhood. Her children are never named, as if they were not for her embodiments of passion and love. When Father Time kills her offspring and himself, on the most obvious level he is simply calling her radical bluff – exposing the fact that her trendy nihilism is 90 per cent talk, and reminding her that for an impressionable child, shunted from one parent to another, it can all be too grievously real. On an even deeper level, as the progressive doctor says, the suicide is part of the coming universal will not to live, part of an ever-growing tendency in modern life. Whereas the young Jude Fawley failed to manage a suicide on the ice-pond, his son is made of sterner stuff. It is clear, however, that that son dies less by his own hand than by Sue's neglect, by her failure as a mother, by her refusal of tenderness, and by her masochist's sensitivity to her own exquisite misery, which far exceeds any concern of hers for the sufferings of the children. The fundamental selfishness of her complaint against life is manifest in the fact that it is finally more a performance of suffering than the real thing. Her suffering has grown histrionic, indistinguish-able from its own self-approving performance, like Beckett's Hamm who yawns and asks: 'Can there be misery – (yawn) – loftier than mine?' There can and there is; but Sue, clearly, does not believe so deeply in her own nihilism as to commit suicide. Not even the death of her own children can drive her to that. Only a child takes human complaints literally.

Sue's lack of real interest in her children is the most obvious indication of her fundamentally narcissistic personality. Her noble rejection of sexist role-stereotyping becomes in the end a rejection of sexuality itself; and this, in turn, is an expression of her conviction that society has no future. In this, she contrasts utterly with Jude, who joins an Artisans' Improvement Society to ensure the fulfilment of his dream of poor boys at Christminster. As his misfortunes increase and multiply, Jude's sense of the future paradoxically grows more and more clear. He senses that his struggle will be successful, even though he may not himself live to witness that success. To his fellow artisans in Christminster, he asserts that the university was not built for the wealthy but for people like him: 'It was my poverty and not my will that consented to be beaten. It takes two or three generations to do what I tried to do in one.'

Jude began as a committed Christian, but ends as a convinced radical, one who would rather go hungry than redecorate the walls of a decaying Christianity and its churches. (This response throws a new light on Sue's willingness to work on Anglican illuminations in whose value she did not believe.) Jude is, in the deepest emotional and intellectual sense, a self-educated man, one who has been massively changed by his experiences; while Sue is just an ever-increasing accumulation of opinions and dogmas. So Jude divests himself of innumerable illusions, on the principle enunciated by the Marx who wrote that the demand to give up illusions about a situation is nothing other than the demand to give up a situation which can feed off such illusions. Jude emerges as the authentic radical whom Sue had only played at being.

His tragedy is that the price of such knowledge, because it is lived out as a high-risk experience rather than a cozy theory, is physical collapse and social ostracism. Worse still, his rate of emancipation never did fully coincide with Sue's, for theirs was always a problem of synchronisation. By the time he is a committed agnostic, her own radical ideas have collapsed under the assault of a conventional society, having no real conviction of their own based on experience. At root, Sue lacks a real interest in other people, that interest which is the origin of all true socialism. So it is finally left to Jude to extend her insights into the limits of bourgeois marriage and the constrictions of the nuclear family. What makes Jude one of the most credible characters in English fiction is his creator's capacity to show this growth from within, not as an espousal of radical abstractions, but as a gradual loss of illusion under the pressure of new situations.

Jude's is the socialist radicalism endorsed in the end by Hardy. Sue's radical dogma is more a form of self-therapy than an honest struggle for social change. Like a phoney fellow-traveller on the fringes of a revolution, she treats politics not as a means of social advance but as a form of self-realisation. Her obsession with her private personality is merely a confession of despair about the future of society. She is 'an epicure in emotions', someone who runs from one experimental adventure to the next, in search of new excitements, for her tenuous selfhood can only express itself in an endless stream of new sensations. 'I do like to do things this way', she whispers to Jude as she forces him to rehearse the wedding-role of his rival Phillotson; and later still, by way of explaining this perversity, she says: 'I do like to hunt up a new experience.' In a book called *The Culture of Narcissism*, Christopher Lasch alleges that this endless search for new sensations is the desperate ploy of an over-bred and anxiety-ridden society, whose members fear they have lost the ability to feel and are driven in consequence to seek reassurance in extreme situations. 'People have erected so many psychological barriers against strong emotion', says Lasch, 'and have invested these defences with so much of the energy derived from forbidden impulses, that they can no longer remember what it feels like to be inundated by desire – rather they tend to be consumed by rage.'[18] There could be no fitter description of the narcissism of Sue Bridehead, or of that inner rage which prompts her to humiliate her men when she is not punishing herself. For, as Lasch shows, the true basis of narcissism is not self-admiration but self-hatred; and the paradox of Sue Bridehead lies in the fact that although she has turned her back on her fellow humans, she still lacks an authentic inner life.[19] All she has is a set of roles, each a phase in her self-conscious enactment of the drama of the New Woman. For her, as for many fairweather left-wingers of the 1960s, radical ideas are not a high-risk challenge, but instead a cosy retreat from the complexities of life.

Sue stands caught between the old world of Marygreen and the modern values of city life, but belongs to neither. Her behaviour in this predicament interestingly reflects the characteristic psychological disturbances of the last century and of this. According to Freud, the characteristic ailment of the nineteenth century was the vice of repression, the self-censorship and sublimation of hidden conflicts. In keeping with this model, Sue repeatedly checks her own libertarian impulses and turns finally to sublimate them in a crackpot religion. According to Lasch, however, in the twentieth century this character has been replaced by the chaotic, impulse-ridden personality, who acts out conflicts instead of repressing them, and who, lacking the capacity for sublimation, depends on others for approval.[20] In certain of her moods and whims, Sue also fits this description. Her overtures to Jude are no sooner made than checked; her every letter to him includes a repudiation of all she said at their last meeting; and she blows as hot and cold with Jude as she had earlier done with Phillotson. She needs to reject an admiring male at regular intervals in order to feed her self-esteem. In that sense, she prefigures the pansexuality of the modern narcissist, who discourages deep attachments because he cannot cope with the risk of self-revelation, but who finds in an endless series of strangers the approval needed to inflate his always tenuous self-esteem.[21] Sue is no bed-hopper, but in the society of her time she is the next best thing. She can never expose herself sensually to another, because a man like Jude or Phillotson will always seek an ever-deepening openness. So Sue can abandon herself only to the roses at the Flower Show, because they do not demand a response, because there the one-way relationship is under her control. Yet such a gesture is maddening to Jude, as any young man who has ever seen a beautiful woman caress a flower on a tall stem will know. Sue's evasion of sexuality in human relationships means that it must find expression in other forms, like caressing flowers in the company of a man, with a tenderness which she can never hope to bestow on him.

In that sense, too, Sue seems to anticipate another kind of New Woman, not the radical feminist but her polar opposite, the seductress of modern advertisements. She prefigures a culture in which real giving is a rarity, but in which modern woman nevertheless gives herself in a thousand indirect ways on billboards, where half-naked ladies purvey anything from cars to aftershave, on films and records where heavy breathing and sighs indicate a surrender that is promised only in public, but all too seldom made in private. She prophesies the world of mini-orgasms, the world which offers a climax with every advertisement, but a world in which true intimacy is less and less possible, because of the violation of private experience by such advertisements, films and records. Sue Bridehead is the first lady of a culture which has conspired to make passion a thing of the past, and Irving Howe has brilliantly discerned the underlying strategy: 'She is all feminine charm, but without body, without flesh or smell, without femaleness. Lacking a focussed sexuality, she casts a vaguely sexual aura over everything she touches . . . '[22] It is a perfect description not just of Sue, but of a culture which has saturated itself in various displacements of sexuality, but only because it is scared stiff of real passion.

Christopher Lasch's most potent allegation against modern culture is that it offers only an endless parade of experiences, each usurping the last at breakneck speed, with the result that experience in the old sense no longer exists, but has been degraded to the level of mere sensation. All too often, experience plays little or no part in the education of a character or a sensibility. This is what is so modern and so distressing about Sue Bridehead – the fact that for her, as for many of us, experience plays an increasingly minor role as a source of information and judgement. Her judgements are all based solely on theory, and in the end she lacks the experience that might enable her to validate one theory and reject another, with the result that she abandons all pretence of judgement and submits herself to a superstitious distortion of Christianity.

The dreary, programmatic nature of much modern sexuality, so unerringly depicted by T. S. Eliot in *The Waste Land*, is the inevitable outcome of a society where experience has been unsurped by the agony column and the sex manual as the primary source of wisdom. Sue Bridehead makes great play of her reading and reels off a list of the most progressive authors, but, like most moderns, she has already read far too much. The reading list, far from being a proud boast, is a confession of defeat – the defeat of her capacity to learn from what happens to her. From now on, everything will be 'learned' at one remove from the flux of a life, and a perniciously critical distance will be maintained from what were once instinctive and unself-conscious activities, like conversing with a friend or walking into a railway station.

The inevitable result of a culture in which people learn more from books than from experience is a diminution of their sense of reality.[23] *Everything* becomes a self-conscious performance and even the most innocuous statements have to be placed in inverted commas by a change of tone or a trick of the voice. Lasch sees this penchant for self-deprecation and self-irony as the over-sophistication of a culture that no longer believes what it is saying.[24] That malaise also afflicts Sue Bridehead, most notably in the fateful scene in Jude's room, just after she has silenced him with her daring ideas and daring booklist. In his myopic and honest way, he has just tried to explain his Christian beliefs, but the superior agnostic radical deflects his intensity, preferring to see it as a phase in a performance which she had long since mastered and abandoned: ' "You are in the Tractarian stage just now, are you not?" she added, putting on flippancy to hide real feeling, a common trick with her. "Let me see – when was I there? – in the year eighteen hundred and . . ." '

At the root of these evasive ironies and contrived flippancies is Sue's half-honest concession that she has found no authentic self to speak a sentence that would be truly her own. That sense of personal inauthenticity often assails Jude, too, but he never indulges it and always battles hard to fight it off. Even on the streets of Christminster, when pedestrians look through him as if he is not there, he insists on the reality of his life and proves it by learning from all experiences. Sue, on the other hand, does not; and those repeated references to her as 'a sprite', 'a fairy', 'a vision', though intended as compliments, finally serve only to convince the reader of her inauthentic being. But . . . if it is Sue's inauthenticity which haunts the reader as he puts down the novel, that is because it is a very modern inauthenticity strangely like his own.

5   W. B. Yeats: Robartes' Quarrel with the Dancer

> I think a man and woman should choose each other for life, for the simple reason that a long life with all its accidents is barely long enough for a man and woman to understand each other; and, in this case, to understand is to love . . . The man who understands one woman is qualified to understand pretty well everything.
>
>   John Butler Yeats to his son

Although a reactionary in politics, W. B. Yeats was a radical on questions of sex, for what he sought was nothing less than a revolution in the relations between men and women, a major reform of the educational system to bring this about, and an end to all forms of sexual repression in Ireland. In a speech to the Irish Senate, he complained that it was a universal habit to discourage any enquiry into the emotional relations between men and women. In his poetry, he asserted the right, already won by the scientist, to fearless investigation of the entire contents of the human mind. He claimed that the two most important things in life are sex and death – and, as any man grows older, he comes to realise that they are alternative versions of the same thing. The young Yeats was an impassioned critic of bourgeois domesticity, offering the comment that he had seen more men destroyed by a wife and children than by drink and harlots. Of one failed poet he cuttingly observed that 'the harlots in his case finished what the virtues began, but it was the virtues and not the harlots which killed his knack of verse.'[1] The older Yeats in the Senate was a scathing opponent of censorship, but he never lost his humour and joked that the three monuments in Dublin's main thoroughfare O'Connell Street were all encouraging – the epic lecher Daniel O'Connell himself surrounded by bullet-scarred angels, Admiral

Nelson, whom James Joyce had dubbed 'the one-handled adulterer', and finally Charles Stewart Parnell, the Galahad *in extremis*.

The beginnings of Yeats's career as a sexual radical were not auspicious. A visiting boy sat with the nervous youth in a hayloft in Sligo and explained the mechanism of sex. Yeats almost fainted and was miserable for weeks, afterwards complaining that the boy's clinical description was devoid of emotion. At home, Mrs Yeats taught her children to feel disgust at all displays of emotion and, in particular, she denounced the lack of reserve of English tourists kissing in the railway station at Sligo. From his father, however, Yeats learned that only those who have deep emotions experience the need to control them – it was not the forwardness of those tourists which appalled John Butler Yeats, but the shallowness of an all-too-visible emotion.

The young poet filled his early work with untamed and superb women, without homes or children, but in the presence of most girls he was shy and awkward.[2] His only real friendship was with the poetess Katharine Tynan, with whom he discussed the technique of verse. It was a purely intellectual liaison, yet such were the conventions of the time that Yeats came to believe that these frequent meetings imposed the obligation to seek her hand in marriage. She sensibly discouraged such lunacy – all the more reprehensible in a penniless poet – but she continued to value the friendship, proving to Yeats that it was easier for a man to have an open discussion with a woman than with another man, who usually offered only a competing thought. Indeed, Yeats's use for male friends was strictly subordinate to his involvement with women, for he wrote: 'We poets would die of loneliness but for women, and we choose our men friends that we may have somebody to talk about women with.'[3] There is little evidence that Yeats reached any great degree of intimacy with other males. His one recorded visit to a pub, in the company of F. R. Higgins, lasted all of five minutes.

It was this early *rapport* with an intellectual woman like Katharine Tynan which gave Yeats the courage to launch into a whole range of friendships with some of the most advanced New Women of his age, with writers, actresses, dancers and political activists. Their self-assurance seemed to contrast fascinatingly with his own timidity. The self-sufficient woman was to become a dominant protagonist in some of his major poems, which seek obsessively to penetrate the mind of a Maud

Gonne or Con Markievicz immersed in revolutionary politics, of a professional dancer like Louie Fuller lost in the patterns of her dance, of the Virgin Mary at the mystic moment of her impregnation by the Holy Ghost. It was as if, in seeking out these superb ladies, the poet was searching for his anti-self, a point neatly illustrated by his first affair with a married lady whom he called by the fictional name 'Diana Vernon', making her sound like a robust schoolgirl straight out of a mystery story by Enid Blyton. She was, in fact, Olivia Shakespeare, and she played the role of confident seductress to Yeats's timid accomplice. On their first expedition to buy furniture for the love-nest, the poet was anxious to end his embarrassment by purchasing the first double-bed on offer, but Olivia insisted on viewing bed after bed, with all the cynicism of a long-standing expert (which she was not). In the face of a leering shop assistant, she drew Yeats into an excruciating conversation about the desirable size of the bed and her bashful consort was suitably appalled when the salesman pointed out that every extra inch would increase the price. Mrs Yeats would scarcely have approved of Mrs Shakespeare, who chose to seduce the poet in a railway station, albeit in England. He recalled the fall wryly: 'I do not think that I knew any way of kissing, for when on our first railway journey together in Kent she gave me the long passionate kiss of love, I was startled and a little shocked.' He was twenty-nine at the time.[4]

It was from such early affairs that Yeats came to an awareness of the need for a reform in the relations between the sexes. The doctrine of the time was, in the words of Wilde's Lord Darlington, that 'between men and women there is no friendship possible – passion, enmity, worship, love, but no friendship'. For Yeats the great flaw in traditional notions of courtly love was the way in which passion denied lovers the capacity to enjoy a friendship of equals. He saw, earlier than most, that placing a woman on a pedestal was simply a convenient way of impressing and ignoring her, of seeming to esteem her while really refusing to take her seriously. To the actress Florence Farr he explained his own feeling: 'You cannot think what a pleasure it is to be fond of somebody to whom one can talk – as a rule any sort of affection annihilates conversation . . . To be moved and talkative, unrestrained, one's own self, and to be this not because one has created some absurd delusion that it is all wisdom, but because one has found an equal – that is the best in life.'[5] What attracted him to Florence Farr was her assault on the insulting code of gallantry and her unsparing mockery of timid suitors who longed to kiss her but hesitated for want of courage. Her technique was to seize the stammering male firmly by the wrists, jerk him into her arms, say 'Let's get this over', give him his kiss, and then proceed to converse on topics of more interest to herself.[6] This parody of false gallantry was a style adopted by Yeats who signed letters to her: 'Yours always, shall I say affectionately, or would that arouse too much scorn?'[7] That deep suspicion of the debased vocabulary of courtly love was increased by his failure to win Maud Gonne in an old-fashioned courtship and he grew even more scornful of it in old age, when he wrote to the dancer Margot Ruddock:

> I understand what you feel about the word 'love'. I, too, hate that word and have, I think, avoided it. It is a name for the ephemeral charm of desire – desire for its own sake. I do not think that it is because I have grown old, that I value something more like friendship because founded on common interest, and think sexual pleasure an accessory, a needful one where it is possible.[8]

He goes on to say that Paris and Helen were probably romantic fools, but, as for himself, he prefers Odysseus and Penelope. It is no accident that the mature Yeats should finally endorse the myth of heroic ordinariness beloved by Joyce, for both men were arch-critics of romantic humbug and staunch believers in the androgyny of the full personality.

Yeats despised an educational system which trained young men to be merely rational and virile and young women to be merely emotional and pretty, for he held that men should enrich their personalities with emotion and women strengthen theirs by self-reliance. Those traits of the New Woman which he most admired recalled to his mind the fierce female warriors of the ancient Celts. In a play written in his thirties, *On Baile's Strand*, he had the hero Cuchulain voice his admiration for Aoife, the queen whose character was modelled on that of Florence Farr:

> You call her a 'fierce woman of the camp',
> For, having lived among the spinning wheels,
> You'd have no woman near that would not say,

'Ah! how wise!' 'What will you have for supper?'
'What shall I wear that I may please you, sir?'

This speech is uttered to Conchubar, the king who has brought
peace to the land, but Cuchulain has no time for such tame living
or for the seductive comforts of family life. The critique of
domesticity is bitterly expressed when Cuchulain berates his
former comrades for their acquiescence to the new regime:

It's you that have changed. You've wifes and children now,
And for that reason cannot follow one
That lives like a bird's flight from tree to tree.

The poet who believed that Synge would never have written a
worthwhile play if he had settled down and married, now causes
Cuchulain to express his predilection for the superb woman who
spurns family life:

You have never seen her. Ah! Conchubar, had you seen her
With that high, laughing, turbulent head of hers
Thrown backward, and the bowstring at her ear,
Or sitting at the fire with those grave eyes
Full of good counsel as it were with wine,
Or when love ran through all the lineaments
Of her wild body – although she had no child,
None other had all beauty, queen or lover,
Or was so fitted to give birth to kings.

Cuchulain can only conceive of love as a kiss in mid-battle,

A brief forgiveness between opposites,
That have been hatreds for three times the age
Of this long-'stablished ground.

So he can love only the woman who is already his military foe,
on the Blakean principle that sexual love is spiritual hate. The
masculine will to power can manifest itself only against resistances,
as Nietzsche taught, and thus it seeks out that which resists it,
the woman who is most aggressive in her attitude to men. In the
words of David Lynch, 'the real stuff of the Yeatsian drama is
the murderous ambivalence women feel toward the men they

love best, a drama of adoration and loathing that is summed up visually in the pillar-stone to which Aoife binds Cuchulain . . . '[9]

Cuchulain chooses Aoife as his lover in deference to her very ambivalence, which guarantees a sexual encounter which will never be conditional upon a surrender to the restrictions of family life. But he is vanquished even in this, for a young emissary arrives from Aoife who so wins the warrior's fancy that he refuses to engage him in single combat. The reason is simple, for the boy's red hair reminds the androgynous hero of the woman he once had loved. 'The very tint/Of her that I was speaking of but now', he explains to his baffled king. Despite repeated exhortations to fight the youth, who has challenged all Ireland in challenging her foremost man, Cuchulain refuses and resorts with the boy to the tame domestic life which so recently he had scorned. The king puts all this down to witchcraft, but Cuchulain denies it is so:

> No witchcraft. His head is like a woman's head
> I had a fancy for.

At the close of the play, Cuchulain is goaded into fighting and killing the youth, who turns out to have been his own and Aoife's son. Maddened by grief, he dies fighting the waves. And so Aoife exacts a double revenge on the enemy of her people and on the warrior who loved and left her. The triumph of the New Woman is complete.

The self-reliant woman is not just a fascinating image in Yeats's poetry and plays, but a practical aspiration of his political life as well. In an unjustly neglected Senate speech of 1925, he staunchly defended the rights of women to work on equal terms with men in the new civil service of the Free State. Remarking that the actresses and dancers whom he knew did not retire from the stage on marriage, he complained that the senators were endangering the very institution of marriage by their refusal to allow married women to remain in the service. The effect of such legislation would be to rob the public service of many gifted women *and* to make it difficult for many women to marry.[10] Later, Yeats was to apply the same logic in an undelivered speech in defence of divorce, for again he accused the senators of eroding rather than enhancing the ideal of marriage. 'The price you pay for an indissoluble marriage', he warned them wickedly, 'is a public opinion that will tolerate cynical and illegal relations between the sexes.'[11] On such questions Yeats was no reactionary, but a thoroughgoing liberal. Remarking that he believed as little in an infallible book as an infallible church, he insisted that marriage was not a sacrament, but, on the other hand, the love of a man and woman was sacred.

It is this whole debate about the proper relations between male and female which, as Donald Davie has shown,[12] underlies the important poems in the volume entitled *Michael Robartes and the Dancer*. The title poem offers an exchange on that topic between a couple who embody Yeats's ideal of future sexuality, an emotional and imaginative man, Michael Robartes, and a self-reliant strong-minded New Woman, a professional dancer. She seeks to master the life of the intellect and put herself to college, but Robartes argues that women attain knowledge only through the body. Lest anyone think that Yeats is being sexist here, it is only fair to add that at all times he applied the same principle to men, and especially to himself in old age, when it took some courage to assert his dependence on his own wasted body. Here, however, the poet is joyously sexual in his imagery. The act of love is seen as a physical attempt by man to quell the rising tide of thought in woman. The knight

> . . . grips his long spear so to push
> That dragon through the fading light . . .
>   . . . and it's plain
> The half-dead dragon was her thought.

Robartes goes on to say that a vigorous thigh grants a knowledge superior to that offered by any book, but the Dancer is unconvinced, for she has been told at school that there is great danger in the body. However, Robartes is too clever for her in the end. As Yeats was often to do, he cites the mystery of the Incarnation in an attempt to use the imagery of Christian tradition against the latter-day Christian prudes. With a ferocious simplicity, he reminds her that Jesus chose to reveal himself in the mystical body rather than in abstract form. He ends by suggesting that if women will banish every thought, except that of their own reflections in a mirror, they will attain knowledge as well as happiness, and lead men to it too. But the Dancer says no and Yeats seems to suggest that this is a repudiation of her own sexuality.

On the surface, it seems like the old story, a deeply sexist poem in which Yeats denies women access to higher education and urges them instead to preen themselves in mirrors. However, a deeper analysis will show that the poet is in good faith and makes no demands on the Dancer that he had not already made on himself. Yeats did not follow his father to Trinity College and cordially despised its professors, whom he described as men who talked in other people's sleep. He disliked the academic habit of retailing opinions at second hand and saw in it an assault on true culture, which consists 'not in acquiring opinions but in getting rid of them'.[13] Hence the opening assertion of Robartes, 'opinion is not worth a rush', for that is all the Dancer will learn if she goes to college. This had been Yeats's conviction from his early days in Dublin, where he once complained to a schoolmaster that the ordinary system of education strengthened the will, but only because it weakened the impulses, offering the pedantry of facts instead of a feeling for life. It was for this reason that he sought to shield women – and men – from the atrophied emotions of university life. Yeats once compared universities to old people's homes, adding darkly that more people actually die in universities.

Yeats admired the New Woman, but foresaw the danger that she would mistake liberation for a share in the rationalist bondage of men. Of George Eliot he commented acidly: 'If she had more religion, she would have less morals. The moral impulse and the religious destroy each other in most cases. I was once afraid of turning out reasonable myself. The only business of the head in this world is to bow a ceaseless obeisance to the heart.'[14] Elsewhere he wrote that 'a simple round of religious duties, things that escape the intellect, is often so much better than its substitute, self-improvement'. As early as 1889, long before he had been frustrated by Maud Gonne's immersion in political opinion, he confided in Katharine Tynan that the higher education of women was a poor delusion. 'Men have set up a great mill called examinations to destroy the imagination', he complained, 'Why should women go through it? Circumstance does not drive them.'[15] (The trick, as he had already demonstrated in his own career, was to fail the entrance qualification.) Then his anger grew magnificent: 'These women come out with no repose, no peacefulness, their minds no longer quiet gardens full of secluded paths

and umbrage-circled nooks, but loud as chaffering market-places.'
Then he proceeded to dissect the latest specimen: 'Mrs Todhunter
is a great trouble mostly. She has been through the mill and has
got the noisiest mind I know. She is always denying something.'
Indeed, neither of the Yeats boys relished the great educational
mill, for the young Jack Yeats told his startled grandmother that
he had deliberately come last in a school examination, because
he could not bear to look into the faces of the boys whom he had
beaten.

Both boys had been warned by their father that educators
believed too much in the intellect, whereas all valuable education
should be a stirring up of the emotions. This did not entail
excitability, but serenity, an insight which the poet applied to
the protestors against *The Playboy of the Western World*, who
reminded him how base at moments of excitement were minds
without culture. According to John Butler Yeats, excitement was
the mark of an *insufficiently* emotional nature, 'the harsh vibrating
discourse of but one or two chords', whereas 'in the completely
emotional man, the least awakening of feeling is a harmony in
which every chord of every feeling vibrates'. It was for such
reasons that John Butler Yeats regretted the failure of his friend,
Edward Dowden, to achieve his potential. By becoming a
professor, Dowden opted for a safe career assessing the opinions
of others, mostly his inferiors, when he should have trusted his
own nature. Like the Dancer of the poem, he could have chosen
beauty, but instead opted for a life of mere instruction.

On his trip to America in 1903, the poet got a first-hand
glimpse of a system of education which taught girls how to grow
rather than how to accumulate facts. A teacher at Bryn Mawr
told Yeats that she prepared her girls to live their lives, whereas
in England they were making them all teachers. What this meant
in practice could be quite interesting, as the same teacher went
on to boast that 'fifty per cent of my girls get married and sixty
per cent have children'.[16] Her formulations, however hilarious,
vindicated Oscar Wilde's famous complaint that in England those
who had forgotten how to learn had all taken to teaching. 'People
never think of cultivating a girl's imagination', wrote Wilde, 'that
is the great defect of modern education.' In *The Importance of
Being Earnest* he launched his own assault on the great mill of
examinations and memory, a tyranny epitomised by the hateful
Miss Prism, who tells her student Cecily to read her Political

Economy, but 'the chapter on the Fall of the Rupee you may omit. It is somewhat too sensational.' Cecily makes the very Yeatsian point that books do not generate ideas. As far as she is concerned, like a certain lady before her, all her best ideas come to her in the garden. In the play, Wilde goes on to indict the new university extension scheme, from which Gwendolen cannot come away 'without having excessively admired'. Yeats came to conclusions similar to Wilde's during a visit to the Catholic College of Chicago in 1903, where he found that the course of literature prescribed for the girls showed 'no real grasp of ideas', just 'mere prettiness getting the foremost thought'.[17] He contrasted the cloistered lives of these girls with the abundant freedoms enjoyed at Bryn Mawr. Always a disciple of beauty, Yeats was never a lover of mere prettiness.

So the Dancer is urged to shun the temptations of college and submit herself to the heroic discipline of the looking-glass. The discipline is heroic – not vain – because although pretty girls are ten-a-penny in every street, real beauty demands a painful daily service no less rigorous than that of the artist to his art. That is the theme of 'Adam's Curse', where the poet's apparent ease is deceptive, for it is the outcome of meticulous rehearsal:

> I said: 'A line will take us hours maybe;
> Yet if it does not seem a moment's thought
> Our stitching and unstitching hath been naught.

This nonchalance was learned from Wilde, who seemed to speak perfect sentences with no effort, but who practised for hours even his most trivial one-liners. The strain of such a performance was immense, proving Goethe's dictum that art is art because it is not nature. The steps and shapes of the ballet dancer were painful because unnatural, but it was because they were unnatural that they were beautiful. Hence the equation between an artist and a beautiful woman, for both live under Adam's curse, the need for labour:

> To be born woman is to know –
> Although they do not talk of it at school –
> That we must labour to be beautiful.

It is no accident that a very similar phrase – 'they say such

different things at school' – is uttered by the Dancer in her reply
to Michael Robartes, who comments:

> Your lover's wage
> Is what your looking-glass can show.

For a beautiful woman, to look into a mirror is quite literally
a discipline which she would rather avoid, since that mirror can
only chronicle her decline and summon her to an art which
repairs the defects of nature. Nature, as Wilde said, has good
intentions, but it is the artist who must carry them out. In the
Gaelic lore studied by Yeats, beauty was more often a curse than
a blessing, because a beautiful woman could never know whether
she was loved for herself alone or for her yellow hair. It was for
reasons such as this that the Deirdre of Yeats's play threatened
to mar her beauty, in hopes of initiating a more honest relationship
with the world. Yeats never ceased to marvel at how hard life
was for a beautiful woman – hence his shrewd fatherly prayer
that his daughter be beautiful, but not too beautiful. He slyly
noted that Maud Gonne seemed to hate her own beauty, not its
effect on others but its image in a mirror.[18] She was the classic
New Woman who repudiated her impersonal beauty and wished
to assert her self. 'A woman can scarce but hate her beauty',
remarked Yeats, 'for not only does it demand a painful daily
service, but it calls for the denial or dissolution of the Self.'[19] Such
a call was anathema to the woman who sought the very opposite
state of self-sufficiency. Robartes, on the other hand, insists that
wisdom can only come when the self is lost in the service of
beauty, just as the real personality of the dancer is lost for a
moment in the ideal patterns of her dance. Yeats himself is not
so sure of this and so he leaves the last word to the Dancer. The
debate is still open.

That moment of disciplined ecstasy when the real and the
ideal, the self and the beautiful, the dancer and the dance, are
one, is thrown even more deeply into question in the next poem,
'Solomon and the Witch', which may be an account of Yeats's
early married life with his wife Georgina Hyde-Lees. In the poem,
Sheba of the famous legend cries out in a strange tongue at the
moment of her ecstasy, but Solomon – ever the calculating male –
gruffly points out that this sound has been made not by her, but
by a cockerel which

Crew from a blossoming apple bough
Three hundred years before the Fall
And never crew again till now.

Clearly, the subject of this remembered moment is Maud Gonne, whom Yeats first saw beside an apple-tree in blossom. The cockerel, thinking that another perfect coupling has been achieved, crows again. But the cockerel has misinterpreted the moment – choice (what a person would want) and chance (what he actually gets) are never one. Maud Gonne is not Georgina Hyde-Lees and so Yeats celebrates with tragic honesty not the moment of perfect passion, but the subtler pleasures of the near-miss:

And when at last that murder's over,
Maybe the bride-bed brings despair,
For each an imagined image brings
And finds a real image there.

Freud put the same idea somewhat differently when he said that there are four persons involved in every act of love, two real people and the idealised versions of each other to which the partners make love.

Such an idea in such a poem could have hurt Yeats's wife deeply, but he rises above hurtfulness in his celebration of the woman's will to try again, which is finally more moving than the lover's disappointment. If chance and choice *were* finally one, the universe would end and there would be nothing left to strive for. This is all somewhat reminiscent of Wilhelm Reich's famous argument that nobody has achieved absolute orgasm since the Middle Ages, but Yeats would add that, all things considered, it is probably just as well. The dignity of man and woman in this splintered world lies in the energy of their uncertain search. Their littleness, far from being a liability, becomes the very condition of their greatness. In sex, more than anything else, that greatness is achieved, for in the act of love man's soaring aspiration is forced to come to terms with the imperfections of the body. One of Yeats's greatest poems to Maud Gonne, 'Broken Dreams', is great precisely because it celebrates a flaw in her loveliness, her small ill-proportioned hands. Yet the final effect of the flaw is to set off the beauty when measured against an everyday physical disfigurement, the very defect offering a reassuring touch of personality in the midst of such chilling impersonal beauty.

What this means is the old cliché that nobody is perfect, but more deeply it hints that beauty is the lover's gift – that the lover, by seeing beauty in his beloved, actually brings it into being. So every young lover thinks his girl more beautiful than she is, because to his subjective eyes she is beautiful, but also because she may truly look more beautiful to objective eyes, when she is inspired by the presence of her beloved. The flaws of the body, like Maud Gonne's misshapen hands, are a challenge to the lover's imagination and to the strength of his love. This recalls for us the truth of the anti-self and the need to study to become the opposite of all that one is, by nature and inheritance, in daily life. That, ironically enough, is usually the attempt to reshape oneself into conformity with the expectations of one's lover and with the ideal image nursed in that person's heart. In a passage from his diary in 1909 – which is the real source of the poem – Yeats outlined his theory of sexuality:

> It seems to me that true love is a discipline, and it needs so much wisdom that the love of Solomon and Sheba must have lasted, for all the silence of the Scriptures. Each discovers the secret self of the other, and refusing to believe in the mere daily self, creates a mirror where the lover or beloved sees an image to copy in daily life.[20]

In other words, the ideal image is not a lie, but a revelation of that deeper self which has lain undiscovered in the beloved, a hidden self which its owner may never have suspected to exist, but which a true lover can bring to the surface of being. This was a theme in Synge's *Playboy of the Western World*, where Christy Mahon liberates the tender eloquence which the barmaid Pegeen Mike had to conceal beneath the hard exterior of a sharp-tongued bitch. So there is hope for Yeats, as the ideal Maud Gonne of his imagination may be the undiscovered self of Georgina Hyde-Lees.

This is exactly the process described by C. G. Jung in his famous essay on marriage as a psychological relationship, where he says that every man carries within himself the archetypal image of woman. This he calls the *anima* – erotic and emotional in character, as defined in Chapter 4, it is what Yeats would call the feminine element in man. At the outset, according to Jung, the *anima* is merely a *collective* image of 'all the ancestral experiences of the female, a deposit, as it were, of all the impressions ever made by woman'.[21] This is in keeping with Yeats's own idea that at first a man falls in love with a type, not an individual: 'and when we love, if it be in the excitement of youth, do we not also . . . exclude character . . . by choosing that beauty which seems unearthly because the individual woman is lost amid the labyrinth of its lines as though life were trembling into stillness and silence?'[22] In confirmation of this idea, Yeats once assured Katharine Tynan that the Maud Gonne whom he loved was not a specific person, but 'a myth, a symbol'.[23] Jung argues that at a later stage, however, this collective ancestral image is unconsciously projected onto a single woman, being one of the chief reasons for passionate attraction or aversion. 'Hence', he observes rather archly, 'most of what men say about feminine eroticism and the emotional life of women is derived from their own *anima* projections and distorted accordingly.'[24] Such a projection is fraught with risks – that the woman cannot embody the qualities of the projected *anima*, that the man will find in the woman not a complement but a rival. If the experience is fruitful, however, 'the projection, though dangerous in itself, will have helped him to pass from a collective to an individual relationship. This amounts to a full *conscious* realisation of the relationship that marriage brings.'[25] This is what the reader witnesses in 'Solomon and the Witch', the spectacle of a fifty-five-year-old man who marries in haste, on the rebound from a lifelong lover, but soon finds himself falling deeply in love with his wife.

This resolution was not achieved without some pain, for the spectre of Maud Gonne haunted the bridal bed in 'An Image from a Past Life'. In this context Yeats wrote: 'Those whose passions are unatoned seldom love living man or woman but only those loved long ago, of whom the living man or woman is but a brief symbol forgotten when some phase of some atonement is finished.'[26] Full marriage is only achieved after arduous expiations of the past: 'It is therefore only after full atonement or expiation, perhaps after many lives, that a natural deep satisfying love becomes possible, and this love, in all subjective natures, must precede the Beatific Vision.'[27] This is in accord with Jung's account of the psychology of marital relationships. In an exemplary model, Jung describes a husband whose complex personality provides a wholly absorbing focus for the passion of his wife, whose less fragmented personality allows her to adapt readily to the conditions of marriage. Not so the husband, who has some unfinished business to transact in his subconscious, as part of his still ambiguous relationship with his parents. His nature is problematical and many-sided and feels the need of integration in individual love for another; but it is frustrated by the very simplicity of his spouse's emotional structure, which cannot contain his own and reflect it back in all its complexity as an image of unity. The more the spouse clings, the more the husband feels shut out of the relationship and the more painful is his awareness that unity has always been lacking. The spouse, like Mrs Yeats or Aline Solness, 'discovers that in the rooms which apparently belonged to her, there dwell other, unwished-for guests',[28] that is, the *anima*-projection or 'image from a past life'. Her acceptance of this is the very basis of her recovery, for she learns that the security which she was seeking in him may be found first and foremost in herself. In achieving this, she discovers in her own nature all those complexities which her husband had sought in vain. Equally, his unity is achieved only by admitting his own fragmentation, which is healed by the completion of his disintegration. 'All the powers that strive for unity, all healthy desire for selfhood, will resist the disintegration, and in this way he will become conscious of the possibility of an inner integration, which before he had always sought outside himself. He will then find his reward in an individual self.'[29] Only the most extreme fragmentation of the self, which can be contemplated without despair, rouses the will to reconstruct the self in a pattern of genuine unity.

In marriage Yeats found the nearest human approximation to his ideal of a restored unity of being. Novalis had written that the beloved alone can give that knowledge of nature necessary for a restoration of the primitive unity, because he or she alone reflects the self. 'Since the soul can perceive itself only if it is reflected in nature', said Novalis, 'and since nature can be known only through love and sympathy, a beloved person alone effectively sends back the image of the self, which can then be adored and cherished.'[30] Yeats's early intimations of such unity were achieved with Maud Gonne on a spiritual rather than bodily basis, as the poet recalls in 'An Image from a Past Life'. This often occurred when the couple were separated by hundreds of

miles. Maud Gonne wrote of one dream which she had in July
1908: 'We melted into one another till we formed one being, a
being greater than ourselves, who felt all and knew all with
double intensity.'[31] So, the perfect being, whom Zeus divided in
order to create the sexes, is reconciled with itself in such moments
of astral union; and the impulse which animates all sexual desire
is seen by Yeats as the impulse to recover the undivided self. At
about this time, therefore, he celebrates the marriage of Maud's
daughter as a wedding of the man-in-woman to the woman-in-
man: 'Iseult picked this young man . . . when he seemed almost
imbecile to his own relations. Now he is her very self made
active and visible, her nobility walking and singing. What an
inexplicable thing sexual attraction is . . . '.[32] All marriages are
now seen by the poet as reenactments of the love of Solomon and
Sheba, of light and darkness, sun and earth, wherein opposites
fuse and, in fusing, reveal the androgyny of the full personality.
According to the myth, the masculine Solomon represents solar
energy, which will fade if left to itself. Thus it enters the feminine
darkness of Sheba, whereby it is returned again to its original
power, 'but now the energy is organised in a different way from
the way it was when it first emerged at its own birth. What was
born out of the *chaos confusum* has been subjugated to the principle
of order.'[33] Solomon and Sheba, personifications of Sol and Luna,
form the classical alchemical SYZYGY or complementary pairing,
where the qualities of each are interpenetrated by those of the
opoosite. Yeats had always held to the view that without contraries
there is no progression, but what he meant by 'progression' may
be deduced from his lifelong aphorism that 'talent perceives only
differences, genius unity'. He saw that the universe only *seemed*
to be split into dualities of mind and body, male and female,
sacred and profane love, but that a real visionary could perceive
the underlying unity of all creation.

It is in the context of these poems on male–female relations
that 'Easter 1916' may be read as a love lyric, rather than being
seen solely as the great political poem that it is. After all, its lines
were written by a man in order to soften a rigid and unyielding
lady. The man who wrote the poem was in the grip of a powerful
emotion which had been unrequited, leaving him childless and
loveless in his fiftieth year. In 'The Wild Swans at Coole' he had
sought to come to terms with that disappointment, contrasting
the passion of the coupling swans with his own lonely mortality.

That poem is a direct rehearsal of the major themes of 'Easter 1916' and those themes are only incidentally political. The deeper question concerns the costs in human terms of an abstract ideal. The coupling swans become in 'Easter 1916' the hens calling to moorcocks; and the poet who has loved too long becomes the victim of a dilemma no different from that posed by the rebels:

> What if excess of love
> Bewildered *him* till he died?

That is simply the last of four questions in the closing stanza which the poet asks but cannot answer. The questions are ultimately so painful that they cannot even be discussed, but are merely suppressed. The personal interrogations of the poet are drowned out by the public voice of the national bard, who performs his ancient duty and lists the names of the warrior dead. That device of the suppressed question is a favourite of Yeats's middle period:

> Was it for this the Wild Geese spread
> Their grey wing upon every tide? . . .
>
> But let them be, they're dead and gone,
> They're with O'Leary in the grave.

Yeats wrote in the belief that there are no answers to any question worth asking and so his questions are agonised, too agonised to be entertained for long:

> What is it but nightfall?
> No, no, not night but death.

The very stridency of the triple negatives indicates just how much forcing is needed to suppress the private questions, if the public bard is to perform his duty.

Of course, the public bard is trying to write a poem that will please the nationalist Maud Gonne, but the private questioner is trying to cure her of political rigidity, to make her forget the stone for the flashing life of the stream. The outcome is a poem which enacts once again the quarrel between Robartes and the Dancer, between the irrational man and the all-too-logical woman. The result is a series of questions, so searing as to throw the very refrain into some doubt. This is worth mentioning, because the refrain, like the poem itself, has often been ripped from its context and acquired canonical status, being ritually intoned by politicians in times of catastrophe as a source of reassurance. In fact, the self-confidence of the refrain is increasingly thrown into question, as the poem examines the costs to their sexuality of the political campaigns of Maud Gonne and Con Markiewicz. At the start it is declamatory enough, but by the end of the third stanza, that refrain is entirely omitted, as if the poet were no longer sure that he had anything to celebrate. When the refrain returns at the end, it comes back shame-facedly, as a crude rhetorical device to suppress the terrifying questions. It should be voiced hesitatingly by a skilled reader, as if it is the terror, rather than the beauty, which is uppermost in our minds. If this is truly a love poem, then the refrain must be interrogative rather than declamatory – ironic as well as literal. The very fact that it is based on Maud Gonne's recorded response to the Rising – 'tragic dignity has returned to Ireland' – should be enough to alert us to the fact that it will never be fully endorsed by the poet.

The later poems in *Michael Robartes and the Dancer* develop this theme. In 'On a Political Prisoner' Yeats implies that Con Markiewicz is more caged by her arrested sexuality than by her enemies, the British occupiers of Ireland. She feeds a bird which has alighted on her cell window and the poet asks:

> Did she in touching that lone wing
> Recall the years before her mind
> Became a bitter, an abstract thing? . . .

In the subsequent 'A Prayer for My Daughter' he elaborates:

> An intellectual hatred is the worst,
> So let her think opinions are accursed.

Yeats declared that women, 'because the main event of their lives has been a giving themselves and giving birth, give all to an opinion as if it were some terrible stone doll . . . They grow cruel, as if in defence of lover or child, and all this is done for something other than human life.'[34]

Once again, the superficial convictions appear to be sexist, a principled opposition to women's involvement in politics. But Yeats is not preaching one law for men and another for women; rather, he believes that there should be no abstract laws binding either. What he is opposed to is politics as a form of sexual sublimation; just as earlier he had criticised Arthur Griffith and the male protestors against *The Playboy of the Western World*, so now he directs the same allegations against Maud Gonne and Con Markiewicz. And far from being a reactionary or non-political stance, Yeats's response is profoundly political, a critique of the system which prescribed reason as the sole preserve of men, emotion of women. He understood that Maud Gonne's abstract politics was the protest of a free New Woman against being stereotyped as a pretty debutante and social butterfly. While he could admire the energy of her protest, he felt that it was not so much a response as a reaction; and that her reaction was as distorted as the very system which she opposed, for it led to a substitution of extreme abstraction for extreme emotion. Both were needful to the full woman and the full man, rather than a mere devotion to abstraction at the expense of the human body. Hence Yeats's delight on the publication of *Lady Chatterley's Lover* by D. H. Lawrence. The coarse language of the gamekeeper, accepted across the social divide by the titled lady, became for him 'a forlorn poetry uniting their solitudes, something ancient, humble and terrible'.[35] In a letter to a lady friend, he remarked very uprightly that he found the whole book interesting, and not just the sexual parts. 'They', he said, 'are something that Lawrence sets up against the abstraction of an age that he thinks dead from the waist downward.' However, he came to the conclusion that Lawrence's search for happiness was as hopelessly physical as Maud Gonne's had been hopelessly abstract; and so he asserted that 'we are happy only when for everything inside us there is an equivalent something outside us'.[36] Body and soul must consort in the integration of a personality.

Most critics believe that Yeats finally found such integration in the figure of the Dancer, at the end of what may be his greatest poem 'Among Schoolchildren', when he asks 'How can we know the dancer from the dance?' There, so it is said, the labour which epitomised 'Adam's Curse' is transformed into the effortless patterns traced by the lady. Some even go so far as to pivot the poem on a contrast between the painful beauty achieved by the poetic artist and the effortless beauty attained by the Dancer.[37] This is a reading which should be challenged. From the beginning in Yeats's poetry, Robartes had warned the Dancer that she must *labour* to be beautiful; and from the outset the Dancer had shown a troublesome mind of her own. Moreover, as a poet Yeats has always addressed her as a fellow-artist, someone who shared his painful efforts. If there is a contrast in the poem, it is between the painless growth of the tree to beauty and the excruciating discipline of the dancer's path to loveliness. The underlying subject is the pain of being a woman, as experienced by the nun and mother who worship images whose consistent unreliability breaks their hearts. Yeats wonders if the pain of his own mother in childbirth is justified by the withered scarecrow he now feels himself to be. If the flesh is easily broken, then the images worshipped by the nun are more durable; but they are only statues, made of stone, as cold and forbidding as the stone worshipped by Maud Gonne in the earlier poem. Many of these poems from Yeats's middle period pivot on a choice between the fleshly delights of birth and copulation and the fixed, heart-rending immobility of the stone. Even the nuns have their hearts broken by their chosen images, which chronicle the tragedy of suffering in the figure of a crucified Jesus, who trusted men enough to become flesh, only to experience the disappointments of the human body. Lover, mother and nun all worship an ideal rather than a real image; and these ideal images live on as mere dreams to mock the decaying body.

That is the meaning of the final stanza, which brings together the various levels of the poem:

> Labour is blossoming or dancing where
> The body is not bruised to pleasure soul,
> Nor beauty born out of its own despair,
> Nor blear-eyed wisdom out of midnight oil . . .

The body is bruised by nuns who deny the physical self for the sake of a beautiful soul; but it is bruised also by mothers in the pangs of childbirth and by lovers as they wrestle in a bed of passion. The wisdom of the poet himself, as he toils by the midnight lamp, is won only at the cost of bleary eyes. So even art, the ultimate worship of images, is created only out of suffering and the poet has the honesty to include himself in the tragic picture, as the wasted son of sixty years, but also as the blear-eyed sage. Most critics see the concluding image of the stanza as the resolution of these conflicts, with the poet turning from the world of rotting bodies to the durable beauty of art captured by the Dancer:

> O body swayed to music, o brightening glance,
> How can we know the dancer from the dance?

This is to say that most see the question as rhetorical – not so much a serious question as a clever way of making a statement about the enduring identity of the artist with the pattern he creates. A closer inspection, however, would show that the status of art has already been thrown into question by the poet's bleary eyes. There are no rhetorical questions in the major poems of Yeats, if by a rhetorical question is meant an alternative way of making a statement, a question asked because the answer is already known. In Yeats's poems, the concluding question is asked in terrified uncertainty.

The Dancer is the ideal image of woman brought to the marriage-bed by a man who goes on to find a real image there in the very moment of love. Eventually, a beautiful child is born out of the lovers' despairing search for a moment of ecstasy in which the ideal and real might merge. Unfortunately, it is Yeats's belief that such a perfect fusion is never achieved. Instead, as he explained in another context, 'we beget and bear children because of the incompleteness of our love'.[38] Yeats insisted that for Solomon and Sheba there *is* a real image, a real dancer who takes knocks and bruises as she rehearses her seemingly ideal dance. 'Suffering has affected my poems, my true self, no more than the character of the dancer affects the movements of the dance',[39] he wrote in 1930, but in that sentence is an admission that the suffering left its mark on the character of the man who created the poems. He had admitted all this years earlier in 'The Choice':

> When all the story's finished, what's the news?
> In luck or out the toil has left its mark.

Or, as T. S. Eliot put it, an artist suffers in creating, but never allows that suffering to show through directly in his art: there will always be a necessary distinction between the man who suffers and the mind which creates, for otherwise art would become a version of self-pity. So the line rehearsed with difficulty for hours, lasts for seconds. So also the dance breaks not just the hearts of others, but the dancer's own. That is what the critics, with their nineteenth-century search for a happy ending to the poem, will not concede – that it really does end with a question. The poet's heart is broken by the ideal beauty of the dance, which reminds him as a fellow-artist that such beauty is attained at a great cost, and only for a few moments. It is extraordinary how many great critics who are tough-minded about life become sentimental about art. They have turned that closing question into a statement to the effect that the dancer becomes the beautiful pattern which she creates; but Yeats has actually asked himself 'Does she?' For a few seconds, yes, but those seconds cost her a lifetime of sacrifice. The Dancer is the epitome, and not the resolution, of Adam's curse.

In a famous essay in *Essays and Introductions* Yeats contrasted the apparent spontaneity and playful joy of Spanish dancers with the sobering thought that 'their training had been long, laborious, and wearisome'.[40] Those who invest the final image of 'Among Schoolchildren' with such transcendental significance should never forget that Yeats abandoned the Dancer for the more enduring beauty of sculpted stone in his later poetry. Those stones which epitomised hardness and imperviousness to the author of *On Baile's Strand* and 'Easter 1916' now symbolise the artistic permanence which he seeks in 'The Statues' and 'Lapis Lazuli'. Their resistance to imposed form, because it is even greater than that of the human body, enhances the glory of the artist who subdues recalcitrant stone to his will with passion and calculation. In so far as the Dancer does embody a truth, it is not the transcendence of time but rather the transcendence of sex by art. For the duration of the dance, the dancer lacks not only character, but sexual differentiation. She who was unambiguously female in the poems in *Michael Robartes and the Dancer* is not necessarily so here – and this may be part of the meaning of that closing question. 'The absorption into the dance carries the dancer away from everyday sexual roles and evokes the seductive power of the androgyne',[41] writes Elémire Zolla in celebration of Nijinsky's swirls in the *Scheherazade*. Such swirls seemed to endow male dancers with female contours. They remind us that the Dionysian revels from which Greek tragedy and comedy first emerged often demanded a ritual exchange of dress between the sexes. Many students of the Siva dance have found in the patterns which erase sexual difference an embodiment of 'the androgyne as living motion . . . as both the dancer and the dance'.[42] So the Dancer in Yeats's poem transcends the painful sexuality of the mother in a manner more absolute than that achieved by the nun, but this victory is won only for a few moments, before she is returned to the world of physical decay and sexual difference.

That famous closing question has another dimension and that is Yeats's recurring envy of a woman's self-sufficiency – his obsessive desire as a mere male to know what thoughts course through a woman's mind in a moment of ecstasy and to sense what the dancer is feeling in the midst of her dance. The self-sufficiency of the New Woman maddens the poet now just as it had frustrated Robartes in the earlier poem, her self-sufficiency as a professional woman, but also, more importantly, as a woman in the grip of a mysterious emotion. Yeats's later poems, such as 'Leda and the Swan', show a poet tortured by the unknowability of a woman in a moment of excitement. When Leda is raped by the swan, he asks another question: 'Did she put on his knowledge with his power?' This is a version of the Incarnation, where spirit expresses itself in body; and for Yeats, the mystery of the Incarnation was never merely religious, but primarily a truth of sex. For him, as for Joyce, the artistic process is a mystery of incarnation: 'you cannot give a body to something that moves beyond the senses, unless your words are as subtle, as complex, as full of mysterious life, as the body of a flower or of a woman'.[43] The trouble is that the poet has no access to his desired knowledge. His tragedy is to be the powerless external witness of the incarnation, a man who can report the impregnation of matter with spirit but cannot fathom the mystery. Christ took on this knowledge in taking upon his shoulders the sins of the world. The decadent artist, Aubrey Beardsley, took upon himself not just the consequences but the *knowledge* of sin, remarked Yeats with admiration, 'and by so doing he enabled persons who had never heard his name to recover innocence'.[44] But not this poet. As in 'Solomon and Sheba', his own mind never fuses with his body, but remains a troublesome and separate entity. This explains the essentially sexual nature of all his disappointment. 'The tragedy of sexual intercourse', he admitted, 'is the perpetual virginity of the soul',[45] the fact that two souls never do truly fuse on earth and the knowledge that the heart itself is lonely in the lover's kiss. Instead, we must bear children as physical proof of the fact that we have been momentarily one.[46] (Hence, no doubt, the baffled look which Yeats often gave his own children, as if he was trying to remember how they got there – a curious reversal of the difficulty which most children have in believing that their parents really went to bed and conceived them.) That same imperfection may be found also in the experience of God himself, whose unsatisfactory relationship with the world gave rise to the need for the Incarnation of Jesus in the womb of Mary, a mystery summed up in the peasant adage, 'God possesses the heavens, aye, but he covets the earth.'

Once again, it is the self-sufficiency of Mary's sexuality which baffles the poet. She can conceive of herself, while her soul remains virgin, and yet somehow a god has made love to a mortal:

> The threefold terror of love; a fallen flare
> Through the hollow of an ear;
> Wings beating about the room;
> The terror of all terrors that I bore
> The Heavens in my womb . . .
> What is this flesh I purchased with my pains,
> This fallen star my milk sustains,
> This love that makes my heart's blood stop
> Or strikes a sudden chill into my bones
> And bids my hair stand up?

On the basis of this poem, Marina Warner has gone on to argue that 'Mary cannot be a model for the New Woman';[47] but it is precisely as a 'fierce' New Woman that Yeats repeatedly celebrates her:

> The Roman Empire stood appalled:
> It dropped the reins of peace and war
> When that fierce virgin and her Star
> Out of the fabulous darkness called.

So, also, in the case of Leda, Yeats is baffled to know if she put on a god's 'knowledge' with his power – did she, like Mary, become divine, even as the gods took human form? As always, Yeats badly wants to know the thoughts of a woman in crisis, for he was unsure whether he could separate the woman who was violated from the woman who engendered new life. He was convinced that no male poet had ever penetrated the mind of an independent woman and complained that the heroines of Swinburne, Morris and Rossetti were essentially men's heroines, with no separate life of their own.[48] Many of the great poems of his middle and later periods have as their aim nothing less than the desire to share the experience of a woman in the defining moments of her life.

This creates a problem. If the poet is to penetrate the minds of Mary, Leda or the Dancer, he will have to *become* a woman. The impossibility of this maddens and frustrates him and so he resolves to do what *is* possible, to write words in which he confronts that part of his personality which caused him to seek such knowledge. So he composes a wide variety of poems – the Crazy Jane lyrics and the verses of 'A Woman Young and Old' – in which he adopts the female voice and tries indeed to 'make a woman express herself as never before'.[49] This sentence is a reference to the Muse as *anima*, the inspiratrice who must be invoked by the poet before he begins to create. Sir Philip Sidney, after falsely seeking inspiration in the world outside himself, was sharply rebuked in his own famous line: 'Fool, said my Muse, look in thy heart and write.' Yeats goes one better, and takes this in literal earnest, as a warning that poetic inspiration is derived from the female element in man, who must render himself androgynous in order to create. 'A mind can never create until it is split in two', he wrote as a grateful son of Zeus.

The same underlying principle explains the adoption of the pen-name 'Fiona Macleod' by one of Yeats's friends and fellow-artists, William Sharp. In a letter to Ethel Mannin, Yeats explained that men achieved androgyny through art:

> You are doubly a woman, first because of yourself and secondly because of the muses, whereas I am but once a woman. Bitterness is more fatal to us than it is to lawyers and journalists who have nothing to do with the feminine muses. Our traditions only permit us to bless.[50]

What the *anima* did for the poet, the *animus* could do for the poetess – or so Yeats argued in a letter to Dorothy Wellesley:

What makes your verse so good is the masculine element allied to much feminine charm – your lines have the magnificent swing of your boyish body. I wish I could be a girl of nineteen for certain hours that I might feel it more acutely.[51]

Indeed, at this late point in his career, Yeats began to associate not just his art, but all the more creative moments in his life, with that instant when sexual difference is transcended. He tells Lady Dorothy in the same letter: 'My dear, my dear, when you crossed the room with that boyish movement, it was no man who looked at you, it was the woman in me. It seems that I can make a woman express herself as never before. I have looked out of her eyes. I have shared her desire.'[52]

For Yeats, this admission of the female element to full consciousness was a breakthrough which it had taken almost an entire lifetime to achieve, as James Olney has shown. His early work had shown him to be an unconscious slave to his *anima*, precisely because he was (like so many Victorian males) so intent on keeping it suppressed beneath the level of consciousness. As Frances Wickes has explained in an analysis of Jungian psychology, the *anima* may become 'she who must be obeyed – this can make the man an artist or only a womanish creature incapable of asserting himself'.[53] Having had an unstable relationship all through his childhood with a dominant but often absent father, the poet may have been too timid in his twenties to assert his masculinity in a heterosexual relationship. He seems equally to have denied himself wholeness by failing to confront the female dimension within himself.[54] The *anima* will not be denied and so she 'exerts a power that often defeats his ego choices, making them denials of the very decisions that would reinforce his masculine nature, if he could let *anima* become a friend of choice'.[55] In contrast, William Sharp, though consciously invoking 'Fiona Macleod', was not usurped by his *anima* in his daily masculine existence. 'Through his inner marriage to his social image', says Wickes, 'he could, as a completed personality, live his man's life more fully.'[56] Not so Yeats, who became an early slave to his *anima*, as he later admitted in a letter to George Russell: 'I cannot probably be just to any poetry that speaks to me with the sweet insinuating feminine voice of the dwellers in that country of shadows and hollow images. I have dwelt there too long not to dread all that comes out of it ... Let us have no emotions, however abstract, in which there is not an athletic joy.'[57] The celebration of the 'harsh' and 'masculine' will in Yeats's later poetry is his reaction against his early enslavement to the dreamy moods of the *anima*. There are times when the later Yeats seems to protest his masculinity too much, but Wickes is correct in asserting that a conscious recognition of the *anima* has the inevitable effect of ending this enslavement and liberating the masculinity of the male. It is no accident that Yeats writes his most aggressively masculine poems in the decade which also produces Crazy Jane, for it is in this period that he achieves a full integration of his own personality as a poet.

Many men dispose of the *anima* 'by projecting all her evil power upon the outer woman and so feeling justified in getting rid of her', but, according to Frances Wickes, others 'remove her to the world of pseudospirituality where, from a safe distance, her image may be worshipped',[58] much as Yeats worshipped Maud Gonne. In projecting his *anima* demands onto the figure of Maud, the poet was in effect asking this woman to live out on his behalf the femininity which he had been suppressing within himself. Like most men, Yeats expected his beloved to be gentle, soft and warm and to abjure the harsh world of public affairs. He was deeply disappointed when Maud confessed to a horror of physical love and to a relish of the hurly-burly of politics. Frustrated in the wish to have Maud embody his own repressed femininity, Yeats was compelled to return and confront those elements in himself. June Singer has given a valuable description of this universal stage in the male's development to emotional maturity:

> At some point in the process of coming into the fullness of his own being, a man will have to withdraw these expectations from the woman or women in his life. This is not to say that a woman should not behave in the so-called 'feminine' ways. What I am saying is that the man has to cease *expecting* that from her. The woman must be and has every right to be the person she is, and a man in working out the problem of the contrasexual opposites must learn to stop projecting his own confused and unrecognised contrasexual qualities upon women. If he feels a need for tenderness, then let him be tender himself, and see what that evokes from the world.[59]

In other words, no man is ever truly ready for marriage until he has first wedded himself to the female within his own personality.

The idealised image of Maud Gonne could only postpone that moment of confrontation, when Yeats would liberate his *anima* into full consciousness. Only when he became both male and female could the poet be certain of finding a woman whose feelings he fully understood, whose needs he could fulfil even as she answered his own. The longer a man remains unconscious of his *anima*, said Jung, 'the less is marriage a matter of free choice, as is shown subjectively in the fatal compulsion one feels so acutely when one is in love'.[60]

Jung was forever at pains to emphasise that this confrontation with the *anima* in man or the *animus* in woman could be a painful and even a dangerous process. The negative connotations which still surround the word 'animus' are proof enough of that. 'There are mobs in every personal psyche – savage emotions, inferior and despised potentials', writes Frances Wickes, 'that can be either roused to violence or, when accepted and consciously acknowledged, redeemed by the newly awakened consciousness.'[61] Yeats knew to his cost just how unruly such mobs could be. Jung had demonstrated that the unacknowledged *anima* leaves a man a prey to unappeasable *moods* – and it is those very moods which accounted for the 'unmanly' poetry of 'longing and complaint'[62] which Yeats later disowned, a point first noted by James Olney. Wickes argues that many a man might have averted such early psychological calamities 'had he possessed the mood instead of letting the mood possess him'.[63] The same is equally true of the *animus* in women, which Jung saw as the source of dogmatic *opinions* – that 'intellectual hatred' in Maud Gonne which caused the poet to pray that his daughter would 'think opinions are accursed'. If *anima* and *animus* can wreak such havoc from their unrecognised bastions in the human psyche, it is no surprise that there is a marked reluctance in most people to bring them out into the open. June Singer accounts for this by explaining that 'these very personal qualities are bound to emerge in a raw and unrefined state in an individual because they have been so long repressed and denied their natural development'.[64] Many years after he had confronted his own *anima*, Yeats could still be so unnerved by her raw and unruly power that he felt obliged to write to his wife: 'I want to exorcise that slut, Crazy Jane, whose language has become unendurable.'[65]

Further sanction for the use of the female voice in these later books of poetry would have been found by Yeats in the Gaelic poetic tradition. From the seventh to the seventeenth centuries,

Gaelic bards regularly adopted the persona of bridegroom to the chief who was their patron. A poet like Tomás Ó hUiginn could dramatise his uncertainty about whether to accept the official patronage of Ó Ruairc or Costelloe in a poem, 'Féuch fein, an obair-se, a Aoidh', which generations of critics read as a literal account of a woman wavering between two lovers. James Carney, the first scholar to 'crack the code' of this text, has gone on to suggest that Gaelic poetry thus offers a plausible and very ancient model for themes and techniques of the type found in Shakespeare's sonnets.[66] The Gaelic bard demanded as of right a seat next to the prince he loved and even the privilege of sharing the royal bed. The beautiful lament 'Géisidh Cuan' sees a poet keening 'an laech ro laiged liom' ('the warrior who used to lie with me'). Carney tentatively suggests that one of the most famous of all Old Irish poems 'The Hag of Beare' – in which a ribald old woman recalls with gusto the sins of her youth and prepares for death in a monastery – could have been written by a man:

> The poet, in such an interpretation, was what one may call a 'king-lover': when old age was approaching he took unwillingly to religion; he expresses all his past experiences with kings in the person of an old harlot who after a good spring, summer and autumn found herself rejected by her patrons in the early months of her winter.[67]

The relevance of all this to the Crazy Jane poems is obvious:

> I had wild Jack for a lover;
> Though like a road
> That men pass over
> My body makes no moan
> But sings on:
>
> *All things remain in God.*

To Olivia Shakespeare Yeats wrote justifying this late exercise in ribaldry in the manner of the 'Hag' poet: 'I shall be a sinful man to the end, and think upon my death-bed of all the nights I wasted in my youth.'[68] His soul seemed to be growing younger than yesterday, even as his body decayed into old age. So the man who began his career writing verses of priggish senility ended his life penning passionate celebrations of the body that would have done justice to the most athletic youth. In his sex life, as in all else, Yeats favoured a reversal of the roles usually deemed appropriate for old and young; and so he prepared for a lusty senescence with the aid of monkey-glands implanted during the fashionable Steinach operation. Monkeys had always seemed appropriate acolytes of old age to a poet who had written in youth, against the theories of Darwin, that 'monkeys are degenerate men – not man's ancestors, hence their sadness and look of boredom and old age'.[69]

The androgynous nature of the artist prompted the older Yeats to see all writing as a form of sexual activity, in which male and female grappled themselves into a unity. He was particularly excited by the challenge of reworking a poem by Dorothy Wellesley, to whom he wrote: 'Ah my dear, how it added to my excitement when I re-made that poem of yours to know it was your poem. I re-made you and myself into a single being. We triumphed over each other...'[70] This ideal of two lovers who fuse into a single angel is a borrowing from Swedenborg, which crops up in the ninth song of 'A Woman Young and Old':

> I gave what other women gave
> That stepped out of their clothes,
> But when this soul, its body off,
> Naked to naked goes,
> He it has found shall find therein
> What none other knows,
> And give his own and take his own
> And rule in his own right;
> And though it loved in misery
> Close and cling so tight,
> There's not a bird of day that dare
> Extinguish that delight.

In a letter to Olivia Shakespeare, Yeats seemed to offer a gloss on those final lines by referring to Swedenborg's axiom that 'the sexual intercourse of angels is a conflagration of their whole being'.[71]

Yeats's adoption of the female persona might have been predicted by those early readers who had meditated on his notion of the anti-self, at whose dictate a man tries to be the opposite of all that he is by nature – and, no doubt, gender. 'If we cannot imagine ourselves as different from what we are and assume that second self, we cannot impose a discipline on ourselves',[72] wrote the poet long before he had exchanged the persona of man for that of woman. By nature and inheritance, he felt himself to be emotional, soft and warm; and so he sought to become impervious, hard and cold, on the Wildean principle that the only way to intensify personality is to multiply it. But he could not cultivate the manly virtues until he had first put an end to his thrall to the *anima*, and that could only be done by unleashing her into full consciousness and speaking in the female voice. The struggle between self and anti-self, between man and daimon, was but a part of the deeper struggle at the root of all sexual love. 'When I think of life as a struggle with the Daimon who would ever set us to the hardest work among those not impossible, I understand why there is a deep enmity between a man and his destiny, and why a man loves nothing but his own destiny.'[73] On this principle, the masculine self hates and fears the female anti-self, and endlessly postpones the moment of confrontation between them, only to discover that this confrontation was its deepest desire. So in the world of love, Yeats dreamed of a man who danced and swung his lover so hard that he might have killed her; and Crazy Jane, grown old, sees in the scene an image of true love:

> Did he die or did she die?
> Seemed to die or died they both?
> God be with the times when I
> Cared not a thraneen for what chanced
> So that I had the limbs to try
> Such a dance as there was danced –
> *Love is like the lion's tooth.*

Yet again, Yeats has gone right back to the Blake who said that sexual love is founded on spiritual hate.

What Yeats admired in Blake was his ability to wrap Christian thoughts in a new and unfamiliar dress; and this was what he himself did in his closing battles with Catholic Ireland, during which he never lost a chance to assert the fundamentally sexual nature of the mystery of the Incarnation. He had always been haunted by the fact that God chose a slovenly stable for his birth in human form and a rough beast for conveyance. This gives another, more religious, dimension to Crazy Jane's famous assertion that 'Love has pitched his mansion in the place of excrement', just as it reveals an entirely *sexual* component to the mysteries of Bethlehem as witnessed in 'The Magi', 'the uncontrollable mystery on the bestial floor'. 'To read Verlaine's sacred poems', said Yeats, 'is to remember that the Holy Infant shared his first home with the beasts.'[74] In similar fashion, Jung is often quoted for his remark that when people brought sexual problems to him, they repeatedly issued in questions of religion, and when they brought a religious problem, it invariably turned out to be sexual.[75]

This paradox at the very heart of the Christian mystery was turned to use by Yeats in his assaults on the new puritans who took charge of the Irish Free State. In 1926 the Christian Brothers publicly burned a magazine which, they claimed, contained 'a horrible insult to God and the Holy Family'. When this turned out to be the beautiful 'Cherry Tree Carol', Yeats seized his opportunity and reprinted the words that gave offence, Joseph chiding a pregnant Mary:

> Then up spake Joseph
> With his words so unkind
> 'Let them gather cherries
> That have brought thee with child.'
>
> Then up spake the little child
> In his mother's womb
> 'Lay down you sweet cherry tree
> And give my mother some.'

'There is the whole mystery', said Yeats, 'God in the indignity of human birth' and he went on to show that he believed far more in Christian mythology than the official Christians themselves. 'I have thought it out again and again and I can see no reason for the anger of the Christian Brothers except that they do not believe in the Incarnation. They think they believe in it, but they do not, and its sudden presentation fills them with fear, and to hide that horror they turn on the poem.'[76]

Yeats's indictment of the new censorship law was no less devastating. Again he enlisted the prophets of an earlier Christianity against the latter-day Christian puritans. The government had defined the word 'indecent' as meaning (among other things) 'calculated to excite sexual passion'. Yeats was vastly amused and pointed out that the definition, while merely ridiculous to a man of letters, constituted sacrilege to a Thomist. Whereas Plato had separated soul and body, St Thomas had rightly laid down that on the contrary the soul is wholly present in the body and all its parts. This being so, it was unChristian as well as unkind to condemn sexual passion, a return to the dark ages when Platonic thought dominated the painters of Europe, who depicted Christ with a head of pitiless intellect and a pinched flat-chested virgin holding a stiff child-like doll. Such an art arose from a contempt for the God-given body, and therefore for the Creator who had assumed human form. Yet, within fifty years of the death of Thomas Aquinas, that art had been transformed to a celebration of the body so liberal that nobody complained when Raphael chose his mistress as a model for the Virgin – 'and represented her', said Yeats, 'with all the patience of his sexual passion as an entirely voluptuous body.'[77] It was for a similar reason that Yeats praised Aubrey Beardsley for painting St Rose of Lima ascending into Heaven on the bosom of the Madonna, her face enraptured with love, but (he coyly added) 'with that form of it which is least associated with sanctity'.[78]

As the protegés of the Irish system of education sought to legislate such art out of existence, it was no wonder that Yeats could complain that Catholic schools tended to destroy the great mysteries, symbologies and mythologies which the Catholic faith, more than any other version of Christianity, can give.[79] This point was unwittingly endorsed by James Joyce in *A Portrait of the Artist as a Young Man*, where the sensuality of Stephen Dedalus is aroused by the image of a Virgin swamped in flowers on the May altar, only to be frustrated by the life-denying ordinances of the priests from the same altar.

Yeats's sexual beliefs were not only revolutionary in their time, but, like all the best revolutions, dynamically traditional. They are a call for a return to a fuller way of life when religions were sensual, when men were not afraid of emotion nor women of self-reliance, when sex itself was seen as a gift rather than a threat. But his poetry is also radical in the sense that it confronts the dilemmas faced by the New Woman and registers the problems of a New Man who, in learning how to come to terms with the Dancer, is learning how to live with himself.

6 D. H. Lawrence: The New Man as Prophet

> The self's a fine and private place
> But none, I think, do there embrace.
>
> F. W. Dupee

'To begin with, what is the sex of D. H. Lawrence?',[1] asked one of the earliest reviewers of *The White Peacock*. Lawrence's first novel baffled readers by its intimate analysis of the heroine, in a narrative which is nevertheless written from a persuasively male point of view. For Lawrence, androgyny was not just a theme, but also a crucial part of his narrative method. 'I think the only re-sourcing of art, revivifying it, is to make it more the joint work of man and woman', he wrote, 'I think *the* one thing to do, is for men to have courage to draw nearer to women, expose themselves to them, and be altered by them: and for women to accept and admit men.'[2] This bold experiment has not been universally admired. Many critics will never forgive Lawrence for what often seems like a redeployment of the clichés of the women's magazine. All too often his characters look for something soft and warm and dark, or resort to such timeless ecstasies as the trance or swoon, swamped by the mandatory flood of adjectives. Moreover, the narrative lingers more often and more lovingly on privileged female glimpses of the male loins and buttocks than it does on the female form, to the outrage of one lady reader who complained that whereas Lawrence's men (usually) have legs, his women have only stockings.[3] The result of all this is a strange uncertainty of tone – in the words of Robert Heilman, 'often one page seems to have been written by a man, the next by a woman'.[4]

Lawrence offered an unwitting reply to such a charge by comparing himself to Michelangelo, whom he celebrated as the most perfectly androgynous of artists. The Renaissance genius contained so much of the female in his body that he was 'unable to find any woman who in her being should resist him and reserve still some unknown from him'.[5] The result is that he strives to obtain his own physical satisfaction in his art and in his own flesh, 'for his own body is both male and female'. The child is an androgynous being, of indeterminate sex, and it is the artist alone who maintains that state in adult life. In adolescence differentiation occurs in most personalities and one sex comes to predominate over the other; but in equable, happy or artistic natures the sexual balance is maintained. Such a man, according to Lawrence, will not suffer the torments of desire endured by a more masculine being, for he contains sufficient of the female in himself and tends to voluptuousness rather than passion. If every man can be his own wife (as Joyce implies in *Ulysses*), and live according to the female side of his nature (as Lawrence states in his *Study of Thomas Hardy*), then Michelangelo is the consummate example of the male spirit fulfilled in his own female flesh.

In his life, no less than his art, Lawrence never sought to suppress or conceal the female element in his nature. He enjoyed domestic chores such as baking and cleaning, preferred the company of women to that of men, and actively sought the comradeship of feminists and suffragettes. Like Yeats, he seems to have enjoyed the intellectual frankness of the self-willed New Woman, with whom he could discuss the problems of sexuality. In the suffragette Blanche Jennings, Lawrence confided his thoughts on the redefinition of the notion of 'masculinity', to be seen no longer as a power but as a capacity: 'in lovemaking, do you think the woman is always passive? I prefer a little devil, a Carmen – I like nothing passive.'[6] He saw the act of love as an expression by each partner of his or her androgyny in an ecstatic abolition of the notion of sexual difference. June Singer has written of this attitude in her book *Androgyny*:

This breaking of the boundaries gives each woman and man the freedom to be her or his most natural self. It is akin to a counterpoint in which two independent melodies combine into a single harmonic texture in which each retains its individual character. The Masculine seeks, probes, thrusts, and storms the jasper gates; the Feminine yields to him, and then a moment later, she gently slides out from beneath him and begins to stroke him into tension-filled quiescence. Who leads and who follows is inconsequential and fluid and of the moment . . .[7]

In the highest form of such a union, each lover experiences the joy of the other as his or her own. As in the Tantric ritual, the lover never knows 'whose is the hand that caresses or whose the skin caressed'.[8]

Lawrence's rejection of the strong, stern man, whose strength comes from an imperviousness to the diversity of life, has caused many contemporary feminists to interpret his androgyny as a sly front for a covert homosexuality. Kate Millett senses in his writings a fear of being branded effeminate, with the consequence that 'there is always something prurient about the homosexual strain in Lawrence'.[9] Nothing could be further from the truth. In private letters, as well as in public essays, Lawrence repeatedly denounced homosexuality, but not in terms so strident as to warrant the suspicion that he was protesting too much:

> And the essential blood-contact is between man and woman, always has been so, always will be. The contact of positive sex. The homosexual contacts are secondary, even if not merely substitutes of exasperated reaction from the utterly unsatisfactory nervous sex between men and women.[10]

It was in an attempt to remedy the ills in the relation between men and women that Lawrence cultivated the female in himself. It was in figures of intermediate sexuality, such as artists, that he saw the hope of healing the absolute split between male and female in society – and also in the self. Artists like Lawrence felt entrusted with the mission of reinterpreting one sex to the other, as Paul Rosenfeld wrote in *Men Seen*:

> This is not Don Juan . . . Lawrence seems to us the man who has appeared simultaneously with the individualising, breeched, self-conscious woman of the new century . . . Something akin to what happened to men through women in the twelfth century seems commencing a parallel course . . . The Minnesingers, the type of men who could understand and meet these delicate and scornful dames, and who could interpret them and their world to other men, were developed . . .
> The capacity for satisfactory choice has produced in quantity

a woman at war with her own sex, and a man subject to a woman, incapable of developing beyond a rudimentary state his own masculinity, and unweighted and unconvinced in himself . . .

This new sense is not what the awareness of Shaw and George and other scratchers of the sexual is . . . It is a sort of genius, a power of entering sympathetically into the object and coinciding with it. It is an intuition of what goes on within the woman in her endless cycle of revulsion from and reference to the man; a capacity for following her in flights from her own sexuality, and of meeting her in her strange fluttering returns to it . . . And it is as though the female in man himself had suddenly become useful to him in helping him feel the world of women. He, the man, has dared to feel the secret life of the woman where she is female most.[11]

Not all women – or men – have welcomed such intimate investigation. 'He seems more than a human being ought to see', remarked Vernon Lee of Lawrence, 'perhaps that is why he hates humanity so much.'[12] T. S. Eliot accused Lawrence of craving for greater intimacy than is possible between human beings and of failing to see that even lovers must have private sanctuaries which their partners should never expect to penetrate. Lawrence might have responded to such charges by pointing to *Lady Chatterley's Lover*, where it is made absolutely clear that complete self-revelation is a 'bore', precisely because it is too self-conscious. Lawrence's real interest is not the *conscious* sharing of intimacies between lovers, but the attempt by a man to know a woman in those areas where she has never known herself, beyond sex, beyond individuality. And the attempt is to be reciprocal. It is this which unnerves Kate Millett, for she sees the affirmation of the primal unconscious sexual being as a denial of woman's ego, will and personality – all those attributes which women had only recently developed and of which Lawrence now wishes to divest them. So, she reads his masterpiece *Women in Love* as a study of the New Man arrived in the nick of time to give the New Woman her come-uppance.

It is an influential interpretation and has spawned a dozen others, including the predictable assertion that Lawrence is not an androgynous artist attuned to the inner lives of both sexes, but a male propagandist who invariably examines the male

psyche, using women characters to that end. It is ironical that
an author who set out with the impeccably feminist objective of
writing as a person should be degraded by critics to the status of
a bigoted male. It is even more strange that he should be accused
of the very deficiency of which he was so keenly aware in other
male writers, to one of whom he wrote: 'It seems to me queer,
that you prefer to present men chiefly as if you cared for women
not so much for what they are in themselves as for what the men
saw in them. So that after all in your work women seem not to
have an existence, save they are the projections of men. It's the
positivity of women you seem to deny – make them sort of
instrumental.'[13] 'Instrumental' is one of the dirtiest words in
Lawrence's moral lexicon. In *Women in Love* he reverses the
traditional process, making Gerald the instrument of a masterful
woman, Gudrun Brangwen. Just how radical is the art practised
by Lawrence may be seen in the fact that here it is the woman
who treats the man like a sexual object:

> She lay and looked at him, as he slept. He was sheerly beautiful,
> he was a perfect instrument. To her mind, he was a pure,
> inhuman, almost superhuman instrument. His instrumentality
> appealed so strongly to her, she wished she were God, to use
> him as a tool.

This is the same attitude shown by her sister towards her lover
Anton Skrebensky at the end of *The Rainbow*, the previous novel
which, with *Women in Love*, comprises *The Sisters*. A close analysis
of the emotional lives of the two sisters will show just how partial
and wrong-headed is the current feminist response to Lawrence.
   The Sisters was conceived as a Book of the Future, written 'like
a novel in a foreign language I don't know very well'.[14] Lawrence
was preoccupied with the attempt to invent a language adequate
to experiences so new as to be largely unutterable. Like Jude and
Sue, his lovers spend nine-tenths of their energies trying to
understand and describe their experiences to one another. 'The
book frightens me, it is so end-of-the-world', wrote Lawrence of
Women in Love, 'but it is, it must be, the beginning of a new world
too.'[15] Like his critical essays of the period, it was written 'for the
world that will come after this poor, weak-stomached show'.[16] It
is this attempt to imagine a future sexuality which lies at the root

of the book's power to disturb. Middleton Murry complained in a review of *Women in Love*: 'We should have thought that we should be able to distinguish between male and female, at least. But no! Remove the names, remove the sedulous catalogues of unnecessary clothing – a new element and a significant one, this, in our author's work – and man and woman are indistinguishable as octopods in an aquarium tank.'[17]

At the end of *The Rainbow*, Ursula Brangwen had been defined as an androgynous being, ' beyond womanhood', both 'masculine and feminine', poised 'to blaze a path into the future'. There is no doubt that Lawrence endorsed the aspiration, for he described *The Rainbow* as a book about 'woman becoming individual, self-responsible, taking her own initiative'.[15] In an essay, he offered a profoundly feminist gloss on the theme: 'That she bear children is not a woman's significance. But that she bear herself, that is her supreme and risky fate.'[19] Paradoxically, it is through her involvement with the suffragette movement that Ursula learns the pitiful inadequacy of social change, unless there has been a prior change in the self. 'To Ursula, the vote was never a reality', but 'the liberty of woman meant something real and deep . . . But having more freedom she only became more profoundly aware of the big want.'

The 'big want' is the true subject of *Women in Love*, dominating the book from start to finish. It is not at all clear that the big want can be fulfilled in marriage. In the opening discussion of whether to marry or not, both sisters are amused and amazed at the strength of the temptation not to. Gudrun feels no emotion at the thought of bearing children and Ursula berates other people's. The exchange is paralleled by a similar interlude between the two men near the end of the book, when Gerald asks: 'What *do* women want at the bottom?' and Birkin can only speculate and shrug. Kate Millett has no doubts as to the meaning of all this. Lawrence is the most subtle of sexual politicians, she says, 'for it is through a feminine consciousness that his masculine message is conveyed'.[20] The big want of men like Lawrence, says Millett, is nothing more nor less than Victorian marriage, and so Ursula must be made to conform to her author's requirements. She is so close to the author as to become his rival, her triumphant versatility as child-bearer and worker a challenge to his limited male being. As in the world of Strindberg, the male feels marginalised by a resourceful woman, or so Millett argues:

After all, she is, in the vulgar expression, sitting on a fortune and is never without 'the price of her ransom – her femaleness'. There is a cynical envy in Lawrence's attitude that this is unfair competition – 'what she could not get because she was a human being, fellow to the rest of mankind, she would get because she was female'. As she can always sell herself, earning her living is an indulgence made at his expense.[21]

So the woman who dreamed of leading a movement is punished by failure in examinations, departure from university without a degree and – the unkindest cut of all – life as a contented housewife. This radical misreading of Lawrence's book fails to concede that Ursula is at least as much a projection of Lawrence as is Birkin; and that it is central to Lawrence's art to reincarnate himself as fully in his women as in his men. More important still is Millett's failure to see that the issue broached in *The Rainbow* has not changed at all. The big want is still there and it concerns Ursula's desire to be known and valued as a person rather than as a female. Legislation and votes for women cannot fully fulfil that need, but Rupert Birkin can. It is one of the ironies of his character that long after he has assuaged Ursula's need, he continues to assert his ignorance of what a woman really wants. Perhaps that is Lawrence's way of saying that virtue is never conscious of itself as such.

From the outset, Ursula is reaching towards a new notion of her own character, beyond the external trappings which the public is pleased to call 'individuality'. In that opening conversation with Gudrun, she wonders if the desire for children is merely superficial and not a true longing of the soul. Ideas of 'male' and 'female' may be equally insubstantial, or so the school inspector Birkin seems to think. On a visit to Ursula's classroom, he urges the children to paint the androgynous flowers yellow and insists that they paint the *fact* – 'red little spiky stigmas of the female flower, dangling yellow male catkin, yellow pollen flying from one to the other'. He wants the children to have the fact of the flowers rather than the knowledge of them, because already the culture is narcissistic and book-ridden, its object not passion but the knowledge of passion, not lovemaking but the pornography of watching one's animal actions in mirrors. The subsequent resignation of Ursula and Rupert from their posts as teachers must be seen not as an act of despair in society, but simply as a protest against the false culture purveyed in schools and books. The child must lose the flower to gain the knowledge of it, but Birkin would prefer to have the experience and miss the meaning. 'A book is an underground hole with two lids to it', wrote Lawrence, 'a perfect place to tell lies in.'[22] Or again, 'one is reborn not by taking thought, but by letting go'.[23] So Birkin has come to tell Ursula that he wants not a knowing sensuousness but a mindless sensuality, the dark knowledge that is death to one's self, but the birth of another. It is at this point that Hermione starts 'jeering at him as if he were a neuter'. Yet it is this very androgyny of Birkin which attracts Ursula from the start and teases her with the prospect of a man who could take her by sex into zones beyond the reach of mere sexuality.

The more others despise Birkin for his ambiguous sexuality, the more steadfast is the attraction between himself and Ursula. To Minette he is one of the Bohemian 'half men', unlike such 'real men' as Gerald, who put her in her place. To the Contessa, 'he is not a man, he is a chameleon, a creature of change'. To Hermione, 'he was not consistent, not a man, less than a man'. Gerald, on the other hand, is an exponent of raw masculine power and it is the man in Gudrun who falls in love with that force. Watching Gerald swim, she cries: 'God, what it is to be a man!' For this, she and he are eventually doomed. 'The freedom, the liberty, the mobility!' cries this woman as she falls in love with the male principle. But it is Lawrence's view that 'there is no getting of vision . . . before we get our souls fertilised by the *female*';[24] and Gudrun and Gerald fatally turn their backs on that process. Gerald cannot help but 'strive to come up to her criterion, fulfil her idea of a man and a human being'. In doing so, as when he spurs his horse under his bloody power, he earns the hatred of Ursula, who 'alone understood him perfectly, in pure opposition'. She asks in outrage if it is manly to torture a horse, a creature ten times as sensitive as himself. Here the identification between Ursula and Lawrence is complete, the Lawrence who wrote that 'strong stern men bore and irritate me'.[25] So she turns, as if by magnetism, to the womanly man who wants to save the world by reinterpreting each sex to the other. He tells Ursula that we hate the word 'love', because we have vulgarised it, dirtied it with our sentimental minds in the same way that we have polluted the words 'shit' or 'fuck'. Every word, said Emerson, was once a poem; and if the words now bring a blush of shame, of whom is it that we are reminded? Birkin believes, like Yeats and Joyce, that the word 'love' should be tabooed for years, until we get a better idea. No sooner has he avowed this than Ursula tries to force him to say that 'love' is what he wants, but he reformulates it as 'freedom together'. He will resign from his post, if he can live sufficiently by himself, a phrase used of Ursula in the opening chapter ('she lived a good deal by herself'). So Birkin shows himself female, even in his attempt at self-sufficiency, his initial desire to live without a woman itself balancing Ursula's inability in the first chapter to imagine a life with any man of her acquaintance.

Birkin's attempt to define his new notion of love is hampered by the lack of a ready idiom, with the result that the new dispensation sounds at times suspiciously like the old. It is most unfortunate that, in the presence of Gerald, he should illustrate his theory, for the benefit of a listening Ursula, with the image of a horse. She cannot believe that a horse ever wanted to put itself in the human power, but Birkin sees the resignation of will to a higher being as the ultimate sign of love. Ursula reserves the right to mock his Salvator Mundi touch, while continuing to discuss his notions. Birkin believes that 'there is a real, impersonal me, that is beyond love, beyond any emotional relationship' and that this is true of Ursula as well. 'And it is there I would want to meet you – not in the emotional, loving plane – but there beyond, where there is no speech and no terms of agreement.' Still suspicious, Ursula wonders if all this rhetoric is a mask for the old selfishness, but Birkin insists that he doesn't know what he wants of her, that in coming to her, stripped of defences, he delivers himself over to the unknown. He cares not one whit for her good looks or personality; he is bored by the woman he can see; and he wants an invisible presence:

> I want to find you where you don't know your own existence, the you that your common self denies utterly. But I don't want your good looks, and I don't want your womanly feelings, and I don't want your thoughts nor opinions nor your ideas – they are all bagatelles to me.

It sounds remarkably like Yeats all over again. It will be recalled that Yeats believed that the ideal image worshipped by the male was the secret undiscovered self of the female, which only a true lover could bring to her awareness. The female in the male helps him to articulate the woman in herself; and the male element in woman does no less for the man. When this consummation is finally achieved in Sherwood Forest, Lawrence is at pains to insist that, in the ebb and flow of a relationship, either Rupert or Ursula may seize the initiative and dominate:

> And he too waited in the magical steadfastness of suspense, for her to take this knowledge of him as he had taken it of her. He knew her darkly, with the fullness of dark knowledge. Now she would know him, and he too would be liberated.

There are, however, major differences between the doctrines of Yeats and Lawrence. Philip Sicker has pithily defined the difference – for Yeats, love is a mirror by which we behold ourselves in the inmost self of the beloved; for Lawrence, it has been likened to a lamp, by which we illuminate for the beloved a self that is entirely external and strange.[26] Moreover, while the *anima* in a man might attach itself to the hidden self of a woman, according to the Yeatsian system each person remained fully androgynous after the transaction; and it was *this* which allowed the love to flourish. But for Lawrence, androgyny is only a means to a very different end. He desires no mystical melting of the partners into union, but rather that they retain and augment their sense of difference, like two stars which remain at once separate yet mutually dependent in a dynamic equilibrium. In his *Study of Thomas Hardy*, he described how there can be no coming together without a falling asunder; and argued that the sense of separateness is actually reinforced by the process of falling in love:

> . . . in the act of love, that which is mixed in me becomes pure, that which is female in me is given to the female, that which is male in her draws into me, I am complete, I am pure male, she is pure female; we rejoice in contact perfect and naked and clear, singled out unto ourselves, and given the surpassing freedom.[27]

For Lawrence, androgyny ceases to be a final resting-point, or a mere qualification for the artistic life; instead, it becomes a prerequisite for all who wish to become themselves. No longer an end, it is the means by which an absolute differentiation into pure male and female is achieved in the very act of love. No longer a victim of the Platonic myth, no longer an abject half earnestly desiring his opposite, the pure male is freed of all sexual desire, a being sufficient and whole unto himself.

A notion of character which annihilates all forms of individuality and freedom of will is anathema to the modern liberal. At the very phase of history when the New Woman and the Democratic Man have won a measure of personal freedom, Lawrence asks them to admit that it is a frivolity, a trapping. Kate Millett was not the first to question his motives, for he asks the same questions of himself, by placing them in the mouth of Ursula. His art has room for the opposing self, for he knows that in tales, as in love, there are two sides to every story. The greatest art, he said, must always contain the essential criticism of the morality to which it adheres; and Ursula is the source of that liberal critique of the totalitarian radical in *Women in Love*. Birkin's assumption of male superiority makes her cross, for she sees it as a lie, no different in kind from Gerald's bullying of a horse. She wonders if men with labour-saving devices, comfortable lodgings and kind landladies need wives any more; but Birkin welcomes such developments as a way of testing the authenticity of the wedding vow. He is disgusted by those who, in the past, married for a home and glad that such motivations are no longer important. Sex without the ulterior motive of procreation or housekeeping becomes a truly free action, a version of the *acte gratuit*. A man has little practical need for a woman, except to share his bed and bear children, and it is just as well, for it leaves a couple free to define the deeper needs, the big want. Ursula suspects that all this is an elaborate way of saying that he loves her, a radical presentation of the traditional view of marriage. As a conscientious feminist, 'she was reluctant to yield there, where he wanted her, to yield as it were her very identity'. Ursula, like many creative women, experiences what June Singer has called the need 'to go through a period of anger, of rebellion, against the men who, she believes, have oppressed her'.[28] Later, she will realise that most women are bound only because they have allowed themselves to be, but that bondage is not what Birkin asks of her. His desire for androgynous fusion is exciting in its promise of a Third Heaven, but unnerving in its possibility of a confusion of sexes and a surrender to the formless chaos whence man came. For such reasons, Mircea

Eliade felt the need to distinguish spiritual androgyny from interpersonal sexual confusion.

Every attempt to transcend the opposite carries with it a certain danger, This is why the ideas of a *coincidentia oppositorum* always arouse ambivalent feelings; on the one side, man is haunted by the desire to escape from his particular situation and regain a transpersonal mode of life; on the other, he is paralysed by the fear of losing his 'identity' and 'forgetting' himself.[29]

Ursula fears that Birkin is asking her to yield up her very identity; but he is not seeking of her anything he has not already asked of himself. 'I don't want love, I don't want to know you', he says; 'I want to be gone out of myself and you to be lost to yourself, so we are found different.' He does not want a clinging, dependent woman, but a proud and separate being, who has a self to give and a self to lose. There is nothing antifeminist in that. What he has to offer is exactly what Ursula wants and she is critical only because she has already decided to give her assent. He will respect her manly self-reliance, just as she will respect his womanly sensitivity. She has already admitted the justice of his conviction that free will is a myth, that men kill and die not by accident, but by some hidden design of a deeper self that wills its own destiny. It is that self which she now wishes to know and Birkin says that he can reveal it to her.

In making this promise, Birkin echoes the claim which Lawrence made for his art in a famous letter to Edward Garnett: 'that which is psychic – non-human, in humanity, is more interesting to me than the old-fashioned human element – which causes one to conceive a character in a certain moral scheme and make him consistent'.[30] The ghost of Strindberg haunts those lines, in their redefinition of character as a multiple self, with a right to inner contradiction. In *Women in Love* each of the major characters contradicts himself or herself, and usually for the same reasons as obtain in *Miss Julie* – because the initiative in a relationship flows one way and then the other, or because a person 'borrows' an idea from another. Critics have often complained that both Hermione and Ursula say things which would be far more characteristic of Birkin and have seen this as a failure on Lawrence's part to create psychologically distinct and credible protagonists. But such critics forget that both women are in love with him, and to love someone is to try to see the world through that person's eyes. Strindberg anticipated Lawrence's conviction of the tenuousness of the modern self, but not his belief that there is a deeper self that may be plumbed. In his letter, Lawrence went on:

> I don't so much care about what the woman *feels* – in the ordinary usage of the word. That presumes an ego to feel with. I only care about what the woman *is* – what she IS – inhumanly, physiologically, materially – according to the use of the word; but for me, what she *is* as a phenomenon (or as representing some greater, inhuman will), instead of what she feels according to the human conception.

In this anthropological view of women, Lawrence wishes to celebrate what he elsewhere called 'the tremendous non-human quality of life'. It was this non-human quality which caused Marx, in a notorious passage, to wonder if man was really man and his relation to the world a human one. Marx believed that a force such as money had a malevolent dynamic of its own, which transformed the self into a contingent non-human entity, and which divested the relation between self and world of its human content. The repeated assertions of such diverse nineteenth-century theorists as Arnold and Wilde that a man must be measured by what he *is* rather than by what he *has* lie behind Lawrence's desire to know what the elemental woman is, not the personal trappings (including a personality) which the individual woman has. He may suspect that man is no longer the measure of all things, but at least he is the measurer, of his non-humanity, if of nothing else. This is an aim which Lawrence shares with Joyce – the wish to move in a sexual relationship beyond the all-too-human to that which transcends or denies it. So he concludes:

> You musn't look in my novel for the old stable ego of the character. There is another ego, according to whose action the individual is unrecognisable, and passes through, as it were, allotropic states which it needs a deeper sense than any we've been used to exercise, to discover are states of the same single radically unchanged element. (Like as diamond and coal are

the same pure single element of carbon. The ordinary novel would trace the history of the diamond – but I say, 'Diamond, what! This is carbon'. And my diamond might be coal or soot, and my theme is carbon.)

Ursula is unnerved by the candour of a man who loves her right enough, but believes they 'can go one better'. She fears that he wants to be deathly, but he claims that he only wants them to know what they are. She covers his face with kisses, 'to show him she was no shallow prude' and momentarily he scorns and forgets his 'other self'. Yet it is that other self which claims him as he lies sick in bed in the days that follow. Ursula has not accepted his proposal of a union-in-separateness, and so he turns to Gerald, in hopes that he can assuage the industrialist's suffering after the death of his sister. In 'Man to Man', his hopes are put to the test in a chapter which is less a study of incipient homosexuality than an analysis of applied androgyny.

By now, Birkin is aware that his life rests with Ursula, but he revolts against the prospect of the horrible privacy and narrow intimacy of conventional marriage. As he hates promiscuity even worse than marriage, a liaison to him is just another form of coupling, even more reactionary and derivative than the institution which it flouts. At root, Birkin suffers from the modern flaw of seeking in sex a consummation offered by religion. According to T. S. Eliot, this excessive desire for intimacy is based on a failure to concede that 'the love of two human beings is only made perfect in the love of God' – 'as if', Eliot derisively adds, 'human love could possibly be an end in itself'.[31] Birkin's reply would be as simple as that which he offered to Gerald:

'And you mean if there isn't the woman, there's nothing?' said Gerald.
'Pretty well that – seeing there's no God.'

Lawrence once argued that the religious passion is largely sexual, but it is clear that the problem which agitates Birkin here is the need to treat sex as a sublimated form of religion: 'On the whole, he hated sex, it was such a limitation. It was sex that turned a man into a broken half of a couple, the woman into the other broken half. And he wanted to be single in himself, the woman single in herself.' Yet the paradox is that he must accept this broken halfness in a sexual relationship, in order to break out of the sexual limitation; just as Ursula must overcome her lust for possession and settle for knowing him in separateness. Birkin wants sex to revert to the level of other appetites, to be regarded as a functional process and not a fulfilment. No longer an end in itself, it must provide the means of its own transcendence, so that each lover attains to absolute self-sufficiency, free of the tremblings of desire. The question asked by Hardy's Jude – are men and women fractions lacking an integer? – is raised now by Birkin:

> It was intolerable, this possession at the hands of woman. Always a man must be considered as the broken-off fragment of a woman, and the sex was the still aching scar of the laceration. Man must be added on to a woman, before he had any real place or wholeness.
>
> And why? Why should we consider ourselves, men and women, as broken fragments of one whole? It is not true. We are not broken fragments of one whole. Rather we are the singling away into purity and clear being, of things that were mixed. Rather the sex is that which remains in us of the mixed, the unresolved. And passion is the further separating of this mixture, that which is manly being taken into the being of the man, that which is womanly passing to the woman, till the two are clear and whole as angels, the admixture of sex in the highest sense surpassed, leaving two single beings constellated together like two stars.

Birkin then goes on to evince a nostalgia for the Platonic notion that male and female are two halves of a whole and original being;

> In the old age, before sex was, we were mixed, each one a mixture. The process of singling into individuality resulted in the great polarisation of sex. The womanly drew to one side, the manly to the other. But the separation was imperfect even then. And so our world-cycle passes. There is now to come the new day, when we are beings each of us, fulfilled in difference. But there is no longer any of the horrible merging, mingling self-abnegation of love.

The rhetorical power of this sermon cannot conceal a fundamental contradiction in Birkin's – and Lawrence's – position. In this instance, he presents himself as a man bound on a voyage to pure maleness; but elsewhere, he comes forward as an example of the new intermediate sexuality, one who will mediate the opposing extremes. In defence of Lawrence, it might be argued that he was conjuring up a vision of two counterbalancing androgynes, a male androgyne and a female androgyne, but this is merely hinted in the novel and never refined as an idea, either by Birkin or his creator.

This long passage comes by way of introduction to the realisation by Gerald and Rupert that what unites them is something suspiciously close to love. Rupert is immensely attracted to the knightly ritual of *Blutbruderschaft*, if only because the pure love of man for man is free of the ulterior motive of procreation, which complicates relations with a woman. Gerald's refusal of the proposal reveals his limitation, 'a sort of fatal halfness, which to himself seemed wholeness', unlike the versatility of Birkin. Singled out into complete maleness, Gerald is almost ready for death. He has achieved much because he has imagined little but the efficiency of his mines is now so total that he is hardly necessary any more. The masculine principle is revealed to be finally self-destructive, unless the soul is fertilised by the female. Paradoxical though it may seem, it is to save Gerald from death and open him to the female principle that Birkin offers the *Blutbruderschaft*.

'The possibilities of love exhaust themselves', says Gerald, 'then you die.' So at least he knows what he is up against. In the 'Gladiatorial' sequence, both men flirt with the idea of homosexuality as a possible expression of their love. It is only a mild flirtation, however, a desperate option toyed with by two men, one of whom has been temporarily spurned by the woman he loves, the other of whom fears that he will never be able to love. The account of their naked wrestling is explicit sexual, each driving his flesh deeper into the other, 'as if they would break into a oneness'. Birkin openly voices his pleasure in the beautiful body of his friend, but is at pains to balance this with an assertion of the spiritual nature of his pledge. 'We are mentally, spiritually intimate, therefore we should be more or less physically intimate too – it is more whole.' This need for an equilibrium between body and soul is an obsession in *Women in Love*, for without it man dies. For Birkin, it is just as wrong to live only in the mind as it was for the African lady (depicted in the statue) to have lived solely in the body: 'It must have been thousands of years since her race had died, mystically: that is, since the relation between the senses and the outspoken mind had broken, leaving the experience all in one sort, mystically sensual.'

Even more important to Birkin, however, is the conviction that such a complete friendship with another man would remove some of the terrible pressure from modern marriage. If men and women were less exacting in the demands made on one another, then the love between them might be saved. Equally, in a culture which is saturated in the knowledge of sex, and devoid of true physical tenderness, there is an urgent need for people to touch one another, especially if they belong to the same sex. When men can express their physical attachment to other men, and women to other women, without provoking a leer or a wink, then marriage itself may be freed of the need to carry the intolerable burden of *all* our sensuality. 'You've got to get rid of the *exclusiveness* of married love', says Birkin, 'and you've got to admit the unadmitted love of man for man. It makes for a greater freedom for everybody, a greater power of individuality both in men and women.' The alternative is traditional marriage, a prospect both sinister and chilling: '*Égoisme à deux* is nothing to it. It's a sort of tacit hunting in couples: the world all in couples, each couple in its own little house, watching its own little interests, and stewing in its own little privacy.' Moreover, the very power of the institution has grown self-destructive, for the expectations it arouses can never be met by any one relationship, 'because the relation between man and woman is made the supreme and exclusive relationship, that's where all the tightness and meanness and insufficiency comes in'.

As Birkin takes pleasure in his friend's blond body, he considers it as different from his own as a man's from a woman's; but this beauty reminds him of Ursula, who regains ascendancy over his being. It is almost as if he has made love to the man by way of preparation for the later hour when he may make love to the woman. His invitation to Gerald to make a bond of pure trust may be seen as an attempt to open the other man to the possibility of being loved by a woman. At the very outset, he had confided in Gerald that if there isn't woman, there's nothing. 'Have you ever really loved anybody?' Gerald asked on that occasion, the question to which he returns again and again in conversation

with Birkin. After the wrestling, he seems to have reached a kind
of solution:

> 'I've gone after women – and been keen enough over some of
> them. But I've never felt *love*. I don't believe I've ever felt so
> much *love* for a woman as I have for you – not *love*. You
> understand what I mean?'
> 'Yes. I'm sure you've never loved a woman'.
> 'You feel that, do you? And do you think I ever shall?'

The Birkin who looks into Gerald's eyes and is reminded of Ursula
hopes that he can perform a similar service for his friend and
open him to the possibility of a woman's love. In his heart, this
is what Gerald seeks in his bond with the other man. He tells
himself that 'if he pledged himself with the man he would later
be able to pledge himself with the woman: not merely in legal
marriage, but in absolute mystic marriage'. The fact that he
rejects Birkin's offer as soon as that thought strikes him is the
ultimate proof of just how impervious Gerald really is to life and
all that it offers him. The Salvator Mundi cannot even save his
friend and lives to witness the destruction of his hope that the
female in himself could lead Gerald to the love of a woman.

Influenced by the theories of Edward Carpenter, Lawrence
saw Birkin as an example of a new 'intermediate sex', which
might become 'the teachers of future society' interpreting men
and women to one another,[32] like the Navajo *nadle*, those ferrymen
who traverse the rapids between river-banks and who mediate in
quarrels between husband and wife.[33] Edward Carpenter believed
that such a man, 'while possessing thoroughly masculine powers
of mind and body, combines with them the tenderer and more
emotional soul-nature of the woman', in an exciting blend of
sensibility and perception. Havelock Ellis wrote in support of the
theory that 'genius carries us into a region where the strongly
differentiated signs of masculinity or femininity, having their end
in procreation, are of little significance'.[34] Mrs Havelock Ellis
pointed out that the doctrine was, in part, based on a conviction
of the *superiority* of women and on the capacity of certain privileged
males to share in this charisma through 'the woman in man'. She
wrote in open admiration of her hero, James Hinton, 'this
muscularly strong man with the tenderness of a woman'.[35] An
apostle of free love, Hinton seems to have endured the usual

afflictions which beset the Salvator Mundi. 'Christ was the Saviour of Men', he complained, 'but I am the saviour of women, and I don't envy him a bit.'[36] Men like Hinton and Ellis were dubbed by Carpenter as members of the 'intermediate sex', 'inventors and teachers of arts and crafts, or wizards and sorcerers; they became divines and seers, or revealers of the gods and religion; they became medicine-men and healers, prophets and prophetesses'.[37] Thus Birkin and his attempt to reconcile the sundered sexes. His attempt fails, but it dominates many of the classics of modern literature, where it more often meets with success. The hero of Thomas Mann's *Tonio Kroger* becomes obsessed with a blond bourgeois for a time, but much later recognises the same attributes in a girl and falls in love with her. In *The Magic Mountain*, another work by Mann, Hans Castorp falls for Claudia Chauchat and is suddenly struck by her close resemblance to a boy whom he had once loved.[38] And in Evelyn Waugh's *Brideshead Revisited*, Charles Ryder is prepared for the mature love of an adult woman by purging himself of all adolescent silliness in his initial relationship with Lord Sebastian Flyte.

It may well be that Lawrence submitted Birkin to the humiliation of a rejection by Gerald because he was even more repelled than fascinated by the ritual of *Blutbruderschaft* anyway. When he was working on the last sections of the novel, he wrote to Dollie Radford in June 1916: 'And even this terrible glamour of camaraderie, which is the glamour of Homer and of all militarism, is a decadence, a degradation, a losing of individual form and distinction, a merging in a sticky male mess.'[39] The fact that this was written just after a physical examination by the army does not entirely invalidate its sincerity. The man who had dedicated himself in 1912 to 'sticking up for the love between man and woman'[40] renewed the vow four years later (in the year of *Women in Love*) by adding that 'in this relation we live or die'.[41] In the intervening period, he wrote to Henry Savage in 1913 that 'one is kept by all tradition and instinct from loving men, or a man – for it means just the extinction of all purposive influences'.[42] This extinction was not necessarily a bad thing, in Lawrence's opinion, for the ulterior motive of procreation had often impaired the purity of commitment between men and women. The trouble is that the warrior bond is a pact of death. That longing for death is seen as a grave disease which afflicts all four major characters in the book, most obviously Gerald, who fears the end as deeply as he desires it. Even Ursula, the most homely and purposeful of the four, is a prey to such thoughts: 'One can never see beyond the consummation. It is enough that death is a great and conclusive experience. Why should we ask what comes after the experience?' Nor is it coincidental that she imagines the hereafter in terms of the 'illimitable space' in front of Sappho as she prepared to dive. 'To die is also a joy', she thinks, but the reference to Sappho at the cliff at Lesbos has linked the homosexual urge with death, the fatal plunge of the priestess who sought to assuage the sorrows of love and transcend her own sexuality. After the dive in mythology, those souls which survived returned as new men and women, androgynes; and their androgyny was signified by sacrificing a boy and girl to the waters,[43] motifs adumbrated in the chapters called 'Diver' and 'Water-Party'.

Yet Ursula is even more attracted by life. She can respond to the attraction of Birkin's notion of a world without humanity; she can share Sappho's hope that the beginning comes out of the end; but she can see, more than anything, that Birkin wants them to know death, that he is death-eating. And she is right. Birkin is obsessed by the statue of an African woman who 'knew what he himself did not know', the experience of a bestiality unchastened by an act of the mind. This process may take thousands of years, but always it comes after that moment when the death of the creative spirit is marked by the separation of body and mind. The protruding buttocks of an African woman imply for Birkin 'great mysteries to be unsealed, sensual, mindless, dreadful mysteries, far beyond the phallic cult'. This knowledge of dissolution he eventually shares with Ursula in moments of their lovemaking:

> She had thought that there was no source deeper than the phallic source. And now, behold, from the smitten rock of the man's body, from the strange marvellous flanks and thighs, deeper, further in mystery than the phallic source, came the floods of ineffable darkness and ineffable riches.

Later, when the lovers holiday on the continent, there is a much less tender account of a similar ritual. On this occasion, Birkin is full of 'mocking brutishness' and 'sardonic suggestivity', his eyes narrow, but Ursula cannot refuse so repulsively attractive a proposal:

> Wasn't it rather horrible, a man who could be so soulful and spiritual, now to be so – she baulked at her own thoughts and memories: then she added – so bestial? She winced. But after all, why not? She exulted as well. Why not be bestial, and go the whole round of experience? She exulted in it. She was bestial. How good it was to be really bestial. There would be no shameful thing she had not experienced.

Later still, when Birkin is asked by Gerald what a woman really wants, he suggests 'some satisfaction in basic repulsion'; but the reader of *Women in Love* cannot agree. For one thing, Ursula's pleasure in the act is no longer innocent but knowing, the pleasure that comes from transgression of an accepted code. Moreover, the lovers have broken Birkin's golden rule, for they are watching themselves commit the act of violation, the excitement is not truly in their bodies but in their heads. In fact, they are at this very moment in the classic British 'state of funk', for, as Lawrence wrote in the famous essay of that name, 'bravado and *doing it on purpose* is just as unpleasant and hurtful as repression, just as much a sign of secret fear'. They are guilty of pornography, of watching their naked animal movements in the mental mirror. Their 'letting go' is neither sincere nor successful nor sufficient unto itself, because it can only define its freedom in terms of the code which it negates. The lovers leave England, as lice crawl off a dying body, because in England you cannot let go; but Lawrence wickedly insists that England is a state of mind which they bring with them wherever they travel. Gudrun senses in Gerald the provincial English contempt for the foreigner and even Birkin is English in spite of himself, never more so than when he responds with some hesitation to the invitation to the Reunionshaal: 'I suppose we'd better – break the ice.' Quite so.

There is nothing inherently wrong with a love that comes from deeper than the phallic source. The feminist in Ursula could only welcome Birkin's staunch rejection of phallus-worship, just as she has, on other occasions, respected his desire for kisses and nothing more. (The old idea that it is the lady who always says no is just one of the myths punctured by Lawrence in this book.) The absolute difference in tone between the two accounts of the buggery, the one tender and wide-eyed, the other brutal and knowing, must be deliberate. In Lawrence's world, there is nothing good or bad but thinking makes it so; and sex-in-the-head is always bad. Most critics assume that Birkin's actions in these scenes are shameful proof that he is himself a citizen of Sodom, but that, unlike Gerald, he can dive into the depths of dissolution and still come up safely on the other side. Frank Kermode justifies the acts of buggery on the grounds that Birkin goes wrong in order to go right. 'It is necessary for those on the side of life to comply with dissolution', says Kermode, 'in such a way that it is hard to distinguish them from the party of death'.[44] This is close enough to what Lawrence wrote in 'Pornography and Obscenity', where he insisted on the necessity and difficulty of the distinction:

> The sex functions and the excrementory functions in the human body work so close together, yet they are, so to speak, utterly different in direction. Sex is a creative flow, the excrementory flow is towards dissolution, decreation, if we may use such a word. In the really healthy human being the distinction between the two is instant, our profoundest instincts are perhaps our instincts of opposition between the two poles.
>
> But in the degraded human being the deep instincts have gone dead, and then the two flows become identical. *This* is the secret of really vulgar and pornographical people: the sex flow and the excrement flow is the same to them. It happens when the psyche deteriorates, and the profound controlling instincts collapse. Then sex is dirt and dirt is sex.[45]

This passage is sometimes used – though *not* by Kermode – to suggest that Birkin's buggery is a dissolute confusion of the sexual and excrementory, while his more conventional copulation with Ursula in Sherwood Forest is all right, a reenactment of the manly diversions of Merrie England. This reading takes no account of the growing conviction among British and continental sexologists at the turn of the century that 'copulation *a posteriori* was the natural way'. Exponents of such phallocriticism forget that the river of dissolution and decreation flows through the penis, as well as the river of life. It is far too trite to see the penis as always and only the source of vitality, and the anus as the vessel of corruption. The Yeats who recalled that love has pitched his mansion in the place of excrement saw in the paradox the

challenge of a humorous God to the imagination of his creation.
And in most cases his creatures have seen the joke. One could
cite Joyce's gentle rebuke to the lover who put his hand on his
heart – 'The seat of the affections is lower down.'

One writer who could never respond with such laughter was
Swift. His failure to live at peace with that instant distinction
between the sexual and the excrementory provoked Lawrence to
witty scorn, in an essay written in the same year as the long
passage just quoted:

> There is a poem of Swift's which should make us pause. It is
> written to Celia, his Celia – and every verse ends with the
> mad, maddened refrain: 'But – Celia, Celia, Celia shits!' Now
> that, stated baldly, is so ridiculous it is almost funny. But when
> one remembers the gnashing insanity to which the great mind
> of Swift was reduced by that and similar thoughts, the joke
> dies away. Such thoughts poisoned him, like some terrible
> constipation. They poisoned his mind. And why, in heaven's
> name? The *fact* cannot have troubled him, since it applied to
> himself and to all of us. It was not the fact that Celia shits
> which so deranged him, it was the *thought*. His mind couldn't
> bear the thought. Great wit as he was, he could not see how
> ridiculous his revulsions were. His arrogant mind overbore
> him. He couldn't even see how much worse it would be if Celia
> didn't shit.

At the root of Swift's disgust is a disproportionate emphasis not
so much on the body as on the mind's experience of the body.
What for Yeats is a baffling miracle becomes for him a recurrent
terror. Of course, Lawrence feels sorry for Swift, but even sorrier
for Celia, doomed always to be measured against a rarefied
woman who exists only in men's heads. Lawrence is never more
feminist than in his desire to dismantle the myth of male and
female fantasy, and to reveal the unaccommodated man and
woman. Celia does shit; Birkin doesn't always feel like making
love. Like Yeats accusing the Christian brothers of not really
believing in the Incarnation, Lawrence accuses the Christian
Swift of not allowing himself to imagine the resurrection of the
body – 'and if that doesn't mean the whole man, what does it
mean?' What distressed Swift was the implication of Celia's

shitting, the fear that culture itself is a fraud which cannot conceal the savage facts.

Norman O. Brown has cited a theory of Freud to telling effect in this precise context. Freud held that the coprophic elements in the sexual instincts of primitive man proved less and less attractive from the moment when he 'developed an upright posture and so removed his organ of smell from the ground'.[46] But such developments affect only the higher layers of man's structure. 'The fundamental processes which promote erotic excitation remain always the same. Excremental things are all too intimately and inseparably bound up with sexual things; the position of the genital organs – *inter urinas et faeces* – remains the decisive and unchangeable factor.'[47] According to Brown, Freud would therefore see Swift as a typical exponent of 'the sexual repression that marches with culture, the organic defence of the new form of life that began with the erect posture'.[48]

There is also the possibility that a covert self-hatred and shame lie behind the awful 'But' of 'Celia shits'. Germaine Greer has seen in those words the 'transferred epithets of loathing for sex undignified by aesthetic prophylaxis and romantic fantasy'.[49] Sophisticated men who laugh at Swift's discomfiture may still say 'fuck you' as an insult, says Greer, or use 'cunt' as the most degrading of epithets. At the root of such usage is the same desire as Swift's – to project the male sense of shame onto the degraded woman, who is asked to bear *all* the burdens of a flawed and incomplete humanity. 'Being forced to play the role of woman in sexual intercourse is the deepest imaginable humiliation', says Greer, 'which is only worsened if the victim finds to his horror that he enjoys it.'[50]

It is in the light of that sentence that one must salute the achievement of Lawrence, who created in Rupert Birkin a new kind of hero who could fulfil that role with pride. Many of his most poignant love-scenes are based on a reversal of traditional sexual roles: 'And she cleaved close to him. He kissed her many times. But he too had his idea and his will. He wanted only gentle communion, no other, no passion now. So that soon she drew away, put on her hat and went home.' By her gentle respect for his moods, Ursula shows herself to be as emotionally versatile a lover as he. Although Ursula momentarily agrees with Hermione that Birkin 'is not quite man enough to make a destiny for a woman', it is ultimately this very passivity in him which she comes to love. He is man enough to allow this New Woman to make her destiny for herself. As he remarks to her father, after his formal proposal of marriage has gone disastrously wrong, 'it's much more likely that it's I who am at the beck and call of the woman, then she at mine'. Like all fathers, Mr Brangwen wants to rear a New Woman, having married a traditional wife.

In the event, he rears two, one of whom triumphs, while the other moves to disaster. The contrast between the balanced androgyny of Ursula and the increasing worship of the male principle by Gudrun is stark. Like Strindberg's Bertha, like Hardy's Sue, she secretly envies the man his very limitations, for she shrewdly sees that they are the source of his strange power. Like Lady Macbeth, Gudrun expects her lover to live out for her the maleness which she has always refused to confront directly in herself; and because she had denied and repressed her own masculinity, she is fatally in thrall to the same elements in Gerald Crich. She knows that the specialist male never falls into traps which he has not the intelligence to perceive; and Gudrun, the 'man's woman', envies this safety, for Gerald is free of a thousand obstacles which beset a woman. She takes out a boat at the water-party, 'having given her word like a man' that she is an experienced hand at the game. Later, an injured Gerald feels sheepish about being rowed home by a woman, but Gudrun 'was subtly gratified that she should have power over them both', a true account of the nature of the relationship between them. When Gerald's father dies, their love comes to its crisis in his utter dependence on this masterful lady. Gerald has too much death in him to be able to face his father's passing without hysteria. He never reckoned with death and suddenly realises that it was there in him all the time, so that when he 'was really left alone, he could not bear it'. This is the ultimate vindication of Birkin's belief in separateness, in the need for lovers to learn to live alone if there is to be any meaning to their love. Birkin has grasped the meaning of the Chekhovian paradox that those who contemplate marriage must first learn how to be lonely, for otherwise they will have no self to surrender to the beloved.

Birkin lives every day of his love for Ursula as if it were her last, and as if he must reincarnate in himself all those female elements which might be snatched from him forever, if she were to die tomorrow. June Singer sees such 'imminence of death' as the ultimate test of love, something which proves that 'each party to it must be whole in herself and himself so that, when the inevitable parting comes, tomorrow or in fifty years, preparation will have been made'.[51] One must not only cherish the beloved in any full relationship, but also one's aloneness. In part, this is necessary because the androgyne must transcend the merely personal and live with a sense of eternity. Singer distinguishes interpersonal romantic love, existing in linear time, from transpersonal androgynous love, whose time-sequences are cyclical and eternal.[52] There must be a withholding as well as a merging in any true love. This is a doctrine most often found in the east, and often as a warning against the excesses of Tantric ritual. The story is told of a beggar Siva, who smoked so much hashish that he could not make his rounds and so he sent his wife Parvati instead. She took his place, performed his tasks, collected and fed him his usual food, and so pleased him by this devotion that 'he embraced her violently and became one with her'.[53] Yet such Tantric fusion ultimately precludes any sexual activity, since desire can only be excited by the notion of sexual difference. Wendy Doninger O'Flaherty has studied the Siva myth and shows that the lovers are forced to separate in order that they may come together. Otherwise, they are caught in the plight of Siva, who has so fused with Parvati that he cannot even take pleasure in her loving face:

> Let the god's delight have been unsurpassed that bearing your slender body joined to his, he receives, Oh Gamri, your tight embrace; still, Siva's heart must often grieve to think your glance cannot by him be seen, sweet, loving, innocent, and motionless with love.[54]

Tantrism holds that only when the sensual longings are satisfied and internalised is lust actually conquered – only when male and female unite fully in the self, or in bodily fusion, is there an end to desire. But O'Flaherty finds in the poem a tragic questioning of this doctrine, an implication that 'the greatest longing may be felt in complete union, when satiation is so near and yet so far'. Hence her wry conclusion that the androgyne may symbolise 'satiation without desire (as in Tantra) or desire without satiation (as in the poem)'.[55] Even the mechanics of bodily love endorse Lawrence's view that there can be no coming together without a prior falling asunder, a view which was particularly current among the exponents of intermediate sexuality in the England of his time. Mrs Havelock Ellis explained the success of her own marriage in *My Life*: 'the beauty and intimacy of our relationship was built on our separations, separations without which the relationship might perhaps have dissolved'.[56]

So, Gerald's inability to be alone is the sign of his early death; and it finally provokes in Gudrun an outburst which would have won the assent of Birkin: 'Try to love me a little more, and to want me a little less.' But the gloomy trail of mud which he leaves in walking from his father's grave to Gudrun's bed is the seal of his own death. There will be moments, even in that first coupling, when she will achieve a kind of serenity, become contained by him in the androgynous communion which Lawrence described as 'in the beloved, and she in me'.[57] However, the pair will never achieve harmony, for always one will lie awake, resentful of the slumber and serenity of the other. In the end, it will be Gudrun, and no longer Ursula, who feels 'a want within herself', who will be left 'jealous, unsatisfied' in comparing her fate with that of her sister.

In her desperation, Gudrun abandons Gerald for the sinister Jewish artist Loerke, in the belief that he will not cling to her as fatally as did Gerald. Loerke seems 'complete' to her, with an 'uncanny singleness, a quality of being by himself, not in contact with anybody else, that marked out an artist to her'. He is a type of the androgynous artist and has the passive, female elements which Lawrence attributed to the Jews, after his reading of Otto Weininger's *Sex and Character*. Weininger's theory of the Jews as womanly men lies as clearly behind the portrait of Loerke as it does behind Joyce's presentation of Leopold Bloom; and, indeed, Molly Bloom's justification of her choice of husband ('because he knew what a woman was') is very close to Gudrun's explanation to an outraged Gerald of what she sees in Loerke: 'It's because he has some understanding of a woman, because he is not stupid.' The sad machismo of Gerald is not enough because it leaves him incomplete; 'however much he might mentally *will* to be immune and self-complete, the desire for this state was lacking'. But Gudrun 'was sufficient unto herself, closed round and completed, like a thing in a case'. She is, in short, an artist, a man as well as a woman, complete unto herself. Loerke finds in her that same self-sufficiency which he seeks in the modernist work of art, for to him a picture is a picture of nothing but itself.

Although Gudrun believes that she has found a more versatile man than Gerald, it is clear from all this that she is still a slave to the male principle, having merely exchanged a specialist in industry for a specialist in art. And Loerke, fa'r from being a fully androgynous artist with an understanding of women, is himself a slave to the same masculine tyranny as Gerald, believing that art should interpret industry as it once interpreted religion. The pure art of modernism is, for Lawrence, the most vile triumph of the male principle, a product of the same inorganic forces which brought war, machines and death. It is left to Ursula to voice his authorial resentment:

> 'As for your world of art and your world of reality', she replied, 'you have to separate the two, because you can't bear to know what you are. You can't bear to realise what a stock, stiff, hide-bound brutality you *are* really, so you say "it's the world of art". The world of art is only the truth about the real world, that's all – but you are too far gone to see it.'

Gudrun becomes infatuated with Loerke, because 'the world was finished now for her' and she sought only 'the obscene religious mystery of ultimate reduction', which for Lawrence was modernist art. In the years after *Women in Love*, this feeling grew stronger still and he denounced all self-conscious art with a capital A. By 1925 he could write to Carlo Linati: 'even Synge, whom I admire very much indeed, is a bit too rounded off and, as it were, put on the shelf to be looked at. I can't bear art that you can walk around and admire.'[58] It is part of Gudrun's corruption that she should be 'closed round and completed, like a thing in a case', too knowing, self-conscious and deliberate. Far closer to Lawrence's heart would be the primitive wisdom of the Balinese who say 'we have no art; we do everthing as well as we can', or even the healthy scepticism of a Keats denouncing the art that has too palpable a design on us and praising the violet for not asking us to dote upon it.

What Ursula says to Loerke is nothing more nor less than what she has been saying to Birkin all along – that there is only this world and that we must recall ourselves to it. They must take the world that is given, because there isn't any other; but Loerke, with his cult of art, has taken Gudrun over the precipice into a world of specialist deceit. Ursula's mission is to save for the world the Salvator Mundi who thinks he is saving her. His religion of love is in danger of growing as self-conscious and self-congratulatory as Loerke's religion of art. There are times when he seems to want to force the flowers to come out, times when he seems to want not so much a woman as the fulfilment of his ideas in her. But Ursula sees that he is serious in his desire to transcend the clinging, self-sacrificial form of love which he rejects in the all-too-abject Hermione. The impulse to death was the source of his fascination with the pornography of Hermione, for she too was a specialist who had driven all sex into the head. The desire for destruction which overcomes most of the casualties of the book is the impulse to violate the self by denying its wholeness and developing only a fragment to an unnatural degree. Birkin is as guilty of this as anyone, but always he has Ursula at his side to diagnose his illness: 'I think it's *criminal* to have so little connexion with your own body that you don't even know when you are ill.' If Ursula can save Birkin from the corruption of specialists, he in turn can fulfil her long-standing desire to know herself as a person and not as a woman. He teaches her the limited importance of the individual, the knowledge that humans live according to a few great laws and are essentially alike, and that to know the personality is to know nothing. This is part of the radical critique of modern marriage which Lawrence developed in 'A Propos of *Lady Chatterley's Lover*':

> Modern people are just personalities, and modern marriage takes place when two people are 'thrilled' by each other's personality: when they have the same tastes in furniture or books . . . Now this, this affinity of mind and personality is an excellent basis of friendship between the sexes, but a disastrous basis for marriage. Because marriage inevitably starts the sex-activity, and the sex-activity is, and always was and will be, in some way hostile to the mental, *personal* relationship between man and woman. It is almost an axiom that the marriage of two *personalities* will end in a startling physical hatred . . .[59]

So Ursula and Birkin divest themselves of furniture and books, of house and home, in the attempt to annihilate personality and rediscover character. As they move away to Europe, the New Woman marvels at how far she is projected from Cossethay and the farmhouse childhood. She sees herself, like Stephen Dedalus, as a changeling, made but not begotten: 'she had no father, no mother, no anterior connexions, she was herself, pure and silvery, she belonged only to the oneness with Birkin, a oneness that struck deeper notes, sounding into the heart of the universe, the heart of reality, where she had never existed before.' The experiment has been a success, the uprooted tree has been replanted in the good earth, and she has known herself beyond sexuality:

'Your mouth is so hard', he said in a faint reproach.
'And yours is so soft and nice', she said gladly.
'But why do you always grip your lips?' he asked, regretful.
'Never mind', she said softly. 'It is my way.'

She knew Birkin loved her and found joy in her self-abandonment. 'And she enjoyed him fully. But they were never *quite* together, at the same moment, one was always a little left out.' It does not matter, however, for he is patient and, anyway, they have moved beyond love. When Gudrun complains that she cannot love, Ursula's mind is seized by the thought: 'Because you never *have* loved, you can't get beyond it.'

*　　*　　*

The objective of Ursula and Birkin in *Women in Love* is to use sex in order to transcend sexuality, to move beyond notions of sexual difference to a higher state of unity, which Gudrun mockingly calls the Third Heaven. This is the preserve of the Holy Ghost, a being at once male and female, who can make two souls one and therefore, in the careful words of Donne, it. In her sense of oneness with Birkin, Ursula discovers a self which is quite independent of her womanhood, and she fulfils that self. Her partner is not so lucky. He is glad at 'having surpassed oneself, of having transcended the old existence', but in annihilating 'this I, this old formula of the age', he uncovers a deeper self that is not so easily fulfilled. For Birkin, though sexually fulfilled as a *man*, feels that he has not fully achieved himself as a *person*. Ursula is enough for him as far as a woman is concerned, but he wanted something more, which he sought and failed to find in Gerald. Ursula dismisses this as a mere obstinacy, a theory, but it is not.
Birkin is suffering from the selfsame lack which afflicts Kate

Leslie in *The Plumed Serpent*, when she discovers that the needs of her self and her womanhood do not coincide. In a masterly essay, T. E. Apter has shown how Kate grows disenchanted with the hollowness of the notions 'male' and 'female', becoming certain that she could perform the male role far more impressively than the men she knows. Apter finds in this story the proof that Lawrence was a psychological realist, who scorned the sentimental assumption 'that the fulfilment of one's need for love will overcome one's need for a self'.[60] From first to last, Birkin shows this tragic awareness of the residual need which can never be fully met, of that part of him which is always 'a little left out' in orgasm with Ursula.

To give her her due, Gudrun shares that wish to lose all awareness of her own sexuality. She has a horror of all knowing lady-killers, like the Lawrence who complained that the memoirs of Casanova 'stink'. Gudrun's rejection of Gerald is based on the realisation that he is a Don Juan, who can never hope to know his lover as a person, because he can never allow himself to forget that she is a woman. 'His very ignoring of women is part of the game. He is never *unconscious* of them', complains Gudrun. 'But really, his Don Juan does not interest me. I could play Don Juanita a million times better than he plays Juan. He bores me, you know, his maleness bores me.' It is a denunciation remarkably close in its terms to the unspoken thoughts of Birkin, as he sees the corpse of the man he loved, 'a dead mass of maleness, repugnant'. Gerald's true obituary is spoken by Loerke: 'Vive le heros, vive . . . ', a fitting send-off for the only male chauvinist in this book.

In *The Study of Thomas Hardy* Lawrence outlined two male attitudes to love and in *Women in Love* he dramatised those attitudes in the figures of Gerald and Birkin. The first is male supremacist and says: 'I am the one, and the woman is administered unto me.' The second is less assertive; 'She is the unknown, the undiscovered, unto which I plunge to discovery, losing myself.'[61] The first makes a man proud and splendid, words often used of Gerald, but for Lawrence the second is the attitude of real love. It is a fear of the unknown which makes for the male chauvinist: 'and because they wanted to retain the full-veined gratification of self-pleasure, men have kept their women tightly in bondage'.[62] Only a man like Birkin can accept Ursula not as a woman, but as a daughter of man, a versatile and independent person. 'The supreme effort each man makes, for himself, is the effort to clasp as a hub the woman who shall be the axle, compelling him to true motion, without aberration.'[63] No sooner is this done than the wheel is in spin. 'But it must first be seen that the division into male and female is arbitrary, for the purpose of thought. The rapid motion of the rim of wheel is the same as the rest at the centre of the wheel. How can one divide them? Motion and rest are the same, when seen completely.'[64] This is the view of a divinity, neither male or female, of which true lovers partake. 'In marriage, in utter interlocked marriage, man and woman cease to be two beings and become one, one and one only, not two in one, as with us, but absolute One, a geometric, timeless, the Absolute, the Divine.'[65]

This was a development of the doctrine outlined by Jules Bois in *L'Eve Nouvelle* (1896) that true marriage creates 'une véritable troisieme personne formée des deux que nous voyons, un être superieur complet qui existe au-dessus d'eux, d'une vie divine.'[66] It is to this perfect state that the imperfect Birkin aspires; and he is necessarily flawed because, as Busst observes, the androgyne must exist only as an ideal, never as a reality.[67] (Even today, many tribes execute infants of intermediate genital sexuality.) In heaven alone can an ideal androgyny be found. The only hint of such a fusion on earth is the moment when both parents search for traces of the beloved in the face of a new-born child.

7   Joyce's *Ulysses*: Past Eve and Adam

> Jesus was a bachelor . . . and never lived with a woman. Surely living with a woman is one of the most difficult things a man has to do, and he never did it.
>
> > James Joyce to Frank Budgen, on his reason
> > for rejecting Christ as a model for the
> > all-round man,   Leopold Bloom

If it is a surprise to learn that Lawrence originally conceived of *Women in Love* as a money-making pot-boiler, it comes as an endearing shock to read that James Joyce submitted some of his early work to the firm of Mills and Boon. There is no record of the reader's report, beyond the fact that he rejected *Dubliners* as unsuitable material for the unique imprint of that publishing house.

For his part, Lawrence had no doubt that the author of *Ulysses* was the real smutmonger of modern fiction. 'My God, what a clumsy *olla putrida* James Joyce is!', he wrote to Aldous Huxley, 'nothing but old fags and cabbage-stumps of quotations from the Bible and the rest stewed in the juice of deliberate journalistic dirty-mindedness.'[1] To his wife Frieda he wrote, after reading *Ulysses*, that 'the last part of it is the dirtiest, most indecent, obscene thing ever written';[2] and he later complained that Joyce had degraded the novel to the level of an instrument for measuring twinges in the toes of unremarkable men.[3] Joyce's reply to the charge that he was just another pornographer doing dirt on sex was to claim that at least *he* had never made the subject predictable or boring. He denounced *Lady Chatterbox's Lover* – his title for Lawrence's notorious novel – as a 'lush' production in 'sloppy English' and dismissed its ending as 'a piece of propaganda in favour of something which, outside of DHL's country at any rate, makes all the propaganda for itself'.[4] It is a minor irony of literary history that both men were married at Kensington Register Office in London, although, unlike Lawrence, the Irishman allowed a decent interval of twenty-five years to elapse before the solemnisation of his nuptials.

It was inevitable that an English puritan like Lawrence would have been incensed by a book which deliberately set out to be the artistic affectation of ordinariness. He had already exposed such modern artistic effects in an early conversation between the sisters in *Women in Love*. Gudrun complains

'You'll find that the really chic thing is to be so absolutely ordinary, so perfectly commonplace and like the person in the street, that you really are a masterpiece of humanity, not the person in the street, but the artistic creation of her –'
'How awful!' cried Ursula.

This seems, in retrospect, an uncanny prophecy of rich accountants paying a small fortune in high-fashion shops for corduroy jeans and dungarees, a strange foresight of slick secretaries gliding out of Laura Ashley boutiques to masquerade as humble milkmaids in the city streets. But it is also a denunciation of the intricate and knowing art which sought to celebrate that masterpiece of humanity, the cultured all-round man, Leopold Bloom.

And yet . . . and yet . . . Long after the recriminations have been savoured and forgotten, what strikes the modern reader is the unsuspected affinity between the two writers, not on the subject of art, but on the nature of modern sexuality. Lawrence was convinced that in Joyce he had detected another Loerke, a depraved specialist indulging in self-admiring experiments with a language which had long since lost all touch with the known world. This prevented him from seeing just how closely the two men agreed on the primary importance of the relationship between men and women as *the* crucial subject for modern art. 'After all, it is *the* problem of today', wrote Lawrence in 1913, 'the establishment of a new relation, or the readjustment of the old one, between men and women.'[5] Joyce had said no less in his defence of *A Doll's House*. Both men felt that the deterioration in relations between the sexes had a parallel in the decline in the quality of male friendship, with the inevitable result that men are seen to come together not as genuine comrades, but as victims of the new sexuality, sharing only a sense of maltreatment at the hands of women. If men come together only to talk of women, and if they come together only after defeats in the life of the emotions, then their relationship is less an expression of free solidarity and more a conspiracy of the walking wounded. The man-to-man relationship is no longer sufficient unto itself, but must now define itself solely in terms of the heterosexual relationship which it flouts. This explains Lawrence's distaste for modern homosexuality, which he saw as a mere *reaction* against the unsatisfactory and neurotic sex between men and women.[6] Of all human arrangements, he believed that 'none . . . is quite so dead as the man-to-man relationship'.[7] *Women in Love* was a phase in Lawrence's attempt to 'bring back the old gay English manliness that was England in the past',[8] a code of comradeship binding the modern knights, Birkin and Crich, to a new round table. Regrettably, Birkin's search for 'something more' failed, based as it was on a mere reaction.

The early writings of Joyce record similarly botched attempts at male camaraderie, whether it be the aimless freewheeling of provincial Lotharios in 'Two Gallants' or the crisis-ridden fellowship of Stephen and Cranly in *A Portrait of the Artist as a Young Man*. Indeed, Cranly's famous offer to heal Stephen's loneliness strangely anticipates that of Birkin to Gerald Crich. Emphasising the implications of Stephen's option to be 'alone', Cranly adds: 'And you know what that word means? Not only to be separated from all others but to have not even one friend . . . who would be more than a friend, more than the noblest and truest friend a man ever had.'[9] However, the attempt fails, as it failed in Joyce's life. He eventually turned to Nora Barnacle and confided in her the pain of that failure: 'When I was younger I had a friend to whom I gave myself freely – in a way more than I give to you and in a way less. He was Irish, that is to say, he was false to me.'[10] Yet, even in the new relationship with Nora, the attempt to reconcile sexual and personal fulfilment goes on, the attempt to find a lover who is also a comrade, a man with all the sensitivity of a woman and a woman with all the power of a man. Like Lawrence, Joyce concludes that at the root of man's inability to live in serenity with woman is his prior inability to recognise and harmonise the male and female elements in himself.

If Birkin is proposed as a new 'androgynous superman' with a mission to reinterpret the sexes to one another, Leopold Bloom is presented by Joyce as an 'androgynous angel' who has already achieved that balance of which Birkin merely talked and dreamed. For Joyce, the androgyny of the full person had always been taken as understood. While Nora Barnacle and her friends were dressing up as men and roaming the Galway quays in search of invitations and high jinks, the youthful Joyce in Dublin was burlesquing the manners of operatic prima-donnas in his famous take-off of *Carmen*. He borrowed the gowns for this purpose from Mrs Sheehy, whose name he dubbed 'epicene', a compound of masculine and feminine pronouns. The Gaelic version of Joyce, 'Seoighe', was a derivative of 'Sheehy', or so he claimed, since this confirmed his own self-image as a 'womanly man'.[11] It is no surprise, therefore, to find that many of the traits attributed to the females in Joyce's writings are characteristics of the author. In *A Portrait*, 'Eileen had long thin cool white hands too because she was a girl', but so had Joyce, who wore sparkling rings in order to advertise their elegance. At the root of such devices lay the younger Joyce's distrust of the absolute Victorian distinction between male and female; and in *Ulysses*, the mature artist set forth the androgynous hero of the future.

But not before he had defined the needs of the modern male in the figure of Stephen Dedalus, a youth in flight from the sad machismo of his father's Dublin world. In *A Portrait*, when the young child at Clongowes was asked 'What is your father?', he had replied promptly 'A gentlemen'; but some years and a couple of hundred pages later, his tune had changed:

> A medical student, an oarsman, a tenor, an amateur actor, a shouting politician, a small landlord, a small investor, a drinker, a good fellow, a storyteller, somebody's secretary, something in a distillery, a tax gatherer, a bankrupt, and at present a praiser of his own past.

Joyce's own father was such a poor provider that, according to Oliver St John Gogarty, he once had to chop down the banisters of the house in Cabra, in order to make fuel for the living-room fire. The Stephen whom we meet again at the start of *Ulysses* has fled his father, in search of an alternative image of authority. 'Why did you leave your father's house?', asks his saviour much later, only to receive the reply 'To seek misfortune.' Underlying Joyce's art is the belief, voiced by Stephen, that 'paternity may be a legal fiction', that fathers and sons are brought together more by genetic accident than by mutual understanding, and that most sons are compelled, sooner or later, to rebel against their own fathers. A delegate to a recent conference of the Irish Labour Party took this idea a step further, in proposing that the state set up a 'paternity register' of all those males who had fathered children. This was done so that any child, who had reached the use of reason and was dissatisfied with his situation, could dispose of his genetic father, scan the register in any post office and select an alternative parent. It was a piece of sheer political whimsy, designed to outrage the staid leaders on a right-of-centre platform, but the implicit assumption would have been endorsed by Stephen Dedalus. 'Who is the father of any son that any son should love him or he any son?', he asks and desperately concludes that 'a father is a necessary evil'.

Stephen's life is a bitter illustration of Nietzsche's aphorism to the effect that when a man hasn't had a good father, it becomes necessary to invent one. For a time he may find a surrogate father in Bloom, but ultimately, as an artist, Stephen will have to give birth to himself, on the himself-his-own-father principle by which Shakespeare recreated himself in the doomed father *and* avenging son of *Hamlet*. On the same basis, Joyce in this book reincarnates himself both in the middle-aged Bloom and in the youthful Stephen. This modern concept of the artistic hero was adumbrated by Oscar Wilde, who taught that every man must form a stylised conception of himself, that is, quite literally, conceive of a self. Whereas Victorian literature had been obsessed with establishing questions of origin and paternity, modernism sought to abolish notions of heritage and to usurp or even murder the father. So its heroes were men like Jay Gatsby, whose inherited name was Gatz, but who 'sprang from some extraordinary Platonic conception of himself'; and its heroines are women like Ursula Brangwen, who 'had no father, no mother, no anterior connexions, she was herself, pure and silvery . . .' Such a hero is an orphan, either psychic or real, and his aspiration has been most acutely expressed by Sartre, who spoke for a whole generation whose fathers had died at war. In *Les Mots* Sartre recalled his upbringing at the home of his grandfather: 'Being nobody's son, I was my own cause and was filled with both pride and wretchedness . . .

I always preferred to accuse myself rather than the universe, not
only out of simple good-heartedness, but in order to derive only
from myself.' For his part, Freud explained the 'family romance'
in similar terms. He held that the boy wishes to become quits
with the parent who gave him life, by performing some great self-
sacrificial service such as saving his mother's life. If this fails,
however, he will as readily dream of killing off the father, for, in
the words of Freud, 'all the instincts, the loving, the grateful, the
sensual, the defiant, the self-assertive and the independent – all
are justified in the wish to be the father of himself'.[12]

Stephen only learns to see a father as a necessary evil *after* he
has repented of his refusal to fulfil his dying mother's wish that
he pray at her bedside. As he teaches at the school in Dalkey on
the morning of 16 June, he ponders his dead mother's love: 'Was
that then real? The only true thing in life?' So the basic
groundwork of *Ulysses* is laid when the truth of maternity is shown
to discredit the myth of paternity. The inadequate fathers in
Joyce's world are exponents of a boozy bravado, a moronic
athleticism and a past that never was. Stephen therefore abandons
that zone of fake masculinity for his own destiny of 'silence,
exile and cunnng', which Mary Ellmann sees as time-honoured
strategies of the put-upon woman.[13] The young man is haunted
by the images and bric-a-brac, the tasselled dance-cards and
feather fans of his dead mother, who bends over him in his dreams
as she mouths secret words. Joyce was lacerated by the same guilt
which assails Stephen when he thinks of his dying mother, but
he was also fired by an almost feminist sense of outrage against
her predicament:

> My mother was slowly killed, I think, by my father's ill-
> treatment, by years of trouble, and by my cynical frankness of
> conduct. When I looked on her face as she lay in her coffin –
> a face grey and wasted with cancer – I understood that I was
> looking on the face of a victim and I cursed the system which
> had made her a victim.[14]

Though Stephen's mother is gone, 'scarcely having been', he
is convinced that her mute and secret words contain a liberating
message. 'What is that word known to all men?' he asks. He still
has hours to wait for the answer from another man who will
perch on the same rock and tilt his hat similarly over his eyes.

In the past, Stephen had pondered the idea of titling a book after a letter of the alphabet and this may hint at the ultimate answer to his question. Philo taught that the letter Y was the symbol for the word which pierces the essence of things, both male and female, and, as such, eternal – a belief echoed by the Naassene Gnostics[15] and also by Pierre Boaistuau, who saw a Greek letter Y on the stomach of an androgyne born in Ravenna in 1512 and thereupon deemed the forked letter to be 'double in kind, participating both of man and woman'.[16] Once again, Stephen has the answer within his grasp, but fails to recognise it as such. In the story of 'how the head centre got away, authentic version. Got up as a young bride, man . . .', he unwittingly stumbles upon a hint of the androgynous hero who will befriend and liberate him. But many hours have yet to elapse before he learns the correct reply to Mulligan's opening invocation – 'Introibo ad altare Dei' – and alters the gender of the Almighty God, as he walks into the arms of the harlot, 'Ad dea qui laetificat juventutem meum.' Only then will he begin to learn the truth of the Qabbalah, that the Supreme Creator is female as well as male, a perfect androgyne.

In the meantime, that imperfect androgyne, Leopold Bloom, begins his day. He prepares his wife's breakfast, a deed appropriate to the liberated contemporary husband, but in the Dublin of 1904 an act tantamount to perversion. Moreover, although he serves his wife her breakfast in bed, he prefers to eat his own in the solitude of the kitchen. What we are witnessing here is the institution called in Ireland 'the silent marriage', whereby two people manage to share a house but not a life. It was the great fear which haunted Joyce's own experiment in non-marital fidelity with Nora, an experiment which the writer explained to his brother as being based on the desire 'to avoid as far as is humanly possible any such apparition in our lives as that abominable spectre which Aunt Josephine calls "mutual tolerance"'.[17] To Nora herself, Joyce complained that there was no honesty in Irish sexuality – 'people live together in the same houses all their lives and at the end they are as far apart as ever'.[18] This is true of the Blooms, who dislike dressing together and who manage, by a tacit compact, to spend most of the day apart. Already it is clear that Leopold has a strong element of the female in his personality, as he stays to straighten the bedspread or to flick an offending crumb off a bedsheet.[19] Nevertheless, he is also a red-blooded

Dublin male, whose first thought on entering the street is to catch up with a comely woman and walk behind her, taking pleasure in her 'moving hams'. Yet even this impulse is inextricably confused with Bloom's urge to female impersonation: 'He turned away and sauntered across the road. How did she walk with her sausages? Like that something. As he walked he took the folded *Freeman* from his pocket . . .'

The fascination with female impersonation all through *Ulysses* is an accurate reflection of a similar obsession of late Victorian society. Thousands of broadsheets were sold in London every month on the theme – one, for example, being a detailed account of how a woman had successfully masqueraded for weeks as a barman at the Royal Mortar Tavern in London Road.[20] By 1892 Vesta Tilley had become one of the highest-paid music-hall performers in the city for her impersonations of 'Picadilly Johnnies with monocles'.[21] Similarly in Paris, many leading actresses (including, reputedly, Sarah Bernhardt) tried their skill in the title role of *Hamlet*. Such pranks were not confined to the stage and lasted well into the second decade of the new century, as the transvestite japes of the Bloomsbury set brought the decadence of Paris to the streets of London.[22]

From the outset of his day, Leopold Bloom shows himself fascinated not so much with women as with what it is to be born a woman. Gravely he ponders a life spent fitting pins into hair and clothing, or making adjustments to disorderly skirts under the protective coverage of a lady friend in the street ('esprit de corps'). His fellow-feeling for woman in the momentous labour of childbirth ('Kill me that would') is paralleled by a similar empathy with the lady suddenly taken short in a city whose lavatories, like its pubs, were notoriously built for men only. As he passes the statue of Tom Moore, he ponders: 'They did right to put him up over a urinal: meeting of the waters. Ought to be places for women. Running into cakeshops. Settle my hat straight . . .' All through the day, Bloom has an admirable and rare capacity to see the world through the eyes and mind of others, to imagine, for example, how wine or cigarettes must have a heightened taste to a blind man. It is this, as much as anything, which Lenehan salutes as the touch of the artist in Bloom.

This empathy is nowhere more clear than in his attitude to women who are caught in moments of disadvantage. When he meets Josie Breen in the street, he is less distressed by the lines around her mouth than by 'the eye that woman gave her passing. Cruel. The unfair sex.' Bloom knows that within her every woman has an eye which looks on other women with the insolence of an appraising male, just as current market research shows that most women, faced with an advertisement, will first assess the look of the woman in the picture, and only then the man. In a culture of increasing narcissism, men are no longer immune to such tendencies and so Bloom surveys his own spreading waistline through the eyes of a critical female: 'Body getting a bit softy . . . But the shape is there . . . still.' In the modern world, each person is intimately aware of the experience of the opposite sex, particularly of those elements in that experience which seem to confirm that person's own character. This explains why Bloom, the passive and put-upon male, has a natural affinity with women in their moments of silent suffering or discomfiture.

His obsession with the masterful and disdainful woman is quite different in quality, arising not from sympathetic intimacy, but from feelings of antagonism and remoteness. Such an obsession may even feed his subconscious desire to be dominated like the kitchen mice who amaze him by their failure to squeal in the cruel claws of the cat. 'Seem to like it', he muses fraternally. Bloom himself is married to such an imperious catlike creature and is introduced to the mourners in Glasnevin as the nonentity who married Madam Marion Tweedy, the good-looking soprano. In his imagination, he has fantasies of aristocratic ladies and horsey women who strut, drink and ride 'like a man'. His thoughts are equally excited by Mrs Bandman Palmer, the actress: 'Hamlet she played last night. Male impersonator. Perhaps he was a woman . . .' Frank Budgen was the first critic to show that Bloom's fellow-feeling with Shakespeare is based on a marked similarity in their marital situations.[23] As Stephen so wittily recapitulates the success of another masterful woman: 'If others have their will Ann hath a way. By cock, she was to blame. The grey-eyed goddess who bends over the boy Adonis, stooping to conquer, as prologue to the swelling act, is a boldfaced Stratford wench who tumbles in a cornfield a lover younger than herself.' Likewise, Molly will later recall her own adventure in another field, 'and a bird flying below us he was shy all the same I liked him that morning I made him blush a little when I got over him that way'. In his letters to his brother Stan from Pola, Joyce liked to swagger a little about deflowering Nora, but his passionate epistles to his wife during a later separation suggest that he normally preferred a more passive role: 'I remember the first night in Pola when in the tumult of our embraces you used a certain word. It was a word of provocation, of invitation and I can see your face over me (you were OVER me that night) as you murmured it.'[24]

After the Stratford encounter, Shakespeare lost his sexual confidence and subsequently sent a lordling to woo for him by proxy, much as Bloom loses his social confidence after a sacking and sends Molly to plead for his reinstatement with Joe Cuffe. Both men are branded as chronically passive by these early events. What Stephen says of Shakespeare is exactly true of Bloom: 'He was overborne in a cornfield first (ryefield, I should say) and he will never be a victor in his own eyes nor play victoriously the game of laugh and lie down. Assumed dongiovannism will not save him. No later undoing will undo the first undoing.' The assumption of masculinity on Sandymount Strand later in the day will be no resolution of this problem, but a masturbatory variation on Mulligan's bleak drama, 'Everyman His Own Wife.' It is no wonder that Mrs Bandman Palmer has triumphed as Hamlet for the four hundred and eighth time, for it was in that character that Shakespeare reincarnated his own androgyny. 'Man delights him not nor woman neither', says Stephen, but 'in the economy of Heaven, foretold by Hamlet, there are no more marriages, glorified man, an androgynous angel, being a wife unto himself.'

Once again, in these lines Stephen has the answer to his overwhelming question, but fails to recognise it, just as he fails to identify the androgynous angel who now passes between himself and the loutish Mulligan. The latter coarsely suspects Bloom of harbouring homosexual yearnings for Stephen: 'Did you see his eye? He looked upon you to lust after you?' At that moment, however, Stephen's mind is otherwise preoccupied with the recollection of a dream from the previous night, in the course of which a strange man held a creamfruit melon out to him in welcome. Already the erotic fantasies of the two men are intersecting, for it will later be shown that Bloom likes to caress Molly's buttocks and pretend that they are fragrant melons, a pleasure he may yet offer Stephen. Sensing a new rival for the friendship of Stephen, Mulligan has done his best to heap scorn on Bloom, whom he has caught peering at the mesial groove on the statue of a Greek in the library. 'O, I fear me, he is Greeker than the Greeks', cautions Mulligan; but the implication of homosexuality is lost in the realisation that, in his emotional life, Bloom rediscovers the dilemmas of Shakespeare with far more poignancy than he reenacts the adventures of Odysseus. If we all lived on the earth long ago, as Bloom explained in his theory of metempsychosis, then surely he was Shakespeare, a frustrated father whose son dies and whose bossy wife cuckolds him. Stephen, as usual, unwittingly completes the painful parallel: 'Forgot: any more than he forgot the whipping lousy Lucy gave him. And left the *femme de trente ans*. And why no other children born? And his first child a girl?' It is no coincidence that a mournful Bloom listens to this disquisition in depressed silence or that his shocked sentences which follow should peter out into irresolution and inconsequence.

At a bookstall, some time later, Bloom confirms himself as a passive male, with fantasies of domination at the hands of a forceful woman. While Stephen seeks out a book on how to seduce a woman, Bloom looks for a volume that might please and entertain his wife. Though he spends most of the day away from Molly, she is never far from his thoughts; and though they have not had full sexual intercourse for many years, he is filled with concern for her well-being. Indeed, the underlying reasons for their sexual incompatibility may be surmised from Bloom's stream of consciousness as he turns over the books: 'Tales of the Ghetto by Leopold von Sacher Masoch. – That I had, he said, pushing it by . . . *Fair Tyrants* by James Lovebirch. Know the kind that is. Had it? Yes . . . No, she wouldn't like that much. Got her it once. He read the other title: *Sweets of Sin*. More in her line. Let us see.' It is already poignantly obvious that Molly cannot and will not feed Bloom's desire for domination. Unlike most of the other women in *Ulysses*, she has misgivings about the dictates of male fantasy and frequently refuses to deny her own sexual desires and tastes. 'Sure there's nothing for a woman in that', she remarks of *Fair Tyrants*, being particularly disgusted by an account of how 'she hangs him up out of a hook with a cord flagellette'.

By way of contrast, in the Ormond Hotel the barmaids Douce and Kennedy obligingly transform themselves into fetishes of the male imagination, though not without some saving irony at the expense of the middle-aged Galahads. 'He's killed looking back', Miss Kennedy laughs, 'O wept! Aren't men frightful idiots?'; but she adds a sad recognition of their controlling power, 'It's them has the fine times.' They plead with her to whack her elastic garter against her thigh, which, after the mandatory coy hesitation, she does. The mirrors which dominate the entire scene have been described as extensions of the barmaids who 'act as mirrors to the masculine word'.[25] Only Bloom sees through the deception, as he checks his own impulse to bask in the winsome smile of Miss Douce: 'Think you're the only pebble on the beach? Does that to all. For men.' To him the mirrors merely recall the looking-glass in Eccles Street where, even now, Molly will pat her hair and assess her own profile, with the practised eye of the arriving Boylan: 'Mirror there. Is that the best side of her face? They always know.' These reflections merge with his contemplation of the bargirls who admire themselves in the surrounding mirrors, kept ever young by the approval of male eyes. So Bloom vicariously experiences the world of women vicariously experiencing the world of men.

As Simon Dedalus brings his song to an end, the music further diffuses Bloom's critical faculties and, as Hugh Kenner has acutely remarked, allows him to experience at once Molly's gasp of anticipation in her visitor's arms, Boylan's consummation and the singer's triumphant climax:[26]

–To me!
Siopold!
Consumed.
Come . . .

Earlier that morning, Bloom had marvelled at how Mr Dedalus was 'full of his son' and decided that 'he is right. Something to hand on.' Wondering if there was still a chance that he could impregnate Molly, he recalled her aggressive desire for lovemaking in the early days as a case of 'how life begins'. Now, however, the song and the wine have made him melancholy and the words of *The Croppy Boy* have a personal poignancy. 'Last of his name and race. I, too, last of my race . . . No son. Rudy. Too late now. Or if not? If not? If still? . . . Soon I am old.' If paternity is a legal fiction anyway, then this passage reinforces our sense of the marginality of all the males in the book, Simon Dedalus as much as Leopold Bloom. If the latter has no son, the former has to ask for news of his from passing cadgers of drink. The woman is closer to the real source of power in her traditional capacity to bear children, to love and be loved by them, allied to her modern ability to live on male terms in the world of men. The very scope of traditional male power has proved self-defeating, for, since culture is largely a masculine creation, the increasing education of women has tended to reinforce the male element innate in all females, *without* a compensating extension in the sexual identity of males. So, the Misses Douce and Kennedy can cast a feminine spell over the males of the pub, while at the same time sharing in the privileged ambience of the men. In public they can exercise their sexual power over Boylan, while privately patronising him as 'the essence of vulgarity'. If women can do all that men can do, and more besides, then nothing is intrinsically 'masculine' any more and the broken provincials at the Ormond Hotel know it.

Bloom's later fantasy in *Circe* of being pregnant – 'O, I do so want to be a mother' – is merely an attempt to heal this sense of disability by wish-fulfilment. *Circe* is a midnight carnival; and, in classical mythology, at the carnival of androgynes, men become pregnant. Joyce himself, according to Maria Jolas, 'talked of fatherhood as if it were motherhood'; and his biographer remarks that 'he seems to have longed to establish in himself all aspects of the bond of mother and child'.[27] Such wish-fulfilment is an almost universal phenomenon and suggests that men secretly desire a more central role in child-rearing, a role they still have in most primitive societies. For example, under the 'couvade' system, the father joins the pregnant mother in observing ritual abstinences from certain foods and, indeed, 'when she goes into labour, he may take to his bed too'.[28] In a recent survey in Britain, 57 per cent of husbands reported mysterious symptoms when their wives were pregnant, which defied explanation but which cleared up as soon as their wives gave birth.[29]

If women have usurped traditional male prerogatives, then Joyce, like his hero Bloom, responded by trying to assume the attributes of wife and mother. The attempt was doomed to fail, however, and a bitter Joyce subjected his male friends to endless tirades 'on woman and her urge to rivalise with menfolk in the things of the mind as well as to dominate them socially'. To Frank Budgen he complained that women had usurped all male functions, 'all save that one which is biologically pre-empted, and even on that they cast jealous threatening eyes'.[30] In truth, he had never really expected anything else. His brother Stan noted that Joyce had early resigned himself to the marginality and powerlessness of the male, who did not expect to be the main purpose of a woman's life, knowing that sooner or later children would take his place.[31] In *Ulysses* he showed how that sense of increasing isolation, following the birth of children, is countered in the male by the attempt to reincarnate in himself those female elements which are disappearing from his life. In this respect, Joyce had much in common with Lawrence, whose wife reported that in his heart he was overawed by the sheer versatility of women's functions and believed that 'they were in the end more powerful than men'.[32]

As Bloom walks from the Ormond Hotel, he gives way on the footpath to male pedestrians and ducks into a shop window, in order to avoid the gaze of a passing whore. Later in the day, he will be equally embarrassed by the same prostitute, who will peep into the cabbie's shelter with her haggard face and black straw hat. He seems to have made a timid appointment with her in the past, which he did not honour: 'Too dear too near to home sweet home.' This may explain his discomfiture at being tracked by her. Molly certainly suspects that he has sometimes gone with painted ladies, if only to gratify those kinks which she will not countenance herself. 'O, well, she has to live like the rest', concludes Bloom, who will in *Circe* call the prostitute 'a necessary evil' – the same phrase which Stephen uses to characterise the world's fathers, providing a most suggestive connection between two of life's outcast groups. He even contemplates a career for Molly in such a role with Boylan: 'Suppose he paid her. Why not? All a prejudice.' It may well have been sexual timidity, rather than perverse delight, which first drove Bloom into the arms of a prostitute, for 'No girl would when I went girling. Too ugly. They wouldn't play.' If so, this uniquely equips him to sympathise with the outcast woman in her moments of humiliation: 'If you don't answer when they solicit must be horrible for them till they harden.' Few of their other customers have shown such natural politeness.

It is this gentlemanly consideration for women which discredits Bloom in the eyes of the male boozers of *Cyclops*, who prefer, like Mulligan, to see in it the signs of an incipient homosexuality. Bloom is full of concern for the plight of Josie Breen, married to a paranoid lunatic who is the laughing-stock of the Dublin drinking fraternity. The callous dismissal of Bloom's concern is couched in *doubles entendres* of sinister implication:

–Still, says Bloom, on account of the poor woman, I mean his wife.

–Pity about her, says the citizen. Or any other woman marries a half and half.

–How half and half? says Bloom. Do you mean he . . . ?

–Half and half I mean, say the citizen. A fellow that's neither fish nor flesh.

–Nor good red herring, says Joe.

–That's what I mean, says the citizen. A pishogue, if you know what that is.

Begob I saw there was trouble coming. And Bloom explained he meant, on account of it being cruel for the wife having to go round after the old stuttering fool . . .

As the conversation proceeds, the chauvinist citizen toys ever more closely with the raw nerves of Bloom: 'A dishonoured wife, says the citizen, that's what's the cause of all our misfortunes.' Ostensibly, he is referring to Dermot McMurrough, whose faithless wife, he claims, brought the Saxon to Ireland; but, in point of fact, all the men are closely studying the reactions of Leopold Bloom. They know that Boylan is 'getting it up' for Molly, which explains 'the milk in the cocoanut and the absence of hair on the animal's chest'. The simple explanation by Bloom that love is the opposite of hatred is followed by his hasty retreat. 'That's the New Messiah for Ireland', says the citizen scornfully, little realising that in mythology androgynes are customarily prophets. Six weeks before his doomed son was born, Bloom was spotted buying a tin of baby-food in the south city markets – further proof to the denizens of the pub that he is not a real man. To Jack Power's humane reminder that there were two children born anyhow, the citizen responds with derision: 'And who does he suspect?' It is at this point that the anonymous narrator of the chapter enters into cynical collusion with the suspicions of the men: 'Gob, there's many a true word spoken in jest. One of those mixed middlings he is. Lying up in the hotel Pisser was telling me once a month with a headache like a totty with her courses . . .'

Although this seems like a vicious slander, it emerges in the following chapter *Nausikaa* to be no more than a colourful elaboration of the truth. Gerty McDowell waves her white handkerchief wadding to the dark stranger, but Bloom proves to be as immune to this romantic gesture as he was to the barmaids in the Ormond. Instead of warming to the mandatory sobbing maiden of male fantasy, he ponders the female experience in its own terms and wonders if the wadding means that Gerty is menstruating: 'Near her monthlies, I expect, makes them feel ticklish.' He is certainly near his, for he adds 'I have such a bad headache today.' Bloom wonders how many women in Dublin are menstruating on that date and why, if it depends on the moon, they do not all do so at once. In this case, however, he moves beyond mere empathy to downright fellow-suffering: 'Devils they are when that's coming on them. Dark devilish appearance. Molly often told me feel things a ton weight. Scratch the sole of my foot. O that way! O, that's exquisite! Feel it myself too. Good to rest once in a way . . .' This passage, which must have seemed perverse and outlandish to many of Joyce's early readers, is in fact a realistic account of the monthly experience of great numbers of men. Long before the publication of *Ulysses*, Havelock Ellis had suggested that men 'possess some traces of a rudimentary menstrual cycle, affecting the entire organism';[33] but only in recent decades have the fluctuations in the amounts of testosterone in men's blood been shown to be in no way haphazard, but rather 'a regular cycle, analogous to the female menstrual cycle'.[34] Sixty per cent of men tested at Stanford University had a regular cycle and most were depressed when testosterone production was at its peak. In some cases, the cycle was 'found to coincide exactly with the menstrual cycle of the women they were living with'.[35]

Bloom begins to wonder if the meeting with Gerty was somehow fated by his own fellow-feeling for her condition. 'Daresay she felt I. When you feel like that you often meet what you feel.' Yet again, Bloom tries to evaluate his own face through the eyes of the woman who is watching him. His capacity for empathy is now so great that it merely augments his self-doubt about his looks: 'Ought to attend to my appearance my age. Didn't let her see me in profile. Still, you never know. Pretty girls and ugly men marrying. Beauty and the beast. Besides I can't be so if Molly . . .' That has multiple poignancies, not the least being Molly's later evaluation of Leopold as still a handsome man. Obviously, she never managed to *tell* him so, for he judges himself too ugly to interest women. Even more poignant is the reader's awareness that Gerty has been beset by similar self-doubts in her attempt to attract Bloom, including the same remedy of showing her better profile to full advantage and tilting her hat romantically low over her eyes. That women have no monopoly on such gestures is subtly proven by the fact that Stephen tilted his hat over his eyes at the same rock that morning, just as Bloom does now. (The iconography of Irish nationalism is rich in examples of famous men from Tone to Pearse who present their better profile to the artist or the camera – in the case of Pearse to hide a cast in one eye and, of course, to imply a subconscious equation with Tone. The intended effect is heroic, as of a man too preoccupied with the world of action to pose vainly for a painter or give his undivided attention to the camera, but in fact the process is narcissistic and self-caressing.) All of which convinces us that the characters in *Ulysses* are reenacting not just the lives of past heroes, but the lives of one another. As Yeats explained in *A Vision*, the borders of our minds are ever-shifting and what strikes Stephen in the morning may strike Bloom in the afternoon, for example, the idea that death by drowning is not the worst way to go. This also applies to the borders between the sexes which shift as much as any. Stephen's dismissal of the big words which make us so unhappy is soon to be echoed by Molly's demand to be told things in plain words.

That demand for unadorned language is the source of much of the comic deflation in the book. 'She's right after all', muses Bloom, 'only big words for ordinary things on account of the sound.' One example of such coy periphrasis is the word 'beetotetom', used by Cissy Caffrey to the outrage of Gerty, who would never have endorsed Molly's complaint against a circumlocutory priest: 'O Lord couldn't he say bottom right out and have done with it?' Joyce here presents the contrast between the language of someone avoiding an experience and the language of somebody else confronting it – and this is the pervasive technique of *Nausikaa*. The idiom of sexual pretension is deflated, as part of Joyce's attempt to throw into question the traditional objects of male and female fantasy. Gerty is mocked, as Colin MacCabe rightly says, for ignoring the onset of her period and living a life which is 'an attempt to turn herself into the fetish prescribed by women's magazines'.[36] More subtly, however, she is also mocked for turning Bloom into the male fetish of female fantasy. 'Art thou real, my ideal?' is for her beautiful poetry, but the ideal Bloom who so thrills her is not the real man whom we have come to know. She wants 'no prince charming' but 'a manly man', who would crush her soft body and 'strain her to him in all the strength of his deep passionate nature'. (No wonder that Joyce fancied his chances with Mills and Boon.) She would present herself as 'a womanly woman not like other flighty girls, unfeminine, he had known, those cyclists, showing off what they hadn't got'. The scoffers in Barney Kiernan's pub could have warned her that she was barking up the wrong tree, just as Molly will later give disapproving testimony to Bloom's interest in female cyclists, 'always skeezing at those brazenfaced things on the bicycles with their skirts blowing'.

If Gerty is woefully misled as to the true nature of her strange admirer, his fantasy is shattered by the events which unfold before his eyes. The Roman Candles bursting in the skies and the sight of Gerty's bared legs, as she leans back to watch, drive Bloom to a sexual climax, with an attendant chorus of 'O!O!O!' However, when Cissy Caffrey imitates the boys in the field and whistles for Gerty to leave, the male fantasy is deflated: 'She walked with a certain quiet dignity characteristic of her but with care and very slowly because Gerty MacDowell was . . . Tight boots? No. She's lame! O!' The curt, single echo of the earlier sound of ecstasy ends a line which stops and starts four times, as if in linguistic reenactment of Gerty's limp. Within minutes, this innocent and open sound is replaced by the more knowing and worldly-wise grunt of 'Ah!', to record Boylan's gasp of pleasure in the bed of Leopold and Molly Bloom. The hesitant and broken rhythms of the line contrast markedly with the jaunty self-confidence of Boylan's *martellato* strut: 'Did he knock Paul de Kock, with a loud proud knocker, with a cock carracarracarra cock?' The four cryptic sentences in half a line contrast with the flowing words of Molly at the end, where forty pages of monologue will contain just eight sentences. More than anything, they register Bloom's latest disappointment with the vagaries of the human body. No sooner has he uttered the words than he contemplates limping ladies, girls with glasses, girls with squints, girls with anaemia, him own headache, menstruation, and all this not long after Gerty has bemoaned 'that tired feeling', which was eased somewhat by the Widow Welch's female pills. Their joint despair of the body is echoed by Molly Bloom who inveighs against 'this nuisance of a thing' called menstruation and who finds that even Boylan comes so soon as to 'take all the pleasure out of it'. As for Stephen, he began the day groping in darkness after breaking his spectacles;

his thoughts on the beach were dominated by the shells that pass for teeth in his mouth; and he is grossly embarrassed by a body of which he would gladly dispose, if he could become an unqualified mind. In claiming that *Ulysses* was 'the epic of the human body', Joyce was only telling half the truth. Being that, it is also an epic of bodily frustration. Nobody was more wary or more respectful of the body than Joyce. When an admirer in Paris asked if he could kiss the hand that wrote *Ulysses*, Joyce reminded him that the same hand had done many other things as well. At the root of such wisecracks is a healthy respect for the exactions of the body and a serene sense of bodily limitation.

Joyce must have known that the phrase 'epic of the human body' applied with far more appropriateness to the mysteries of Christian belief, so wittily parodied by Bloom. 'Good idea the Latin. Stupefies them first', he muses as he watches the communicants receive the body of Christ at All Hallows. He is even less impressed by the notion of Christian resurrection, in which he detects more consolation for the living who remain than for the 'fellow in the six feet by two with his toes to the daisies'. He foresees the Day of Judgement as a comedy of errors:

> Knocking them all up out of their graves. Come forth, Lazarus! And he came fifth and lost the job. Get up! Last day! Then every fellow mousing around for his liver and his lights and the rest of his trap. Find damn all of himself that morning . . .

Yet, for all this pessimism, one of the most impressive things about Bloom is just how at home he is with his body and all its functions. His honest relish of the scented urine of inner organs contrasts with Stephen's aversion to the 'urinous offal'. Bloom is shown through the day shitting and pissing, not to shock the reader, but in order to depict a man who has no abstract pretensions about himself. For Joyce, there was always something poignant rather than foolish about the spectacle of a man with his pants down. This feeling was illustrated by his favourite story of a soldier in the Great War who raised his rifle to shoot a German enemy, who at that very moment dropped his trousers to defecate in an open field. Despite the angry reprimands of his officer, the soldier could not bring himself to shoot so exposed a figure, so he waited until the man was finished and decently covered again, and then he shot him anyway.

Frank Budgen saw *Ulysses* as a book written to counter the twentieth-century worship of the body *and* the ninteenth-century worship of the pure disembodied mind.[37] Joyce saw, earlier than most, that the modern cult of the body had been made possible only by a century of coy evasion, but his close analysis of Bloom's daily actions exposed the laughable inadequacy of both attitudes. Like Lawrence, Joyce wanted to afford the body a recognition equal to that given the mind, but, because the Victorians had lost this just balance, both men *appeared* to elevate the body above all else. Devotees of Lawrence have argued that the anatomisation of the body on which the grand plan of *Ulysses* is based, an organ per chapter, represents the ultimate self-conscious abstraction of the body. This is true of the *plan*, but not of the actual experience of reading any chapter, where the interest centres on the way in which the main characters actually experience their own bodies.

Towards the end of *Nausikaa*, Bloom indulges in some uncharacteristically sexist thoughts on the subject of women ('a defect is ten times worse in a woman. But makes them polite') and their alleged rivalry ('That's what they enjoy. Taking a man from another woman'). These outbursts may be attributed to a covert self-hatred and guilt, as Bloom suffers the cold and clammy after-effects of his masturbation. Some time later in the maternity hospital, Bloom will echo Stephen's denunciation of all forms of contraception, only to be rebuked by the narrative voice for hypocrisy: 'It ill becomes him to preach that gospel. Has he not nearer home a seedfield that lies fallow for the want of a ploughshare? A habit reprehensible at puberty is second nature and an opprobrium in middle life.' This pained awareness would explain, if not excuse, his comments on Gerty.

As if by the same guilty instinct, his thoughts turn at once back to Molly and her masculine lips, pursed like Cissy's for a piercing whistle. Paradoxically, it is at this very moment that his identification with Molly seems most complete. Vividly he recalls her first romantic experience as if it were his own: 'First thoughts are best. Remember that till their dying day. Molly, Lieutenant Mulvey that kissed her under the Moorish wall beside the gardens. Fifteen she told me. But her breasts were developed.' In fact, Bloom seems to have come closest to Molly in those moments when he shared vicariously in her womanhood. There was, for example, the day when he asked her if she fancied the handsome man at the corner of Cuffe Street, only to be defeated by her superior woman's instinct, which correctly told her that the fellow had a false arm. If there is a female element in Bloom which takes pleasure in sharing Molly's secrets, it rejoices even more in those male elements of her personality: 'Dreamt last night . . . She had red slippers on. Turkish. Wore the breeches. Suppose she does. Would I like her in pyjamas? Damned hard to say . . .' This dream of Molly in men's clothing seems to intersect strangely with Stephen's dream of an eastern gentleman, who held out the red carpet and melon to the young arrival. In the true androgyne, according to Elémire Zolla, 'the man's female aspect will act like a mirror to women (as will the woman's male aspect to men); but it will also assert its female charm on men themselves'.[38] The promise and fascination of the androgyne is that of 'a disclosure about the unavowed, tentative elements of our own personalities'. So Bloom's fantasy of Molly seems a variant of Stephen's premonitory dream of Bloom and the borders between the sexes seem more ambiguous than ever.

In the subsequent discussion at the maternity hospital on the future determination of sex in children, it is no surprise to find the respective scientific positions outlined most succinctly by Bloom, from Empedocles's view that the right ovary is responsible for the birth of males, through the theory that spermatozoa or nemasperms are the differentiating factors, to the conventional embryologist's opinion that 'it is a mixture of both'. It is pretty clear by now that Bloom himself is a mixture of both sexes, an exponent of the androgyny which Joyce saw as the sexuality of the future, a man who can share uniquely in the wonder and woe of woman's labour.

No prophet, least of all a sexual prophet, is accepted in his own country. In *Circe* Bloom must pay the price of his advanced opinions and confront the deep-seated guilt which they arouse in him. *Circe* is a dream-play in the manner of Strindberg, complete with manly woman and womanly man. For Strindberg, as for Bloom, dreams were an eruption of suppressed phobias and a fantasy of wish-fulfilment in about equal measure. In the Preface to *A Dream Play*, Strindberg noted how each character might turn into his opposite – so a man might turn into a woman, just as in *Circe* Bella Cohen, the moustachioed woman, becomes Bello Cohen, the man with the bobbed hair. 'The characters are split, doubled and multiplied; they evaporate and are condensed; are diffused and concentrated', wrote Strindberg, 'but a single consciousness holds sway over them all – that of the dreamer',[39] a method which will provide the key to *Finnegans Wake*. Indeed, the uncertain, disintegrated nature of modern characters living through an hysterical period of transition in modern sexuality is as fitting a description of the Blooms, as it is of Miss Julie and Jean, to whom it was originally applied by Strindberg. His idea of character as a conglomeration of past and present phases of civilisation, bits of books and newspapers, is the recipe for the fragmented, multiple self of Leopold Bloom.

Like Lawrence, Joyce derived from Otto Weininger's book *Sex and Character* the notion of Jews as womanly men and forthwith applied the phrase to Bloom in a climactic passage of *Circe*. In *The Study of Thomas Hardy* Lawrence had described the Jew as 'the servant of his God, the female, passive', one in whom the female predominated and whose own physique included the woman. 'The secret, scrupulous voluptuousness of the Jew', said Lawrence, 'became almost self-voluptuousness, engaged in the consciousness of his own physique.'[40] Such lines might have featured on a programme note for the sensuous ecstasy of Bloom in his imagined bath in *Lotus-Eaters* or, indeed, for the narcissistic sexuality of *Nausikaa*. Joyce also shared Lawrence's view of the Jews as victims of a new apocalypse and prophets of a new era. *Circe* is therefore devoted to the New Bloomusalem and presents an apotheosis of the hero, which will cost Bloom every last ounce of his self-respect before he attains to prophecy.

Bloom begins his adventures in Nighttown still feeling light in the head, with secret phrases of Gerty MacDowell strangely invading his mind. 'Monthly or effect of the other. Brainfogfag. That tired feeling. Too much for me now. Ow!' So you do indeed 'run into what you feel', as that telepathic exchange with Gerty proved that there had been 'a kind of language' between them. Within minutes, Bloom is being arraigned by the society ladies of Dublin for his perverse and masochistic demands on them. Mrs Talboys complains: 'He implored me to soil his letter in an unspeakable manner, to chastise him as he richly deserves, to bestride and ride him, to give him a most vicious horsewhipping.' It all sounds rather like what Miss Julie did to the County Prosecutor. For his crimes, Bloom is unexpectedly acclaimed by the citizens of Dublin, including a feminist who 'masculinely' roars her approval. Soon, however, the mood of the mob changes to one of arraignment, during which Dr Malachi Mulligan pronounces Bloom 'bisexually abnormal', in keeping with his suspicions of homosexuality earlier in the day. He considers the female element in Bloom to be overdeveloped, giving rise to morbid symptoms of 'chronic exhibitionism' and 'ambidexterity'. But Dr Dixon, a close friend of the accused, protests that Bloom is merely an example of the androgyny of the fully developed personality, both simple and lovable, 'a finished example of the new womanly man'. His desire for the experience of motherhood is his way of protesting against the marginalisation of the male. In his bitterness, he seeks to transcend man-and-woman love, a mere affair of a cork and a bottle. This bitterness is fed by a sense of failure endured by a man who always 'came too quick with your best girl', a weakness which he unwittingly shares with Boylan. However, it is his Hungarian ancestor, Virag Lipoti, who asks the unresolved question left hanging on Sandymount Strand: 'Have you made up your mind whether you like or dislike women in male habilements? . . . From the sublime to the ridiculous is but a step. Pyjamas, let us say?'

The stage is set for the magisterial entrance of Bella Cohen, the massive whoremistress who has a sprouting moustache – a penalty, as Molly will later explain, for those ladies foolish enough to indulge in oral sex. Bella proceeds to diagnose Bloom's domestic ills: 'And the missus is master. Petticoat government.' Within minutes, she has conformed to Bloom's fantasy by turning into a man, while he in turn is transformed into a passive and adoring woman, Ruby Cohen. Bello (as she now is) Cohen twists the new Ruby's arm and has to be begged for mercy. She tells Ruby:

> What you longed for has come to pass. Henceforth you are unmanned and mine in earnest, a thing under the yoke. Now for your punishment frock. You will shed your male garments, you understand, Ruby Cohen? and don the shot silk luxuriously rustling over head and shoulders and quickly too . . .

For Bloom (now a charming soubrette, albeit with daubed cheeks and strong male nose), this recalls a guilty prank in the early days of his marriage in Holles Street, when in order to save money, he washed Molly's clothes and tried them on himself on one occasion. This mild transvestite impulse first revealed itself when he was at the High School, acting as a female impersonator in the annual play titled, appropriately enough, *Vice Versa*. Now

Bloom pleads with the overpowering Bello for mercy, revelling in his own degradation: 'Master! Mistress! Mantamer!', but Bello devises a punishment to fit the crime. By day he must wash and souse all the whores' undergarments, accepting spankings for inefficiency. Instructing him to empty out the pisspots and latrines, Bello does not mince words: 'What else are you good for, an impotent thing like you? . . . Buy a bucket or sell your pump. (Loudly). Can you do a man's job?' In Eccles Street, a man of brawn is in possession, who lies foot-to-foot, belly-to-belly with his lady, unlike the antipodal position favoured by Bloom, who is urged to wait nine months for the issue of this new coupling. In the meantime, he must remain with Molly, either as paying guest or as kept man. Having made his second-best bed, he must lie in it.

In this entire scene, as in the earlier encounters with the denizens of Barney Kiernan's and the Ormond bar, Bloom is seen to be trapped in a painful dilemma. His androgyny allows him to heal his sense of alienation from the opposite sex, but only at the price of losing the respect of his own. The more successful he is in deepening his awareness of the intimate life of a woman, the more he feels himself unmanned. Although it can be an image of harmony and unity, the androgyne is as often the epitome of lost power and manliness. Wendy Doninger O'Flaherty finds much evidence in Vedic texts to suggest that male pregnancy is ritually associated with death, that the human problem of impotence became the myth of androgyny, with the result that there is 'a deep substructure of shadow and terror inherent in the image'.[41] Yet this is to ignore the consolation to be found in the image by men and women in flight from the freakish extremes of nineteenth-century sexuality. In a book entitled *Freaks*, Leslie Fiedler has documented the traditional nightmares of adolescents who feel that their penises and breasts are always too big or too small, leaving them in either case as freaks. The growth of genital hair reinforces this sense of freakishness, but the most telling factor of all, according to Fiedler, is 'each sex's early perception of the other's genitalia in adult form'.[42] Because of his penis, the male is deemed a *monstre par excés*; because she lacks a penis, the woman becomes a *monstre par défaut*. The nub of Fiedler's argument is that 'each sex tends to feel itself forever defined as freakish in relation to the other. And from our uneasiness at this, I suppose, arises the dream of androgyny.'[43] But even Fiedler is forced to concede that this dream can never become real, because it is always 'undercut by a profound fear of being unmanned or unwomaned, and by guilt for desiring such an event'.[44]

On the basis of this analysis at the start of *Freaks*, Fiedler goes on to end the book by arguing that for Joyce androgyny comes to represent 'an ultimate horror rather than an idyllic vision',[45] as passivity in love becomes the occasion for a dire guilt which is projected onto Bloom. This could hardly be further from the truth, as a cursory examination of Joyce's letters will show just how much he relished his own passivity in lovemaking with Nora. Moreover, Fiedler fails to make any discrimination between Joyce and Bloom. Bloom is *not* the liberated Parisian Joyce of 1922, but a timid outcast in the Dublin of 1904, whose tentative attempts at a more honest sexuality are punctuated by bouts of self-recrimination, which prove that it is easier to preach a new doctrine than to practise it. It would, nevertheless, be quite wrong to see the self-recrimination of *Circe* as being ultimately more real for Bloom (or for Joyce) than the massive endorsement of androgyny throughout the rest of *Ulysses*. What is dramatised in *Circe* is what is shown in every other chapter of the book – the recognition that the harmonies of androgyny are accompanied by a dark legacy of fear and self-loathing. Bloom *never* feels himself to be freakish in relation to the opposite sex. On the contrary, his androgyny gives him a unique insight into womanhood, an insight denied to most other males in Dublin, who treat Bloom in the same way as they treat a woman, i.e. as a freak. These males are the real neurotics of *Ulysses*, because they behave as if the sex of their sexual object determined their own sex. The sexual roles which they enact are a result of social definitions – 'men are in all things the opposite of women' – and not an expression of the full complexity of the person within. In their anxiety to repress the female within each man, they constitute a working majority in the Dublin of 1904; and so they can pass for normal and denounce Bloom as an eccentric. But it is they who live out lives of freakish spiritual contortion and Bloom alone who has discovered that the eccentric is merely a man with a deeper than average apprehension of normality. Fiedler's analysis works from a false premise and puts the cart before the horse. He sees Bloom's androgyny as an attempt to heal the painful sense of each sex that it is freakish in the eyes of the other. But for Bloom, androgyny is not an option, but a donné. He is already androgynous to begin with. Partaking of male and female, he can never see either sex as freakish, for when he contemplates the bodies of women, he is looking at a fuller embodiment of an aspect of his innermost self. Yet, despite all this, Fiedler sees in *Ulysses* 'a travesty of the myth of androgyny: a revelation of the sado-masochism, buggery, and impotence which Joyce believed lay behind all of its elegant mythologising'.[46]

Sleep reveals the worst side of everyone, we are told in *Circe*, children perhaps excluded. Certainly, Bloom's suppressed fears seem, for the time being, even more prominent than his deepest wish-fulfilment – fears of detection, of losing his wife, of being father to another man's child. His fantasies have their source in Sacher-Masoch's classic book *Venus in Pelz*, according to Richard Ellmann. Bloom is thus to be seen as a latter-day Severin, tyrannised by a cruel society lady, whipped by an excited woman who forces him to lace her shoes, and finally forced into a contract of perpetual servitude. Ellmann warns against literal-minded readings of *Circe* and reminds us that these masochistic fantasies occur in Bloom's unconscious mind: 'he berates himself, and makes himself worse than he is, because he is conscious of having allowed too much in reality'.[47] So the scene where Bloom leads Boylan to the bed of his wife is intended as an act of pure vaudeville, with Molly comically taunting the artful voyeur: 'Let him look, the pishogue. Pimp! And scourge himself!' It is only as a voyeur that Bloom seems able to summon up the reserves of sexual aggression which would have satisfied Molly: 'Show! Hide! Plough her! More! Shoot!'

Yet it is at this strange and ambiguous moment that Stephen begins to discern the end of his quest. He and Bloom gaze into a single mirror and see reflected back at them the beardless face of William Shakespeare, the perfect and dignified androgyne, whose life-story had brought them to the verge of a meeting earlier that day. Now Stephen's racing mind recalls the premonitory dream of Bloom holding out watermelons in the street of harlots; and he remembers the question which hovered over the start of his journey: 'Tell me the word, mother, the word known to all men.' It is the 'other word' which Martha Clifford feared, the truth about eternal nature and the new androgynous man. Bloom, the womanly hero, is the alternative image of authority sought by Stephen in flight from his father's world of male vanity. It is for his multiple self that Stephen finally accepts the new prophet,

'Christus or Bloom his name is, or, after all, any other' – a sentence strangely similar to Molly's own words of acceptance in Howth, 'as well him as another'. Yet again, a man and a woman, Stephen and Molly, unknowingly share the same thought. For them Bloom is both average and special, an exponent of the multiple self and therefore a master of none, a man with so many selves that his own identity is tenuous and provisional, everything and nothing, the androgynous goal. In the catechism section of *Ithaca*, this human formula is specified:

> What universal binomial denominations would be his as entity and nonentity?
> Assumed by any or known to none. Everyman or Noman.

No-man and no-woman either, but one who knows 'the surety of the sense of touch in his firm full masculine feminine passive active hand'. It is not a sense of touch and that recommends itself to many others on that day in Dublin. In the newspaper office, all the other men had touched, nudged or slapped one another in the amiable transaction of jokes and cigarettes, but nobody had touched Bloom,[48] another chapter in his epic of bodily frustration. In Kiernan's pub, the drinkers had addressed one another by name, even when trading insults, but nobody had so addressed Bloom. In *Circe* even the drunken Stephen is surprised to feel 'a strange kind of flesh of a different man approach him, sinewless and wobbly and all that'. But he goes with the dark stranger and learns from him the word known to all men.

Not all lovers of *Ulysses* have seen Bloom's androgyny for what it is, and some have even endorsed Mulligan's belief that Bloom is bisexual. Frank Budgen attributed Bloom's failure to halt the affair between Molly and Boylan to 'the homosexual wish to share his wife with other men',[49] since this is the only way that Bloom can achieve a sense of fellowship with other males. Bloom's Jewish masochism is denied its traditional outlet in religious observances, says Budgen, and so the indignity of cuckolding feeds his desire for suffering. But androgyny is not bisexuality – as June Singer has pointed out, the former is intrapsychic, whereas the latter is interpersonal.[50] In Bloom's case, the androgyny – even in *Circe* – is a state of mind. Male and female elements within his self have become so perfectly balanced that all sexual desire is slowly melting away. As Lawrence wrote of the Jew in his *Study of Thomas Hardy*, 'he does not suffer the torture of desire of a mere male being and tends to voluptuousness rather than to passion'.[51] This is the process which Bloom has discerned in all previous lovers of Molly, the transformation from desire to fatigue, 'with alternating symptoms of epicene comprehension and apprehension'. This is no great wonder, for if it is, in part, the female in these men which is attracted to the male aspect of Molly, then that passion is the source of its own dissolution into epicene serenity, when sex itself becomes the source of its own transcendence. Few readers of Joyce have appreciated the fundamentally religious nature of his sexual prophecy; and most continue to see Bloom as the victim of an ailment rather than the prophet of a new sexuality.

The serenity of a man who has almost achieved the Lawrentian balance of *yin* and *yang* has been mistaken by Frank Budgen for mere sexual indifference. Budgen's indictment of androgyny is as spirited as it is wrong-headed:

> But when the life force, if that most depressing divinity happens to be in fashion at the time, finds that tabulated knowledge, the good pal girl and the fifty-fifty boy lead only to tweeds for everybody and general indifference, then social and sexual taboos, ignorance, inhibitions, white undies, black stockings, and furtiveness will come in again with all their tensions, as in the days of Gerty MacDowell.[52]

If sexual equality is already killing romance, it will eventually obliterate sex itself, or so Budgen seems to imply in his strange nostalgia for Victorian fetishism. But he has confused androgyny with asexuality, in much the same manner as Shaw, whose life-force seems to haunt those references to the good-pal girl and universal tweeds. Androgyny is not based on a featureless unisex philosophy, nor is it based on a bisexual lack of clarity in gender differentiation. The androgyne is not interested in obliterating the notions of male and female, but rather in fusing male and female in himself. As June Singer says, he is still vitally and richly aware of sexual difference:

> The new androgyne is not in confusion about his or her sexual identity. Androgynous men express a natural, unforced and uninhibited male sexuality, while androgynous women can be

totally female in their own sexuality. Yet neither tends to extremes: men do not need to exude machismo, or women to pretend to a naive and dependent character. Excessively polarised personality types thrive in a culture that demands the repression of certain natural tendencies while people are developing the so-called 'masculine' and the so-called 'feminine' traits, which society considers to be appropriate for each sex. Androgynous individuals allow these repressions in themselves to be lifted; not in order to prepare a way for living out sexual impulses so much as in order to permit what has been repressed to return and to be reintegrated into conscious awareness.[53]

In the return to such an androgyny, there will be many casualties of the transitional phase and the marriage of the Blooms clearly falls into this category. There are marked male elements in Molly, from the desire for a penis and the power it would confer, to the compulsion to whistle in public through her pursed lips. Like most Victorians, however, she has learned to suppress those male elements in herself. In *A Doll's House*, Nora had yearned to be able to say 'damn' in public, just as in bed with Boylan, Molly would like to say 'fuck' and 'shit'; but her shrewd awareness that this would shock her old-fashioned Lothario prevents her from giving vent. Instead, as David Hayman has shown in an analysis of the following passage,[54] she must content herself by privately contemplating her thighs with the clinical detachment of an appraising male:

> ... I bet he never saw a better pair of thighs than that look how white they are the smoothest place is right there between this bit here how soft like a peach God I wouldn't mind being a man and get up on a lovely woman O Lord ...

Such outbursts would have driven Bloom into the seventh heaven and strongly imply that he is her ideal, as well as her lawful, mate. It is not hard to understand the initial attraction which brought them together, nor the excitement of both lovers as Molly overbore Leopold among the Howth rhododendrons. It was the male in her that fell for the woman in him, just as she was moved to meet a man who 'understood or *felt* what a woman was'. Yet this very affinity which made the relationship possible is now preventing its further development, since Leopold has turned out to be a great deal more womanly than his wife is manly. Their levels of androgyny have proved incompatible and it is *this*, rather than the fear of conceiving and losing another Rudi, which explains the sexual arrest of their marriage.

Molly is still old-fashioned enough to want a lover 'just the right height over me', a man who will possess her. She finds Bloom's desire for absolute self-abasement as odious as men who wear earrings. His desire to know what it is to be a woman has been carried too far for her liking; and his probing questions about her sexual fantasies are even more distressing than fascinating. There is a limit to what any woman (or man) wishes to divulge, even to a spouse; and at the root of much feminist unease with the closing monologue may be the feeling that Joyce, no less than Bloom, has transgressed those limits. Bloom wants to know if Molly would do this with a coalman, that with a bishop; but she dismisses such overtures as a shabby attempt 'to make a whore of me', while he reaches his own lonely satisfaction. From the published letters, it is clear that Joyce made no less a demand on his wife, who must accept the 'obscene and bestial', as well as the 'holy and spiritual' dimensions of his thought, because 'all of it is myself'[55] – and she was expected to reciprocate with a similar frankness concerning her own masturbatory fantasies and private confessions to the priest. It was, in its way, a test rather like that imposed by Birkin in his relations with Ursula Brangwen. Joyce's own case is seen by Richard Ellmann as the desire to know another person beyond love and hate, exaltation and shame, sex and society, beyond humanity itself.[56] In the case of the Blooms, however, it was a one-sided pact, for Molly does not desire nor exact a similar candour from her husband. His androgynous balance is in real danger of being lost through an excessive devotion to the feminine. 'While exoterically the feminine, left force (yetzer-ra) is considered by Jewish mystics as evil', writes Elémire Zolla in *The Androgyne*, 'esoterically it is taught that the greater his yetzer-ra, the greater the man, for as he dominates over it, it becomes his auxiliary – and the perfect man comprises the two harmonies together.'[57] In Bloom, that balance is on the verge of being destroyed, at least partly because he has lived so long with a wife in whom it has never been achieved.

Yet the couple's tragedy is that they came so close to perfection without even knowing it, just as they still share far more than they know. Much earlier that day in the Ormond bar, it was

Bloom's intimate understanding of woman which had allowed him to forgive Molly her infidelity, even before the deed was done: 'Too late. She longed to go. That's why. Woman. As easy stop the sea. Yes: all is lost.' In comparing the forces of sexual attraction to the ebb and flow of the sea-tide, Bloom shares unconsciously the very image with which Molly will justify the escapade to herself at the end, just as both mark their acceptance of nature with a shared and simple 'yes'. So, the very line which records the disaster to their marriage also guarantees its final inviolability. These two are married in the depths of the soul and share something as evanescent as a cast of mind and imagination.

The tragedy of the interior monologue is the poverty of its social occasions. Bloom never does manage to put his arms round his wife and forgive her in person, as he has already forgiven her in his mind – and she never tells him what she tells herself, that he is still the finest man in Dublin, and handsome as well. In the world of the outsider, everything is thought, but little is expressed. Instead, an exhausted Bloom clambers into bed beside a restless and frustrated wife. 'Still he had the manners not to wake me', she muses in her determination to be positive, but she is awake anyway. Bloom's latest attempt at tender concern has proved ineffective. Those critics who find in this closing sequence the affirmation of love and life would do well to ponder the tragic situation of a woman who is left with nobody to talk to but herself. This is the 'silent marriage' with a vengeance, where every woman must be her own husband: '. . . . ages ago the days like years not a letter from a living soul except the odd few I posted to myself with bits of paper in them . . .' In that context, her final 'yes' may not be as joyful as it has been made to seem. Her first word of the day was a muffled 'no' to Bloom's inquiry if she would like anything. Now, at the end, her obsessively repeated 'yes' seems less an affirmation of life than a desperate strategy to convince herself that she is actually talking *to* someone. In Dublin the spoken 'yes' may often be a word of negation, used by a fluent person to suppress a comment from another pair of lips, a way of acknowledging the presence of another without permitting him to speak.[58] It can even be used to interrupt the flow of another's conversation ('Yes and . . .'), in order to assert oneself rather than endure the indignities of further listening. In a city of compulsive talkers, it is a useful weapon, but it is not necessarily the affirmation which the professors, with their fondness for a happy ending, seem to think. Oscar Wilde once joked that 'the good ended happily, the bad unhappily, that is what Fiction means', but it is not what Molly Bloom means. There is selfishness, as well as affirmation, in her 'yes', just as there is a basic subversion of the Victorian principle by which all girls were taught to say 'no' endlessly, until a suitably monied suitor gave the hapless wench the right to lie back and think of England. In a book of androgynes, where everthing is inter-penetrated by its opposite, it is no surprise that 'yes' might also mean 'no'. This was a truth hinted back in *Circe*, when Bella Cohen asked Bloom if he remembered her and received the emphatic Dublin reply 'Nes. Yo.'

As they sleep foot-to-mouth in the bed in Eccles Street, Leopold and Molly unwittingly reenact the attempt at alchemical fusion by the saintly couples of early Christianity, who, in the words of Elémire Zolla, 'sought to liberate the animating principles through fermentation and fusion of the subtle bodies'.[59] St Francis and St Claire, St Theresa and St John of the Cross were simply the most famous exponents of a tradition that sought the wisdom of an androgynous godhead. That tradition was sanctioned by the great Irish philosopher, Scotus Eriugena, who took with literal-minded seriousness St Paul's avowal that after baptism there is neither male nor female. Molly is less than enamoured of the practice, and yet the symbols with which Joyce surrounds her suggest that she too conforms. Her sign is the number eight (for her eight sentences and date of birth), but an eight placed on its side to represent infinity, the female principle. There is, however, an even more specific meaning to the symbol. Giordano Bruno, whose work Joyce admired, used two interlocking circles as a sign of androgyny, with the fish's eye at the centre, in which he placed Christ and the Virgin Mary. Even the spectacular dot with which *Ithaca* ends may have its part in the scheme, since in the *I Ching* (on which Bruno modelled his diagram) the secret of the creative balance of *yin* and *yang* lies in the female dot at the centre of the male part.[60]

Molly strongly objects to the antipodal position, if only because it encourages Leopold to make a fetish of her bottom, a privilege for which she considers charging him money in the future. She berates Bloom in her mind for being 'so cold never embracing me except sometimes when he's asleep the wrong end of me not knowing I suppose who he has'. This is a somewhat hypocritical complaint from a woman who accepted her husband with the words 'as well him as another', but the motif of human interchangeability dominates the entire book. With commendable humility, Bloom learns to view himself as just one in an infinite series of lovers of Molly and he smiles inwardly at the reflection that there may be yet another meaning to the word 'metempsychosis':

> ... that each one who enters imagines himself to be the first to enter whereas he is always the last term of a receding series even if the first term of a succeeding one, each imagining himself to be first, last, only and alone ...

In this context, it was no wonder that Gerty proved attractive to Bloom, for 'she felt instinctively that he was like no-one else'. Molly, for a time, concealed her real attitude by pretending to Leopold that she chose him 'because you were so foreign from the others'; but that, as we know, is not what she told herself. Indeed, readers of her monologue are often confused by her promiscuous and vague pronouns, as to which lover she is describing at any moment in time. Mulvey on Gibralter shades into Bloom on Howth; Bloom's straw hat on Howth shades into Boylan's on 16 June. All these devices underline for the reader Joyce's, as well as Molly's, sense of the provisional and tenuous elements which define any personality. If Bloom is the latest in a series which includes Mulvey as well as Shakespeare, Boylan as well as Odysseus, then nobody is anything in particular.

It is this fear of human interchangeability which agitates Molly as she resentfully recalls Boylan 'slapping us behind like that on my bottom'; and her confusion of pronouns indicates just how uncertain of her self she is. 'I'm not a horse or an ass', she says, angry with herself now for laughing so obligingly for Boylan at the time. In her disgust, she joins hands across the book with Gerty MacDowell, who believed that 'the man who lifts his hand to a woman save in the way of kindness deserves to be branded as the lowest of the low'. Molly shares the worldwide fear that she is loved not for herself so much as for her sexual parts; and the respects paid to her hindquarters by Boylan and Bloom seem less acts of affection than violations of her identity:

> ... any man thatd kiss a womans buttocks Id throw my hat at him after that hed kiss anything unnatural where we havent

1 atom of any kind of expression in us all of us the same 2
lumps of lard before ever Id do that to a man pfooh the dirty
brutes the mere thought is enough . . .

Such an outburst is hypocritical, if only because Molly repeatedly
fails to discriminate in men herself. This feature of her personality
may have been coloured by Joyce's reading of *Sex and Character*,
in which Weininger argued that woman has no ability to make
the rational distinctions which are the basis of logic and principle.
(Feminists will be unsurprised to learn that some time after
writing this opinion Weininger killed himself.) 'The mode in
which her tenderness expresses itself is a kind of animal sense of
contact', he wrote; 'it shows an absence of that sharp line that
separates one real personality from another.'[61] In a similar fashion,
Molly lacks any clear sense of the punctuation that should
separate one sentence from another, with the result that her
thoughts pour forth in a stream as uncontrollable as her menstruation.[62] Finding that his own wife scorned normal sentence
structure, Joyce seems rashly to have inferred a similar propensity
in most women, for he commented in a letter to Stanislaus: 'You
will see from this interpolated letter the gigantic strides which N
has made towards culture and emancipation . . . Do you notice
how women when they write disregard stops and capital letters?'[63]
Based on an attitude like this, it is no wonder that the monologue
was written off by Nora Barnacle with the comment that
her husband knew nothing about women. Joyce had privately
admitted as much in a letter to his brother many years earlier.
Yet the closing chapter of *Ulysses* won many famous admirers,
including the psychologist Jung, who remarked to the author: 'I
suppose the devil's grandmother knows so much about the real
psychology of a woman, I didn't.'[64]

In reality, Molly's monologue is a compendium of old-fashioned
clichés about womanhood, many derived from Weininger, such
as the idea that women are incurably self-contradictory. Molly
denounces a priest for coyly refusing to say the word 'bottom',
yet goes on to criticise a priest for using the word 'bumgut'; she
begins by attacking women who are down on low-cut dresses,
but joins their ranks before the end; she complains that Bloom
won't pay for a home help, but is turns out that it was Molly
who sent the last one packing – and so on. Mixed in with this
traditionalist portraiture are some more radical ideas, such as

Molly's wish to bear her mother's rather than her father's name, an androgynous principle endorsed by Joyce who wrote in a letter that 'a child should be allowed to take his father's or mother's name at will on coming of age'.[65] On a somewhat similar kind of reasoning, Joyce saw to it that Bloom's middle name was Paula. In fairness to Weininger, it should also be pointed out that many of these more radical ideas in *Ulysses* may owe a great deal to *Sex and Character*, which asserted that 'man and woman are like two substances which are distributed among individuals in varying mixed proportions, without the coefficient of one substance ever vanishing. In experience, one might say, there is neither man nor woman, only masculine and feminine.'[66]

Nevertheless, the underlying effect of the final monologue is to reinforce the traditionalist stereotype of womanhood which the book as a whole has thrown so magnificently into question. It is no wonder that many feminists feel betrayed by the chapter, which is scarcely the 'string of veritable psychological peaches' praised by Jung, less a depiction of women as they are than a projection of what the male mind of Joyce would like to believe them to be. The undiscriminating flow of Molly's and Gerty's sentences contrasts markedly with the staccato chop-logic of Bloom; and, for all their linguistic power, the effect of many of the interior monologues is to confirm the most dreary stereotype of all, rational man versus irrational woman. By the time Joyce wrote *Ulysses*, Freud had shown that what seems like reason in men is more often rationalisation and that the immense sexual power enjoyed by men was not conducive to male soul-searching. Women, on the other hand, by virtue of their vulnerability and disadvantage, had of necessity developed a penchant for dispassionate self-analysis. None of *that* found its way into *Ulysses*. In a work which so movingly and convincingly demonstrated the androgyny of the full person, the uncritical inclusion of Weininger's stereotypes seems like a betrayal of Joyce's innermost theme.

*   *   *

'For the most part', wrote Stanislaus Joyce, 'women do not interest Irishmen except as streetwalkers and housekeepers.'[67] Having sampled the streetwalkers, his famous brother fled the housekeepers and sought in his art a return to the feminine principle. He endorsed Oliver St John Gogarty's claim that the men of Ireland would have to find some better way of worshipping God than the hatred of women. For that to happen, men would have to admit the possibility that God was as much woman as man, the first androgyne and artist.

8 The Male Response to Feminism

> In fact, when asked, 'What do you think about women's liberation? How has it affected your relationships?', most men said not at all.
>
> *The Hite Report on Male Sexuality*, 1981

It was inevitable that the twentieth-century recognition of androgyny should have been anticipated by the great modernists who wrote between 1885 and 1925. Those early feminists who needed the 'masculine' traits of aggression and reason in order to pursue their campaigns found their situation inverted by the male writers of the era, who needed the 'feminine' gifts of intuition and sensitivity if they were to become true artists. It might have been expected that the achievement of these writers would have encouraged more women to enter the literary mainstream, yet, by a curious paradox, the literature of women's liberation has still to evolve a truly modernist style. Most feminist novels are still propagandist in tone and content, and their narrative methods owe more to socialist realism than to the works of Lawrence or Joyce. The accounts of sexual relationships in post-modern literature, by men as well as women, in no way equal the complex insights and artistic beauty of the modern masterpieces discussed in this book.

This is not to say that the issues raised in those masterpieces have not been clarified in the intervening decades, but these developments have occurred in the area of critical rather than creative writing. In part, this simply reflects a wider crisis in contemporary culture, which has managed to convert novelists like Norman Mailer and Simone de Beauvoir into writers of social criticism and high-class journalism. So the Mailer who began his exploration of modern relationships in *The Naked and the Dead* is compelled to continue it in critical essays of book length such as

The Prisoner of Sex, just as de Beauvoir is already far better-known for an extended essay such as *The Second Sex* than for a novel of modern sexuality like *The Mandarins*. As twentieth-century literature has progressively told us how little it means and lapsed into self-mockery, criticism has taken itself more and more seriously, becoming the preeminent genre for new ideas in our era. And yet, the paralysis which has gripped our creative writers necessarily affects our critics as well. Try as they may, most of them in their essays simply tease out, at one remove, the more original ideas evolved sixty years earlier in the years of high modernism. It can scarcely be a coincidence that the three most influential feminist tracts of the 1960s and 1970s – *Thinking About Women*, *The Female Eunuch* and *Sexual Politics* – were written by women graduates in English, whose work shows just how intense was their exposure to the modern masters. Even the radical attack by Millett on Lawrence is couched largely in a terminology derived from his novels and essays. These feminist writers, and many others, offered a number of interesting answers to the questions posed by Strindberg, Ibsen, Hardy, Yeats, Lawrence and Joyce; but, more often, they simply restated issues defined more pithily and more movingly in the creative works. Far from being sexual reactionaries, the modern masters are now shown to have been half a century ahead of their time, like true prophets who see so deeply into the crisis of their age that the shape of the future becomes discernible. The feminist tracts of recent decades were explicit restatements for a mass audience of ideas implicit in the work of the modernists. In the event, Jude Fawley spoke for all of them in saying that it would take three generations to achieve what he had attempted in one. If the works of art discussed in this book anticipate much of what feminists have had to tell us in recent years, then it is also likely that they contain valuable indications of the male response to feminism, which seems set fair to be a dominant theme of the 1980s. It is with the application of modernist ideas by feminists and their male critics that this closing chapter will now deal.

MEN AND FEMINISM

It is Simone de Beauvoir's fundamental principle that 'to emancipate woman is to refuse to confine her to the relations she bears to man'.[1] So, it is only in the final pages of *The Second Sex* that she allows herself to speculate on the male response to feminism, a severe impoverishment of a book which sets out to be a blueprint for a future sexuality. A deeper challenge was offered, however, by those writers who asked woman to *redefine* her relations to man by opening herself to the male within her own personality. It took Rainer Maria Rilke to argue that 'personhood' need not be confined to that part of a woman which is discovered when she ceases to be dependent on man. His challenge was more complex and exhilarating:

> One day the girl will be here, and the woman, whose name will no longer signify merely the opposite of masculinity, but something in itself, something which makes us think of no complement of limitation, but only of life and existence: the feminine human being. This step forward will (much against the wishes of the outstripped men to begin with) change the love experience that now is full of error, alter it fundamentally, refashion it into a relationship meant to be between one human being and another.

Such bright hopes have not been fulfilled. Some women have mistaken liberation for the freedom to treat sexual relationships with the callous indifference of the traditional male; others have yet to learn that a man who refuses to exploit them is not on that account less virile. Too many women, like Strindberg's Bertha or Lawrence's Gudrun, still secretly worship the male principle and seek to compete with men, instead of becoming fully aware of themselves as women.

It is of crucial importance that women should help men to understand and accept the new sexuality, whose benefits (as Rilke delicately hinted) are less immediately obvious to men than to women. In their explanations, women must concede that there is a great deal more at stake here than wounded male pride, for some anthropologists have argued that at issue is nothing less than the survival of the species. V. C. Wynne Edwards found that reversed sex-roles were manifest only in rare and isolated species, and concluded that 'the evolution of a dominant female sex is invariably something of quite recent origin, and, by inference, therefore a "wrong turning" or side-track likely to end in extinction'.[3] It is not surprising that two of the most prevalent male responses to feminism are a defeatist self-pity or an angry self-assertion.

Both attitudes may be found at various stages in the writings of D. H. Lawrence. His Lady Chatterley is acutely described by de Beauvoir as 'a compensation myth, exalting a virility that the writer was none too sure of',[4] and the phallus-worship of his later writings is seen as a last-ditch defence by the beleaguered male. Lawrence's more private feelings of cultural despair are comprehensively expressed in an essay of 1927 entitled 'The Real Thing'. Here, he concedes that the 'deepest fight for two thousand years and more has been the fight for woman's independence', but confirms that this has now gone too far and become 'a tyranny of woman' in the home and in the world.[5] The power of technology has rendered the physical strength of the male redundant, but it has not yet wholly usurped the reproductive capacity of the woman.[6] Woman's traditional faith in man has weakened and 'we know now that our fathers were fought and beaten by our mothers, not because our mothers really knew what was "better", but because our fathers had lost their instinctive hold on the life-flow':

> It always happens at the end of some great phase, before another phase sets in. It always seems to start, in man, an overwhelming worship of woman, and a glorification of queens. It always seems to bring a brief spell of glory, and a long spell of misery after. Man yields in glorifying the woman, the glory dies, the fight goes on.[7]

That overwhelming worship of the woman began in the 1890s, when the child-like heroines of Dickens gave way in popularity to the amazons of Charles Dana Gibson. Lawrence's passage is a recollection of a decade when women began to enter public life and attend college in numbers, a decade when George du Maurier's Trilby was just one of the many voluptuous heroines, whose Junoesque stature emphasised her increasing social visibility.[8] The 'good-pal-girl' was born as one writer's desperate response to the challenge posed by feminists. While others retreated into Kiplingesque fantasies of comradeship and *Blutbruderschaft*, du Maurier offered, in the words of Fraser Harrison, 'a more sophisticated form of reassurance, one that evidently struck a chord in the public's imagination: he imposed upon his heroine the insignia of masculinity and made these the very qualities which most endeared her to her lovers'.[9] For all her self-possession and power, Trilby would never humiliate a lover, says Harrison, because she was an 'honorary man' and could be trusted. Her male admirers responded by naming a hat after her – and wearing it. One historian of fashion has remarked on the coincidence in the decline of the Victorian top hat with the loss of male authority, and wickedly concluded that 'towards the end of the century men began to wear, so to speak, the very symbol of their bashed-in authority: the trilby hat'.[10] More crucially, perhaps, women began to wear the male hats currently in fashion in the 1880s and 1890s, as if to question the absolute division between male and female.

Lawrence's bleak diagnosis from the retrospect of 1927 was to conclude that this brief period of egalitarian glory had been followed by two decades of male self-pity and retreat. If women had triumphed, they would have to enjoy the bitter fruits of victory alone, for men had no longer any desire to share in them. If many women saw no other option than that of the self-sufficient lesbian or the breezy career-girl, then the sullen withdrawal of men from sexual encounter may be at least partly to blame. Although women continued to win further freedoms in the decades after Lawrence's essay, this was due more to the spread of sophisticated forms of contraception than to any widespread acceptance by men of the desirability of such change.

The refusal of many feminists to face the daunting and depressing task of expounding their case to men has simply compounded the existing problems. From the sidelines, even radical men have been forced to eavesdrop on a campaign whose leaders have assured the vanquished male of his increasing marginality. Moreover, in their zeal as converts to a new radicalism, many feminists have resorted to a triumphalist tone. Kate Millett cannot report the fact that 'the female sexual cycle is capable of multiple orgasms in quick succession', without adding that 'each of these is analogous to the detumescence, ejaculation and loss of erection in the male'. Such multiple orgasms can be achieved 'with proper stimulation', but if the self-doubting male is not adequate to the task, the implication is that there are others (including the woman herself) who can do it better.[11]

Faced with comments and statistics like these, it is predictable that some men have been driven to extremes of impotence and rage. The increase in the reports of male impotence throughout the decade after the publication of *Sexual Politics* is attributable to a growing anxiety about sex in society as a whole, but it may also arise as a consequence of the uncompromising demands of a new generation of hard-edged feminists. Reay Tannahill has marvelled at how times change – 'whereas the arrogant imaginary woman acted as a sexual stimulant to the Victorian male, the flesh-and-blood feminist today often alarms her lover into impotence'.[12] Many scrupulous men have become so anxious to secure full sexual satisfaction for their partners that carefree or playful sex all but becomes a thing of the past. The ghost of Woody Allen haunted the water-bed as well as the marriage-hearse. Confronted with his own inability to deliver all the pleasures promised to women by the sex manuals, the bruised male went on the defensive in the manner of a Leopold Bloom. According to Tannahill, 'researchers in the early nineteen-seventies discovered that he was having intercourse less frequently, resorting more often to masturbation, and developing a taste for pornography'.[13]

THE NEW PHILOSOPHY IN THE BOUDOIR

Not all men remained so quiescent. The growing passivity of males was accompanied by a startling increase in the figures for rape, though whether this was due to a wider definition of rape, or a greater willngness on the part of women to report such assaults, remains unclear. It may also be attributable to the very successes of the women's movement, for, in the words of Christopher Lasch, 'as male supremacy becomes ideologically untenable, incapable of justifying itself as protection, men assert their domination more directly, in fantasies and occasionally in acts of raw violence'.[14] Such violence must be linked in some measure to the wider availability of pornographic films and magazines which, far from allowing men to sublimate their anti-female desires in a harmless fashion, further arouse those desires with no hope of assuaging them. Angela Carter has laughingly pointed to the anomaly of a pornography produced by men for an all-male audience, which nevertheless purports to describe an ideal relation between men and women. 'All pornography suffers the methodological defects of a manual of navigation written by and for land-lubbers.'[15] Indeed, the ideal woman of the pornographers who comes unerringly to a rapid climax is not the flesh-and-blood woman who gets headaches and cares for babies, but 'a man in disguise'.[16] Thus, even the pornographer's model embodies a version of androgyny, representing the *anima* for a man too immature to find her in any real woman of his acquaintance. Perhaps the ultimate condemnation of pornography is not that it inflames male desire, but rather that it teaches men to formulate specific kinds of desire which can scarcely be appeased without violence or distress.

But what of the growing number of men who no longer want to express aggression in their relations with women? Are they merely masochists or prophets of a future sexuality? Will it ever be fully possible to purge sexual relations of all aggressive impulse? And what of the highly combative responses of certain feminists to the passive or even masochistic male? On the one hand, Mary Ellmann can look forward, beyond our nuclear nightmare, to 'a period in which we will have to value passivity, as we have valued aggression in the past, or not be able to value ourselves'.[17] On the other hand, the impulse to aggression may not be disappearing, but simply passing from the once-dominant man to the New Woman. 'A free woman in an unfree society will be a monster', says Angela Carter, because once she has the limited freedom to employ her sexuality as an instrument of aggression, she will use it to seek vengeance for the humiliations which she endured in the past.[18] Hence the fact that so many relationships between progressive men and women take on the quality of a war of attrition. 'I'm sure if I were a woman I'd blow someone's brains out', mused one male liberal in *The Voyage Out* by Virginia Woolf, but now the Terence Hewets are on the receiving end of their own outrage. Some feminists have even gone so far as to assert that the growing passivity of males is the unconscious confession of a guilt which shades into downright masochism. Men's desire to be dominated by a masterful woman is seen as a manifestation of their shame in the face of their own sexuality, and the shame once visited upon women is now taken by men upon themselves.[19] This seems far-fetched. It is much more likely that men are simply rediscovering the 'female element' long suppressed in themselves, and enjoying it as much as Joyce, Yeats and Lawrence. Germaine Greer has expounded the benefits of the female-superior position, which permits women to respond more spontaneously, unrestricted by the weight of a heavier male body;[20]

but, more than half a century earlier, Joyce had also pronounced the method fully gratifying to the male. Greer's demand that lovemaking cease to be a male activity of which women are the passive judges is exemplary, but the decade since the publication of *The Female Eunuch* has seen the proliferation of manuals on total orgasm and sensuous womanhood which have merely augmented rather than challenged the traditional prejudice. There is still far too much emphasis on the workings of the female body and what men can do to it; and many discourses of recent years have heightened rather than questioned the prevailing obsession. Remarkably little is known as yet about the workings of the male body. If sex is to be freed from all forms of aggression, the first step must be a deeper awareness of the sexual character of both men and women, in their similarities and divergences. Much sexual violence and failure is due to what Virginia Woolf called the appalling gap between human conventions and human needs. If men and woman knew more about the rhythms of one another's bodies, they would be more likely to achieve greater physical pleasure, and to show an imaginative and loving tolerance when they do not.

For it is a fact that we *need* our sexual imperfections, just as much as we desire our own total gratification. The Yeats who celebrated the spiritual value of the near-miss knew well the meaning of Joyce's epic of bodily frustration – that the coupling of a man and woman is not just an expression of love but the occasion for more. Love is what allows men to embrace their imperfections and disappointments with the patience and tact which, more than any manual of the body, are the real book of love. We need our yearnings, too, for without them our acceptance of the lesser good would lack all heroism or imagination. To live in culture is to suppress at least as much of the self as we express, and that suppression is no shame, but an intelligent expression of joy in love. As Christopher Lasch has so movingly written: 'The abolition of sexual tensions is an unworthy goal in any case; the point is to live with them more gracefully than we have lived with them in the past.'[21]

THE LIMITS TO MASCULINITY AND FEMININITY

This does not mean an end to the efforts of men and women to harmonise their desires, but first they must know what those desires are. John Stuart Mill declared that what men called 'woman's nature' or 'femininity' was largely the result of social conditioning, and, in saying this, implied as much about 'masculinity'. 'Men indolently believe that the tree grows of itself in the way they have made it grow', he mocked; and he went on to deny that anybody could know the nature of the two sexes, 'so long as they have only been seen in their present relation to one another'.[22] Mill's point was endorsed by some of the foremost artists of his time. 'Women feel just as men feel', wrote Charlotte Brontë in 1847, 'they need exercise for their faculties and a field for their efforts as much as their brothers do.'[23] If femininity is largely a social construct, then so is masculinity, with the result that most lovers are mere impersonators of time-honoured conventions. The sensitive male who tries to simulate a robustness of manner which he does not truly feel is just as oppressed as the forceful woman who must deny herself in playing the role of simpering maiden. There is no doubt that this kind of conflict between personal desire and social convention troubled many a Victorian marriage, and even today, as in Thom Gunn's 'Carnal Knowledge', it retains the power to disturb:

> Even in bed I pose: desire may grow
> More circumstantial and less circumspect
> Each night, but an acute girl would suspect
> My thoughts might not be, like my body, bare.
> I wonder if you know, or, knowing, care?
> You know I know you know I know you know.
>
> I am not what I seem, believe me, so
> For the magnanimous pagan I pretend
> Substitute a forked creature as your friend.
> When darkness lies – without a roll or stir –
> Flaccid, you want a competent poseur
> Whose seeming is the only thing to know.
>
> I prod you, you react. Thus to and fro
> We turn, to see ourselves perform the same
> Comical act inside the tragic game.
> Or is it perhaps simpler: could it be
> A mere tear-jerker void of honesty
> In which there are no motives left to know?

Lie back. Within a minute I will stow
Your greedy mouth, but will not get to grips.
'There is a space between the breast and lips'.
Also a space between the thighs and head,
So great, we might as well not be in bed:
For we learn nothing here we did not know.

I hardly hoped for happy thoughts, although
In a most happy sleeping time I dreamt
We did not hold each other in contempt.
Then lifting from my lids night's penny weights
I saw that lack of love contaminates.
You know I know you know I know you know.

Abandon me to stammering, and go;
If you have tears, prepare to cry elsewhere –
I know of no emotion we can share.
Your intellectual protests are a bore,
And even now I pose, so now go, for
I know you know[24]

But how true is Angela Carter's allegation that this 'spurious charade of maleness and femaleness' still predominates, with the consequence that 'the act is taken away from us even as we perform it'?[25] This is questionable, based as it is on the extreme assumption that maleness and femaleness are always and only charades, attributable to conditioning. Like most conventions, these concepts have an immutable basis in human biology. Feminists may gleefully point out that only one of the forty-eight chromosomes determines the difference between men and women, but the difference is there all the same. That sense of difference may be *reduced*, in the interests of cooperation between the sexes, and in recognition of the scientific truth that 'the male and female patterns of sexual behaviour in man are much less distinctive than in other species'.[26] Corinne Hutt offers a balanced assessment in her finding that 'sexual dimorphism does not mean that certain characteristics are *exclusively* the property of one sex, but simply that they are more *typical* of one sex than the other. Thus, certain elements of sexual behaviour like mounting or lordosis may be shown by either sex, but in general they are shown more frequently, more definitively and more completely by one sex than the other.'[27] Biology may not be destiny, but it is a most powerful force in shaping human fates. 'The sexes are in everything alike', protests Kate Millett, 'save reproductive systems, secondary sexual characteristics, orgasmic capacity, and genetic and morphological structure.'[28] Such a string of qualifications amounts to a tidy sum, especially when taken in consort with their inevitable psychological consequences.

In separating sex from gender, the innate male and female from learned masculinity and femininity, psychologists like Jung made a valuable distinction; but they also sowed the seeds of confusion by fostering the illusion in superficial minds that gender roles could be altered or reversed at will.[29] The wide discrepancy between male demands and woman's desires is mistakenly seen as a mere result of social conditioning, which can be altered with a little cultural engineering. In an uncompromising rejoinder to such optimism, Beatrice Faust has shown just how fundamental are the discrepancies between the aggressive, impersonal, genital and abstract sexuality of the man and the personal, nurturing, tactile and emotional characteristics of the woman.[30] Faust has poured scorn on the glib claim of the Hite report that the differences can be reconciled by willed changes in men's sexuality. She argues:

> There are substantial differences in the way men and women are sexually aroused, significant differences in their erotic styles, and some differences in their sexual biology. These differences are produced by an interaction of culture and biology so complex that it makes no sense to say that either factor is more important than the other. The most important point is that there are differences between man and women and between male and female sexuality that must be accepted – no matter how unfashionable the idea of differences may be.[31]

Modern psychologists and anthropologists suggest that there is a dividing line to be drawn between the sexes, but that it has traditionally been drawn in the wrong place. The problem is now defined in the terms foreseen by Virginia Woolf – how to *extend* femininity rather than alter it, so that women can partake in endeavours from which they have been ritually excluded in the past.[32] For example, it has now been conclusively proven, contrary to Joyce's prejudice, that females excel males in all aspects of verbal ability: they talk earlier, have a wider vocabulary, write and spell better, showing superior competence in grammar and construction. Corinne Hutt, at the end of a systematic review of research, reached conclusions which may surprise feminists in the starkness of the contrast offered between male and female, but will certainly dismay men in disproving traditional assumptions of male superiority in such areas as language, moral sense and consistency:

> . . . the male is physically stronger but less resilient, he is more independent, adventurous and aggressive, he is more ambitious and competitive, he has greater spatial, numerical and mechanical ability, he is more likely to construe the world in terms of objects, ideas and theories. The female at the outset possesses those sensory capacities which facilitate interpersonal communion; physically and psychologically she matures more rapidly, her verbal skills are precocious and proficient, she is more nurturant, affiliative, more consistent, and is likely to construe the world in personal, moral and aesthetic terms.[33]

If women were permitted to apply these skills in areas traditionally dominated by men, they would renew both themselves and their chosen fields, challenging the male vices of competitiveness and specialisation. It will be recalled that Yeats urged all sensitive women to steer clear of universities, for the very reason that their specialist courses were a denial of the free-ranging imagination; but Virginia Woolf answered that the admission of women to colleges would in itself constitute a challenge to the competitive pedant and the rigid specialist.[34] Moreover, she felt that if such evils could not be abolished, then women 'at least should be permitted to suffer their effects on a basis of full equality with men'. Her indictment of scholarly specialists owes much to Ibsen. She castigated distinguished men who passed their lives 'howling about Greek and Latin texts, and calling each other names, for all the world like bookies on a race-course'.[35] Her espousal of androgyny, however, was her most important challenge to the specialist sexuality of male and female.

No matter how much progress is made along the lines commended by Woolf, there will always be differences between male and female sexuality. Our ancestors seem to have coped better with this problem, perhaps because they expected less from the experience of sexuality.[36] But they also brought to that experience a sense of fun which has been lost by modern lovers, who, as Lasch notes, approach their couplings with all the grim determination and anxious self-scrutiny once reserved for work.[37] The manuals which once told a carpenter or a tiler the skills of his craft have been swamped on the shelves by books which reveal the techniques of making love. Some shrewd commentators have explained all this as the attempt by a hedonistic society to purge its persistent feelings of guilt by presenting sex as part of the day's work, to be approached in the same systematic way as efficiency in the office or success on the field of sports. The Anglo-American suspicion of play is nowhere more obtrusive than in the work of certain female psychoanalysts, one of whom has written that 'the sexual act assumes an intense, dramatic, and profoundly aesthetic significance for the woman – but only this under the condition that it is expressed in a feminine, dynamic way and is not transformed into an act of erotic play or sexual "equality" '.[38] The implied equation between 'play' and 'equality' is revealing, since it confirms the suspicion that playfulness is the greatest democratiser of all. Only true equals can trust one another enough to submit together to the anarchic world of play. (Hence the anxiety of racialist regimes to keep negroes out of white sports.) A restored sense of playfulness may, however, be the best hope for a new sexuality. If man cannot purge his sexuality of its aggressive impulses, he might at once contain and express them in a mode of playful parody, epitomising both his ancient need for them and his modern doubts about their desirability. The immutable differences between men and women could be treated in a spirit of fun, with that cheerful acceptance of human limitation which is the basis of all true humour.

HOMO LUDENS, FEMINA LUDENS

C. S. Lewis has observed that it is God's own jape that 'a transcendent passion be linked in incongruous symbiosis with such mundane factors as weather, health, diet, circulation and digestion'.[39] Lewis's protest against the ludicrous solemnisation of modern sexuality is based on the conviction that Venus is a mischievous and mocking goddess:

When all external circumstances are fittest for her service she will leave one or both the lovers indisposed for it. When every overt act is impossible, and even glances cannot be exchanged – in trains, in shops and at interminable parties – she will assail them with all her force. An hour later, when time and place agree, she will have mysteriously withdrawn; perhaps from only one of them.[40]

This is an ancient attitude, but one healthier than our own. Implicit in it is the recognition that love can have no final fulfilment until after death and that the over-solemn expectations which modern lovers invest in relationships are a consequence of the loss of the idea of God.

By expecting less from their sexual experiences, our ancestors may have achieved more. They could accept the inadequacies of their partners as predictable and even funny, without lapsing into recrimination. According to Christopher Lasch, 'an easygoing, everyday contempt for the weaknesses of the other sex, institutionalised as folk wisdom concerning the emotional imcompetence of men or the brainlessness of women, kept sexual enmity within bounds and prevented it from becoming an obsession'.[41]

The solemnity with which gifted men such as Strindberg and Lawrence approach the subject is in marked contrast to all this, and demonstrates just how lacking is the element of play in the culture of high modernism. The laughter which Shakespeare and Molière found in the relations between men and women has no answering echo in the masters of the modern. The allegedly comic elements in the work of Joyce are scarcely playful and are based on a sense of transgression, of breaking down taboos, whereas play paradoxically demands strict obedience to rules and skilful improvisation within their constraints. All this is symptomatic of a civilisation which has dismissed play as a deviation from the norm, whereas, in the judgement of Johan Huizinga, it is in fact the basis for all culture. Culture, he says, does not produce play, but play produces culture. The child plays long before he thinks conceptually, and the adult man needs play in order to achieve a true accommodation with the world. Play is not just a harmless adjunct to, but a basic condition of, a full adult life. For Huizinga, the problem is 'not to define the place of play among all other manifestations of culture, but rather to ascertain how far culture itself bears the character of play'.[42] On the basis of these assumptions, it is possible to take Huizinga's argument a stage further, and to explain the reasons why playfulness has all but disappeared from the culture of the capitalist West. A society devoted to goals has little use for a goal-free activity, for capitalist man is justified by his products, whereas play is concerned with means rather than ends, with the quality of an action rather than its result. Rubem Alves has isolated one of the cultural contradictions of capitalism – the fact that 'a society dominated by the logic of production and consumption, the negation of play, is precisely the one to present itself as uniquely able to deliver play, as one of the products of consumption'.[43] But, in the process, play has been placed in the service of something which is not at all playful and has been degraded to the level of work. The executive who jogs for the sake of his appearance is no longer enjoying the action for its own sweet sake; and the couple who monitor their sexual performance with the clinical precision of body-mechanics are as far from the art of aesthetic loving as it is possible to be. In the permissive society, sex is the only remaining compulsory game.

ANDROGYNY AND SOCIETY

What is needed, more than anything else, is an acceptance of the rich varieties of human sexual experience, a celebration of 'the drunkenness of things being various'. Men will always be men, and women women, but no sooner has the modern critic isolated a 'masculine' attribute than he can think of half a dozen women of his acquaintance who possess that very trait to a greater or lesser degree. How else can we explain the strong masculine element in most conventionally attractive modern women? If aggressive self-assertion is a traditionally male attribute, then there is a strong masculine element in the overt appeal epitomised by many 'sexy' women, because the ideal contemporary woman is not self-conscious. It is widely accepted that many such women resent their own motherhood, since it can spoil their conventional good looks and exhaust their jealously-hoarded energy. For these very reasons, some of the most attractive modern women are amazingly masculine, just as the desirable modern male shows a traditionally 'feminine' concern about his aroma and appearance. Moreover, the traditional 'masculine' values of assertiveness, intrepidity and pugnacity are scarcely in keeping with the lives of most contemporary men, who want only security, love and peace for their gin-and-tonics. Patrick Lee has also pointed to the fact that men and women now live longer and have more years of leisure after retirement – 'since old age is a life stage in which sex differentiation tends to wane', he says, 'enhanced longevity means that our society now has relatively more people who place relatively less emphasis on differences between the sexes.'[44]

It is, therefore, of some importance that our laws should reflect the growing androgyny of our society. It is obvious that, for the foreseeable future, there will be more male engineers, coal-heavers or bus-drivers than women occupants of these posts; but this should not preclude women from equal access to such jobs, if they can provide the necessary competence. Equally, it would be helpful if employers could encourage the practice of job-sharing between husband and wife, so that many men might cease to be virtual strangers to their own children and many women would no longer feel chained to the kitchen sink. Whether employers respond to this challenge or not, the increase in general leisure as a result of a labour-saving technology in the home and at work will confirm these trends. The constant assault by politicians and captains of industry on the futility of the arts degree in a society already saturated with teachers makes little sense in this context, for, with the prospect of unemployment for some, increased leisure for many, and early retirement for all, it is important that people have the cultural resources to make the most of their free time. Our leaders must also begin to envisage a greater variety in the types of family for which they legislate, ranging from the extended family, through the nuclear unit, to the more experimental approach celebrated by Virginia Woolf in her account of the marriage of William Godwin and Mary Wollstonecraft:

> Godwin should have a room some doors off to work in; and they should dine out separately if they liked – their work, their friends, should be separate. Thus they settled it, and the plan worked admirably. The arrangement combined 'the novelty and lively sensation of a visit with the more delicious and heart-felt pleasures of domestic life'.[45]

A society more tolerant of a variety of sexual arrangements would value and respect those who live a single life, either by choice or necessity. Indeed, the attitude of a community to its single members is fast becoming the most accurate measure of its natural cohesiveness. In an ideal society, according to Lawrence, a Sue Bridehead would find a ready berth: 'If we had reverence for what we are, our life would take a real form, and Sue would have a place, as Cassandra had a place; she would have a place which does not yet exist, because we are all so vulgar, we have nothing.'[46]

In her outstanding book *Androgyny: Towards a New Theory of Sexuality*, June Singer has predicted such a society, based on a recognition of the androgyny of the full person. She persuasively argues that the archetype of the androgyne is at the base of much of the anxiety and jealousy surrounding love, 'because it points to the fear of being torn asunder from that other person who is required to be present for the rounding out of one's own personality'.[47] To be intelligently sensitive to the needs of one's lover calls for an ability to imagine oneself in that person's situation. This means that men must draw on the female resources in the self, like Leopold Bloom, or else run the risk that women will continue to complain of loneliness and isolation. An imaginative androgyny would prevent couples from forming unrealistic expectations of one another. In the past, says Singer, many conventional relationships foundered, because lovers were all too often attracted to a person through whom they could vicariously experience all those qualities which they had learned to suppress in themselves. The result was an expectation so intense that it deprived the partner of all freedom; or else 'the expectations that the other person would fill the void in one's personality were frequently not met'.[48] The ability to reincarnate elements of the opposite sex in the self is of crucial importance not only to people who live alone, but also to married persons who lose a partner or a close friend of the opposite sex.

CLOTHING AND SEXUALITY

In the cultivation of a variety of sexual possibility, men have a great deal to learn from women, who have been coopted with success into roles historically filled by males. During the First World War, women donned the trousers and overalls of tram-conductors and munition workers. Outside the workplace, the trend towards a masculine element in women's fashion continued, much to the chagrin of the editors of *Vogue*, who seized on the opportunity to reinforce traditionalist thinking. They advised every sweetheart to 'make it your business to see that he carries away with him on his return to duty a refreshing vision of loveliness, and in particular to avoid the masculine'.[49] Such ploys never fully worked. It is true that, during both world wars, while women donned dungarees for work, high fashions became more feminine than ever. But this is no contradiction – all it proves is that only in time of war were women free to express the full range of their personalities, their innate androgyny. Being allowed to express the male element in their overalls, they were also free to explore the outer fringes of femininity in their frills and dresses. Only the person who is permitted to articulate one whole side of himself without fear or favour has the confidence necessary to probe the other.

After the First World War, Dorothy Parker denounced the traditional employments of cook, nurse and maid as 'positively unfeminine'; and, with two out of every seven eligible men dead or wounded, many women looked to a future in which marriage was not an inevitability.[50] The boyish fashions of women in the 1920s may have carried the implication that 'women were asserting their new-won rights by dressing like men; or, alternatively, that they were trying to replace the young males who had died in World War One'.[51] 'One cannot help wishing for a less independent, less hard, more feminine product than the average twentieth-century girl', bemoaned *Vogue* in 1921.[52] All through the ensuing decade, it carried articles about 'The Modern Rosalind', about the difficulty which the older generation had in distinguishing girls from boys ('Did you say you were going up to Trinity or Girton next term?'), and about the hordes of females now going to men's shops to buy themselves cardigans, cravats, ties, V-neck sweaters, cuff-links and cigarette-holders.[53] If Ben Hecht could pronounce 'the masculinisation of women' as 'the most significant event to happen in my time',[54] Gertrude Stein could call gleefully for an accompanying feminisation of men. 'And what is a "He-man"?', she mockingly asked, 'Isn't it a large enough order to fill out the dimensions of all that "a man" has meant in the past? A "He-man"!' [55] Throughout the 1920s, younger and less overtly virile men took over as leaders of fashion in clothes which were 'no longer designed to make men look as large and powerful as possible'.[56]

Men still have much to learn from the attitude of women to clothing – and this takes us back to the need for a play-element in culture. If men are ever to recapture this lost playfulness, they must learn to emulate the woman's capacity to be intermittently unserious, to withhold a part of herself in ironic detachment. The greater variety of clothing worn by women has been attributed to the fact that men are deemed admirable if they project a stable self-image, whereas women are judged attractive if they are skilful exponents of a multiple self. Erving Goffmann has made a detailed study of these matters in *Gender Advertisements*, in the course of which he contrasts the intense seriousness of the male about his clothing with the childlike or clowning guise so often adopted by female models. This indicates woman's 'readiness to try out various possibilities to see what comes of it'.[57] These possibilities may range from sobriety to self-mockery. Most feminists would infer from this that a sexist advertising cons women into consuming far more products than men and, worse still, into presenting themselves as less serious participants in social situations. Future commentators may judge otherwise and conclude that the dreary predictability of male clothing for most of the twentieth century – even when such caution was no longer necessary in an era of cheap, machine-produced but surprisingly beautiful garments – was merely the vestige of a prim Victorianism which had long disappeared in personal behaviour and social practice. The sudden extremes of long hair, kaftans and multicoloured coats sported by males in the 1960s may have been a protest against a century of dull conformity. If this was, in modern times, a rare sartorial revolt by the female jailed within the male, one can only regret the current return to drab garb as a pathetic regression.

THE PERILS OF ANDROGYNY

In times of affluence or war, when people have the means and the opportunities to express all aspects of their personalities, an androgynous style has flourished; but during economic recessions the sexes are forced back into traditional moulds. It was in the 1930s, after all, that Garbo and Dietrich were denounced when first they appeared in trousers. The reaction of many males to mannish elements in women is often one of hostility and suspicion, though this can be mingled with fascination as well. There may well be an element of narcissism in that fascination, since the male element in woman can act as a mirror to the man, just as the female hidden in the male can find an answering image in the woman. The projection of sophisticated power by a Garbo-style woman is not at all asexual or anti-sexual in its effect, for in issuing a smouldering challenge, it adds to the excitement of the male desire for conquest. Only the greatest obstacle which can be contemplated without despair, said Yeats, rouses the will to full intensity. The woman who is not easily to be won exerts more power and fascination than the one who is merely coy, and this can increase the eventual pleasure of both partners. Unfortunately, much of the evidence in preceding chapters shows that this does not often work in reverse. The man who is continuously passive offers no great challenge to the woman. Many androgynous heroes, from Orsino to Orlando, from Ralph Touchett to Leopold Bloom, have been morally and emotionally admirable while remaining sexually unsatisfactory.

At his best, as in the case of a Jude Fawley or a Rupert Birkin, the androgynous male is capable of passivity *and* activity, for he has rediscovered his own variousness. A. H. Maslow has remarked that healthy people make no absolute differentiation between the roles of man and woman. Such people are so certain of their own maleness or femaleness that they do not mind adopting aspects of the opposite sex role. 'It was especially noteworthy', says Maslow of his research, 'that they could be both passive and active lovers.'[58] At the root of androgyny, therefore, is the need to embrace the 'opposite' in the self. There is always a danger that such a healthy androgyny may decline into mere narcissism; but the true androgyne is alway in communion with the 'other', whereas the narcissist is locked in a self-caressing relationship with himself. That decadence is to be seen in the fact that for many people today the only romance is with their own bodies; and this decline can be charted in the difference between the advertisements of forty years ago, in which a handsome woman beckoned, and the contemporary hoarding, where she is most often in a pose erotically caressing herself. This may reflect an underlying trend in the behaviour of couples, more and more of whom are reportedly enjoying the spectacle of mutual masturbation.[59] All sexuality has become hopelessly reified and Germaine

Greer is right to bemoan the cult of clitoral stimulation as the ultimate 'index of the desexualising of the whole body, the substitution of genitality for sexuality'.[60] 'We still make love to organs and not people' is her just plaint, so that 'far from realising that people are never more idiosyncratic, never more totally *there* than when they make love, we are never more incommunicative, never more alone'.[61]

Equally distressing is the fact that much female narcissism is merely a reinforcement of male hegemony. This is clear from John Berger's account of the convention underlying Tintoretto's painting of Susannah looking at herself in a mirror:

> The mirror was often used as a symbol of the vanity of a woman. The moralising, however, was mostly hypocritical. You painted a naked woman because you enjoyed looking at her, you put a mirror in her hand and you called the painting *Vanity*, thus morally condemning the woman whose nakedness you had depicted for your own pleasure.
>
> The real function of the mirror was otherwise. It was to make the woman connive in treating herself as, first and foremost, a sight.[62]

Berger's bleak conclusion is that woman, 'born into the keeping of man', is continually accompanied by her own image of herself, split quite literally in two. 'Whilst she is walking across a room or whilst she is weeping at the death of her father, she can scarcely avoid envisaging herself walking or weeping.'[63] Yet many women seem to have fallen under the spell of this convention, to the point where they now actually *enjoy* the male fetish which they impersonate, as opposed to merely tolerating it, like the barmaids in Joyce's novel. Beatrice Faust even claims that sex objects may perceive themselves as sex subjects and derive actual erotic pleasure from walking in high heels and corsets:

> Walking in high heels makes the buttocks undulate about twice as much as walking in flat heels, with correspondingly greater sensation transmitted to the vulva. Girdles can encourage pelvic tumescence and, if they are long enough, cause labial friction during movement.[64]

So, Marilyn Monroe's sensational walk is actually an experience in auto-eroticosm and the sex-goddess becomes the unlikely paragon for those militant feminists who deem men redundant to a fulfilled sexuality. Those gawking males who whistled at Monroe are exposed as redundant voyeurs of a self-delighting performance, versions of Michael Robartes lost in admiration for a self-sufficient dancer he can never hope to know.

Many contemporary women, desirous of male adulation, feel only contempt for those men who can so easily be manipulated to give it. The same is true of a growing number of men who have learned, like Leopold Bloom, how to groom themselves to best effect in the eyes of an onlooking woman. Such compulsive narcissism has not brought fulfilment, but the reverse. 'Unable to express emotion without calculating its effect on others', says Christopher Lasch, 'the narcissist doubts the authenticity of its expression in others and therefore derives little comfort from audience reactions to his own performance, even when the audience claims to be deeply moved.'[65] The 'liberated' notion of the body as a mechanism to be serviced and perfected by its narcissistic owner is a far cry from the idealism of John Stuart Mill who preached feminism as a challenge to 'selfish propensities' and 'self-worship'.[66] Yet the impulse to narcissism has never been stronger, and in so far as some feminists preach a gospel of female self-sufficiency, they collude with Mill's enemy.

LOVE AND DEATH

A true feminism would not assert woman's independence of man, but would firmly remind men of *their* dependence on women. 'Dependency' is not a concept favoured by radicals, but in fact it is only through a universal recognition of our interdependence that the dream of a socialist society will be fulfilled. There *is* a biological difference between men and women, and in that lies our greatest hope. 'Division serves a purpose', writes Jeannette Kupfermann, who believes that it promotes notions of reciprocity and exchange.[67] The attempt to minimise the sexual division of labour is seen by her as a misguided assault on the social fabric by 'the first civilisation in the history of mankind to attempt to eliminate all differences between the sexes'.[68] This is surely true. To deny *any* intrinsic meaning to the notions 'male' and 'female' is to deny the very possibility of a balanced androgynous personality and, equally, of a harmonious interdependent society. Margaret Mead had questioned the excessive erosion of sexual distinctions as early as 1962 and had warned that 'simply compensating for differences is a form of denial'.[69] Yet that denial persists in the crazy search for absolute equivalence, which flies in the face of the fact that the male element is most often a minor and subsidiary component of the female personality, and vice-versa. We need to remind ourselves that the men and women who rediscovered our androgyny for us made no stipulations about equivalence. 'Every man comprises male and female in his being, the male always struggling for predominance', wrote Lawrence, 'a woman likewise consists in male and female, with the female predominant.'[70] Nothing could be more inimical to the open spirit of androgyny than the pedantry of a woman who wonders if it is wrong to ask her husband to 'help' with the baby, since the verb seems to assert her maternal priority. Indeed, the recent spate of literature pronouncing motherhood an 'invention' or 'fiction' of corrupt modern societies may well do great harm, if it encourages the delusion that women are not, in some degree at least, the products of their own biology.

Scientific studies of the subject, by men and women, lead inexorably to Corinne Hutt's conclusion that 'a woman's primary role is that of motherhood and most women have some or other of the attributes which fit them for this role'.[71] It could be added that female exponents of such traditionally 'male' virtues as endurance, courage and intrepidity find a more challenging outlet for these in the experience of childbirth and motherhood than in most of the dull office routines to which both men and women are increasingly condemned. Given the biological facts, Hutt finds that 'the pursuit of a career for the mother of a young family is an arduous and conflict-ridden undertaking'.[72] Much pain and conflict would be avoided if working women and their husbands would admit this, rather than maintaining the pretence that the opposite is true. Most women who have tried to reconcile motherhood with another career know that fulfilment in one area of their lives is often achieved only at the expense of suffering and even shame in the other. It need hardly be added that the heart-rending conflicts experienced by such women arise not from stunted self-hatred but from feelings of thwarted love.

The devaluation of motherhood and the assault on family life are telltale marks of a society that has lost its sense of community.

Love is not necessarily innate in the person, but has to be learned through time and experience; and the family is the most likely zone for that learning. To turn over the care and education of children to more public institutions would free woman to be a human being, says Kate Millett;[73] but the evidence of psychologists suggests that in doing so, woman would suppress far more of herself than she would express. The extended community of Engels, Ibsen and Jude Fawley must remain a utopian vision, but also a warning against the *égoisme a deux* and family chauvinism which the capitalist economy so easily breeds. The criticisms of the family voiced by Ibsen, Strindberg, Hardy and Lawrence are certainly representative of the prevailing attitude of a modernist generation which found its motto in André Gide's 'Familles, je vous hais!', but this was inevitable in a generation which had come to see the artistic vocation as a holy calling.[74] By converting the practice of literature into an all-consuming sacred cult, the modernists ensured that it could only be produced by men and women who had virtually all turned their backs on family life. Those like Joyce who tried to pursue a specialist art *and* to support a wife and children found just how painfully incompatible the two were. And yet Joyce died, as he had lived, a simple middle-class man, with an unaffected scorn for bohemian life and a staunch conviction of the family as the only zone where individuals can thrive and at the same time prepare for life in the social world.

There is nothing inherently wrong with the family as a unit where love is learned and training for society begins. It is only when the family is invaded by the capitalist ethic that sex becomes a mode of aggressive exploitation and love is lost. 'Do not think you can make good republicans so long as you isolate in their families the children who should belong to the republic alone', wrote the Marquis de Sade in *Philosophy in the Boudoir*; but the republican utopia of his dreams is a nightmare land where 'human beings, reduced to their sexual organs, become absolutely anonymous and interchangeable', with the same dreary obligation to 'enjoy and be enjoyed'.[75] The enemy of love is not the family but the *laissez-faire* ethic of capitalism, and the enemy of the family is not a true feminism but capitalism itself. The utopia prophesied by de Sade may be an advertising man's dream, but it is a socialist's nightmare.

Love is our only final challenge to time, and so Jung was right to remark, towards the end of his autobiography, that everybody should form a conception of his own life after death. Inevitably, children are the most tangible assurance that something of a man or woman survives their own passing, but without the notion of God or of the socialist community or of some life force, the relation of parent and child may become clutching. Similarly, the relation of man and woman may be crippled by excessive expectation, without the shared recognition that the impulse to love has no final fulfilment until after death. In the act of love, we are not merely ourselves, but representatives of forces older and less personal – whether we call them 'God' or the 'life force' is unimportant.[76] What is vital is that this intimation of death should be implicitly present in all our protestations of love. 'I do not believe I have ever heard a clergyman use as his theme for the wedding the implicit imminence of death', concludes June Singer in *Androgyny*, 'and the importance of living each day, each moment of a marital relationship with the awareness that each party to it must be whole in herself or himself so that, when the inevitable parting comes, preparation will have been made.'[77] So ageing couples seem to grow more and more alike as they near death. If something of the dead partner is left in the one who remains, then doubtless something of the bereaved has been taken by the dead one into another world. It is this which gives rise to Swedenborg's strange but compelling idea that those who have loved truly on earth may in heaven become a single angel.

Conclusion

The obsession with 'personal relations' in modern writing was denounced in recent decades as a defeatist evasion of the social world, but may now be seen to have been the beginnings of an attempt to imagine and build an entirely new kind of society. Ibsen's boast was that he always started with the individual – but he ended invariably with the world, and that is true of all the authors treated here. In retrospect, it seems ironic that those very radicals who, in the 1960s and 1970s, derided the modernists as political reactionaries, should in the same period have loudly applauded the feminist tracts which derived so much honest inspiration from these same writers. This inconsistency marred the case against Yeats and Lawrence from the start. On the one hand, they were accused of save-your-own-soulism, of elevating the personal above the social; on the other hand, they were alleged to have preached neo-fascist social theory. In fact, the real crime of the modernists was to have been so far ahead of their time that they virtually lost touch with it; and now that their ideas have been rendered commonplace by the new wave of feminist criticism, the world is in danger of forgetting just how radical were the sexual theories, as well as the literary forms, practised by these six men.

Notes and References

CHAPTER ONE

1. Bernice W. Kliman, 'Women in Early English Literature: *Beowulf* to the *Ancrene Wisse*', *Nottingham Medieval Studies*, XXI (1977) p. 32–49.
2. W. B. Yeats, 'On Baile's Strand', *Collected Plays* (London, 1952) p. 259.
3. Wendy Doninger O'Flaherty, *Women, Androgynes and Other Mythical Beasts* (Chicago, 1980) p. 288.
4. Ibid., p. 311.
5. Ibid., p. 293.
6. Marie Delcourt, *Hermaphrodite*, trans. J. Nicholson (London, 1961) pp. 82–3.
7. A. J. L. Busst, 'The Image of the Androgyne in the Nineteenth Century', *Romantic Mythologies*, ed. Ian Fletcher (London, 1967) p. 9.
8. Quoted ibid., p. 26.
9. Ibid., p. 27.
10. Elémire Zolla, *The Androgyne: Fusion of the Sexes* (London, 1981) p. 28.
11. Reay Tannahill, *Sex in History* (London, 1977) p. 165.
12. Leslie Fiedler, *The Stranger in Shakespeare* (London, 1973) p. 21.
13. Ibid., p. 33.
14. Juliet Dusinberre, *Shakespeare and the Nature of Women* (London, 1975) p. 251.
15. Ibid., p. 159.
16. See Helen Gardner, 'As You Like It', *Shakespeare's Comedies*, ed. L. Lerner (Harmondsworth, 1967) p. 238.
17. Quoted ibid., p. 241.
18. Quoted by Dusinberre, p.251; see George Meredith, 'An Essay on Comedy', *The Idea of Comedy*, ed. W. K. Wimsatt (New Jersey, 1979) p. 248.
19. C. L. Barber, 'Liberty Testing Courtesy', *Twentieth Century Interpretations of Twelfth Night*, ed. Walter King (New Jersey, 1968) p. 50.
20. Walter King, Introduction, ibid., p. 12.
21. Dusinberre, pp. 257–8.
22. Ibid., p. 263.
23. Ibid., p. 267.
24. Clara Claiborne Park, 'As We Like It – How a Girl Can Be Smart and Still Popular', *The American Scholar*, 42 (Spring 1973) p. 262–8.
25. There is an interesting discussion of this aspect of the play in D. W. Winnicott, *Playing and Reality* (Harmondsworth, 1971) pp. 98–9.

26. Marianne Novy, 'Shakespeare's Female Characters as Actors and Audience', *The Woman's Part : Feminist Criticisms of Shakespeare*, eds Lenz, Greene and Neely (Illinois, 1980) pp. 256–71.

27. Dusinberre, p. 285.

28. This is more fully discussed in its wider mystical context by Elémire Zolla, pp. 30–1.

29. Ian Watt, 'Defoe as Novelist: *Moll Flanders*', in *Twentieth Century Views on Defoe*, ed. Max Byrd (New Jersey, 1976) pp. 117–19. From *The Rise of the Novel* (California, 1956) pp. 108–15.

30. Maximilian E. Novak, 'Conscious Irony in *Moll Flanders*', *20th Century Interpretations of MF*, ed. Robert Elliott (New Jersey 1970) p. 44.

31. Virginia Woolf, 'Defoe', ibid., p. 15; from *The Common Reader* (London, 1933) pp. 121–31.

32. See Jean Hagstrum, *Sex and Sensibility: Ideal and Erotic Love from Milton to Mozart* (London, 1980); and R. F. Brissenden, *Virtue in Distress: Studies in the Novel of Sentiment from Richardson to Sade* (London, 1974).

33. Terry Eagleton, *The Rape of Clarissa* (Oxford, 1982) pp. 14–15.

34. Ibid., p. 96.

35. Ibid., p. 99.

36. Katherine Rogers, *Feminism in Eighteenth Century England* (Illinois, 1982) p. 2.

37. Ibid., pp. 55–6.

38. Quoted ibid., p. 59.

39. Quoted ibid., p. 60.

40. Quoted ibid., p. 60.

41. Ibid., pp. 61–2.

42. Martin Green and Bernard McCabe, 'Herman Melville', *American Literature to 1900*, ed. M. Cunliffe (London, 1973) pp. 228–9.

43. Ibid., p. 250. This entire essay is one of the most incisive, and neglected, analyses of the mind and art of Melville.

44. Tannahill, *Sex In History*, p. 383.

45. Isabelle de Courtivron, 'Weak Men and Fatal Woman: The Sand Image', *Homosexualities and French Literature*, eds Stambolian and Marks (Cornell, 1979) pp. 222–3.

46. Ibid. This summarises the conclusions reached on the basis of research by Robert Stoller and Karen Horney.

47. Frederick Crews, 'Frustration and Guilt: The Ruined Wall', *Twentieth Century Interpretations of The Scarlet Letter*, ed. John Gerber (New Jersey, 1968) pp. 96–7.

48. D. H. Lawrence, *Studies in Classic American Literature* (Harmondsworth, 1971) p. 88.

49. Ibid., p. 94.

50. Ibid., p. 91.

51. Crews, 'Frustration and Guilt: The Ruined Wall', p. 94.

52. There is a brilliant analysis of this element in the relationship in Elizabeth Hardwick, *Seduction and Betrayal* (New York, 1970). See final chapter, pp. 177–205.

53. James T. Fields, *Yesterdays with Authors* (Boston, 1900) p. 122.

54. James Russell Lowell, *Poetical Works* (Cambridge, Mass., 1890) vol. 3,

p. 60. My attention was drawn to this and the preceding quotation by Larzer Ziff, *Literary Democracy* (Harmondsworth, 1982) pp. 137–8.

55. Wendy Doninger O'Flaherty, p. 284.
56. Busst, p. 9.
57. Ibid., pp. 43–53.
58. See Busst, pp. 56ff. for this feature of German Romanticism.
59. Mircea Eliade, *Mephistopheles and the Androgyne* (New York, 1965) p. 100.
60. I owe this formulation to Lionel Trilling who applied it to the vision of E. M. Forster.
61. June Singer, *Androgyny: Towards a New Theory of Sexuality* (London, 1977) p. 34.
62. Oscar Wilde, *The Artist as Critic: Critical Writings of Oscar Wilde*, ed. R. Ellmann (London, 1970) p. 86.
63. The implications of this for literary studies are brilliantly discussed by J. E. Rivers, *Proust and the Art of Love: The Aesthetics of Sexuality in the Life, Times and Art of Marcel Proust* (New York, 1980) pp. 35ff. My application of the idea of the homosexually-oriented person to Wilde is based on the same methodology.
64. Quoted by Rivers, p. 53.
65. Quoted by Ronald Pearsall, *The Worm in the Bud: The World of Victorian Sexuality* (Harmondsworth, 1983) p. 106.
66. Quoted ibid., p. 425.
67. James Laver, *The Concise History of Costume and Fashion* (New York, 1969) p. 54.
68. Virginia Woolf, *A Room of One's Own* (Harmondsworth, 1967) p. 102.
69. Ibid., p. 57.

CHAPTER TWO

1. August Strindberg, *Samlade Skifter*, xxxviii, p. 155–6, quoted by O. Reinert (translator), 'Introduction' to *Twentieth Century Views on Strindberg* (New Jersey, 1971) p. 9.
2. Letter to Georg Brandes, 1890. Quoted ibid., p. 1.
3. See Chapter 8.
4. Germaine Greer, *The Female Eunuch* (London, 1971) p. 90.
5. Joseph Wood Krutch, *'Modernism' in Modern Drama* (New York, 1966) pp. 31–2.
6. August Strindberg, 'Preface to *Miss Julie*', *Seven Plays by August Strindberg*, trans. Arvid Paulson (New York, 1972) p. 69.
7. Mary Ellmann, *Thinking About Women* (London, 1979) p. 127.
8. Christopher Lasch, *The Culture of Narcissism* (London, 1980) pp. 330 ff.
9. Philippe Ariès, *Centuries of Childhood* (Harmondsworth, 1973) pp. 98–124.
10. Michel Foucault, *The History of Sexuality*, vol. 1 (London, 1979) p. 19.
11. Ibid., p. 72.
12. This quotation from Vivisektioner (1887) is translated and cited by Arvid Paulson in his invaluable essay 'Probing Strindberg's Psyche', *The Strindberg Reader*, p. 434.

13. For an extended discussion of this see Lionel Trilling, 'Mansfield Park', *The Opposing Self* (Oxford, 1980) pp. 181–202.
14. Strindberg, 'Preface to *Miss Julie*', pp. 66–7.
15. Quoted by Robert Brustein, 'August Strindberg', *Twentieth Century Views on Strindberg*, p. 35.
16. August Strindberg, 'An Attempt at Reform', *The Strindberg Reader*, compiled, trans. and ed. Arvid Paulson (New York, 1968) p. 8.
17. August Strindberg, 'The Stronger One', *The Strindberg Reader*, p. 12.
18. Letter to Harriet Bosse, 28 August 1901; translated by Arvid Paulson and reproduced in *The Strindberg Reader*, p. 420.
19. Robert Brustein, 'August Strindberg', *Twentieth Century Views on Strindberg*, p. 40.
20. August Strindberg, 'An Attempt at Reform', *The Strindberg Reader*, p. 8.

CHAPTER THREE

1. Quoted by Rodelle Weintraub, 'Introduction', *Fabian Feminist: Bernard Shaw and Woman* (Pennsylvania, 1977) pp. 1–13.
2. Quoted by Michael Meyer, *Ibsen: A Biography* (Harmondsworth, 1971) p. 687.
3. Quoted ibid., p. 46.
4. Quoted ibid., p. 293. Source: Martin Schneekloth.
5. Quoted ibid., p. 799. Source: Bergliot.
6. Ibid., p. 776.
7. Ibid., p. 180.
8. James Joyce, 'Ibsen's New Drama' (1900), *James Joyce: The Critical Writings*, eds Ellsworth Mason and Richard Ellmann (New York, 1959) p. 64.
9. Quoted by Arthur Power, *Conversations with James Joyce* (London, 1974) p. 35.
10. Quoted by Meyer, pp. 345–6.
11. Ibid., p. 817.
12. Quoted ibid., p. 466.
13. John Northam, 'Ibsen's Search for the Hero', *Ibsen: A Collection of Critical Essays*, ed. Rolf Fjelde (New Jersey, 1965) p. 107.
14. Ronald Gray, *Ibsen: A Dissenting View* (Cambridge, 1977) p. 57.
15. Lionel Trilling expressed this idea in the context of an essay on Forster.
16. James Joyce, 'Ibsen's New Drama', p. 64. He is describing Irene in *When We Dead Awaken*.
17. Quoted by George H. Ford, 'The Victorian Age', *Norton Anthology of English Literature* (New York, 1979) p. 940.
18. See Meyer, pp. 635–40; and in relation to Hilda Wangel, pp. 653–4 and 731.
19. F. W. Kaufmann, 'Ibsen's Conception of Truth', *Ibsen: A Collection of Critical Essays*, p. 26.
20. Leo Lowenthal, 'Henrik Ibsen: Motifs in the Realistic Plays', in *Ibsen: A Collection of Critical Essays*, p. 147.
21. Quoted by Rolf Fjelde, Foreword, *Ibsen: Four Major Plays* (New York, 1965) p. xvi.

22. Meyer, p. 661.
23. Meyer, p. 727
24. Meyer, p. 654.
25. Muriel Bradbrook, *Ibsen the Norwegian: A Revaluation* (London, 1969) p. 124.
26. C. G. Jung, 'Marriage as a Psychological Relationship', *The Portable Jung*, ed. Joseph Campbell (Harmondsworth, 1976) pp. 173–4.
27. Ibid., p. 174.
28. Ibid., p. 175.
29. Ibid., p. 168.
30. Ibid., p. 171.
31. Quoted by Lowenthal, p. 153; from Ibsen, *Nachgelassene Schriften*, eds Elias and Koht (Berlin, 1909) vol. 1, p. 206. The idea that Hilda might be 'the daimon which is finally introjected into Solness's psyche so that his personality is extended *ad infinitum*' was first suggested by Richard Schechner, in 'The Unexpected Visitor in Ibsen's Late Plays' (1962), reprinted in *Ibsen: A Collection of Critical Essays*, pp. 158–68. Subsequently, Ronald Gray saw Hilda as an example of wish-fulfilment, 'Solness's own fantasies coming from the outside world to meet him' (*Ibsen: A Dissenting View*, p. 161). But, far from being the embodiment of a wish, Hilda seems to me to be an example of the return of the repressed.

CHAPTER FOUR

1. Lionel Trilling, 'Mansfield Park', *The Opposing Self* (Oxford, 1980) p. 193.
2. Irving Howe, *Thomas Hardy* (London, 1968) p. 144.
3. See Patricia Stubbs, *Women and Fiction: Feminism and the Novel, 1880–1920* (Sussex, 1979) pp. 81 ff.
4. Elizabeth Hardwick, 'Sue and Arabella', *The Genius of Thomas Hardy* (London, 1976) p. 71.
5. Marina Warner, *Joan of Arc: The Image of Female Heroism* (London, 1981) pp. 145–6.
6. Ibid., p. 147.
7. Ibid., pp. 151, 153, 148.
8. Ibid., p. 155.
9. D. H. Lawrence, 'From *Study of Thomas Hardy*', *A Selection from Phoenix*, ed. A. A. H. Inglis (Harmondsworth, 1979) p. 236.
10. Ibid., p. 237.
11. Ibid., p. 242.
12. Ibid., p. 252.
13. Alison Lurie, *The Language of Clothes* (New York, 1981) p. 229.
14. Ibid., p.229.
15. Terry Eagleton, Introduction, *Jude the Obscure* (London, 1974) p. 15.
16. Quoted by F. E. Hardy, *The Later Years of Thomas Hardy* (London, 1930) p. 42.
17. Shere Hite, *The Hite Report on Male Sexuality* (London, 1981), especially pp. 545–7, 'Masturbating with a Partner'.

18. For the modern parallel see Christopher Lasch, *The Culture of Narcissism* (London, 1980) pp. 39–40.
19. For the contemporary evasion of the inner life, see Lasch, pp. 29–30.
20. Ibid., pp. 80–2.
21. Ibid., pp. 326–7.
22. Irving Howe, p. 142.
23. Ernst Fischer, *The Necessity of Art* (Harmondsworth, 1978); see especially 'The Loss and Discovery of Reality', pp. 197–225.
24. Lasch, pp. 174–9.

CHAPTER FIVE

1. W. B. Yeats, *Autobiographies* (London, 1955) p. 485.
2. A. N. Jeffares, 'Women in Yeats's Poetry', *The Circus Animals: Essays* (London, 1970) pp. 78–81.
3. *Letters of W. B. Yeats*, ed. Allan Wade (London, 1954) p. 867.
4. W. B. Yeats, *Memoirs*, ed. D. Donoghue (London, 1972) pp. 86–8. The Jeffares version reads 'Kent', the Donoghue 'Kew'.
5. *Letters*, p. 468.
6. Hesketh Pearson, *Bernard Shaw: His Life and Personality* (London, 1942) pp. 120–1.
7. *Letters*, p. 472.
8. *Ah, Sweet Dancer: W. B. Yeats/Margot Ruddock – A Correspondence*, ed. Roger McHugh (London, 1970) p. 42 (11 August 1935).
9. David Lynch, *Yeats: The Poetics of the Self* (London, 1979) p. 180.
10. 'Women in the Civil Service' (17 December 1925), *The Senate Speeches of W. B. Yeats*, ed. Donald R. Pearce (Indiana, 1960) pp. 104–5.
11. 'Divorce: An Undelivered Speech' (March 1925), *Senate Speeches*, p. 157.
12. Donald Davie, 'Michael Robartes and the Dancer', *An Honoured Guest: New Essays on W. B. Yeats*, eds D. Donoghue and J. R. Mulryne (London, 1965) pp. 73–87.
13. Quoted by Frank Tuohy, *Yeats* (Dublin, 1976) p. 175.
14. *Letters*, p. 31.
15. Ibid., p. 123.
16. Ibid., p. 414.
17. Ibid., p. 423.
18. Quoted by A. N. Jeffares, *A Commentary on the Collected Poems of W. B. Yeats* (Stanford, 1968) p. 101.
19. Quoted ibid., p. 101.
20. W. B. Yeats, *Autobiographies*, p. 464.
21. C. G. Jung, 'Marriage as a Psychological Relationship', *Portable Jung*, p. 173.
22. Quoted by Kermode, *Romantic Image* (London, 1971) p. 92; W. B. Yeats, 'The Tragic Theatre', *Essays and Introductions* (London, 1961) pp. 243–4.
23. *Letters*, p. 117.
24. Jung, 'Marriage', p. 174.
25. Ibid., p. 176.

26. Quoted by Jeffares, *Commentary*, p. 223.
27. Ibid., p.223.
28. Jung, 'Marriage', p. 171.
29. Ibid., p. 172.
30. A. J. L. Busst, 'The Image of the Androgyne in the Nineteenth Century', *Romantic Mythologies*, ed. Ian Fletcher (London, 1967), p. 63.
31. Quoted by David Lynch, p. 31; and footnote 47.
32. *Letters*, pp. 799–80.
33. June Singer, *Androgyny: Towards a New Theory of Sexuality* (London, 1977) p. 246.
34. W. B. Yeats, *Autobiographies*, p. 504.
35. *Letters*, p. 810.
36. Ibid., p. 810.
37. Frank Kermode, *Romantic Image*, pp. 61 and 97 ff.
38. *Letters*, p. 824.
39. Quoted by Kermode, p. 91.
40. W. B. Yeats, 'Certain Noble Plays of Japan', *Essays and Introductions*, p. 223.
41. Elémire Zolla, *The Androgyne: Fusion of the Sexes* (London, 1981) p. 55.
42. June Singer, p. 212.
43. W. B. Yeats, 'The Symbolism of Poetry', *Essays and Introductions*, p. 164.
44. W. B. Yeats, *Autobiographies*, p. 331.
45. W. Rothenstein, *Since Fifty*, p. 242. Quoted Jeffares, *Commentary*, p. 372.
46. *Letters*, p. 824.
47. Marina Warner, *Alone of All Her Sex; The Myth and Cult of the Virgin Mary* (London, 1976) p. 338.
48. *Letters*, p. 46.
49. *Letters*, p. 868.
50. *Letters*, pp. 831–2.
51. *Letters*, p. 875.
52. *Letters*, p. 868.
53. Frances G. Wickes, *The Inner World of Choice* (London, 1977) p. 169.
54. For another Jungian analysis, see James Olney, *The Rhizome and the Flower: The Perennial Philosophy of Yeats and Jung* (Berkeley, 1980), especially pp. 308–15. Noteworthy is the quotation from Jung, p. 312, 'as the *anima* produces moods, so the *animus* produces opinions'. Note also 315, for a parallel account of how Yeats 'succeeded, to a fuller degree than most people, in bringing the feminine aspect of his personality into consciousness'.
55. Wickes, p. 183.
56. Ibid., p. 184.
57. *Letters*, p. 434.
58. Wickes, p. 188.
59. June Singer, p. 147.
60. Jung, 'Marriage', p. 165.
61. Wickes, p. 209.
62. *Letters*, p. 63.
63. Wickes, p. 187.
64. June Singer, p. 261.
65. Quoted by Jeffares, *Commentary*, p. 370.
66. James Carney, *The Irish Bardic Poet* (Dublin, 1967) p. 13.

67. Ibid., p. 38.
68. *Letters*, p. 790.
69. *Letters*, p. 108. To John O'Leary.
70. Quoted by Jeffares, *Commentary*, p. 454.
71. Quoted by John Unterecker, *A Reader's Guide to W. B. Yeats* (London, 1959) p. 239.
72. W. B. Yeats, *Memoirs*, p. 334; *Autobiographies*, p. 469.
73. Quoted by Jeffares, *Commentary*, p. 376.
74. W. B. Yeats, *Autobiographies*, p. 341.
75. June Singer, p. 269.
76. W. B. Yeats, 'The Need for Audacity of Thought', *Uncollected Prose*, vol. 1, ed. John P. Frayne (London, 1970) pp. 462–3.
77. W. B. Yeats, 'The Censorship and St Thomas Aquinas', ibid., pp. 478–9.
78. W. B. Yeats, *Autobiographies*, p. 333.
79. Ibid., p. 500.

CHAPTER SIX

1. Anonymous, Review of *The White Peacock*, *Morning Post*, 9 February 1911; reprinted in H. Coombes (ed.), *Penguin Critical Anthology: D. H. Lawrence* (Harmondsworth, 1973) p. 62.
2. Cited in Coombes, pp. 79–80.
3. Philippa Tristram, 'Eros and Death – Lawrence, Freud and Woman', *Lawrence and Women*, ed. Anne Smith (London, 1978) p. 143.
4. Robert B. Heilman, 'Nomad, Monad and the Mystique of the Soma', *Twentieth Century Interpretations of 'Women in Love'*, ed. Stephen J. Miko (New Jersey, 1969) p. 101.
5. D. H. Lawrence, *A Selection from Pheonix*, ed. A. A. H. Inglis (Harmondsworth, 1971) p. 578.
6. *Collected Letters of D. H. Lawrence*, ed. Harry T. Moore (London, 1962) p. 44.
7. June Singer. *Androgyny: Towards a New Theory of Sexuality* (London, 1977) p. 327.
8. Wendy Doninger O'Flaherty, *Women, Androgynes and Other Mythical Beasts* (Chicago, 1980) p. 293.
9. Kate Millett, *Sexual Politics* (London, 1977) p. 267.
10. D. H. Lawrence, *Selection*, p. 353.
11. Paul Rosenfeld, *Men Seen* (London, 1925) pp. 46–7.
12. Quoted by Aldous Huxley, introduction, *The Letters of D. H. Lawrence* (London, 1932).
13. Quoted ibid.
14. *Collected Letters*, p. 203.
15. Letter to Catherine Carswell, 7 November 1916; reprinted in Coombes, p. 109.
16. Letter to J. B. Pinker, 2 February 1918; reprinted in Coombes, p. 118.
17. J. M. Murry, review, *Nation and Athenaeum*, 13 August 1921; reprinted in Coombes, p. 140.
18. Diana Trilling (ed.), *Selected Letters of D. H. Lawrence* (New York, 1958) p. 71.

19. D. H. Lawrence, *Phoenix I* (London, 1936) p. 446.
20. Millett, p. 239.
21. Ibid., p. 260.
22. D. H. Lawrence, 'Books', *Selected Essays* (Harmondsworth, 1950) p. 45.
23. *Phoenix I*, p. 441.
24. Letter to Gordon Campbell, 21 September 1914; reprinted in Coombes, p. 93.
25. *Collected Letters*, p. 34.
26. Discussed in Philip Sicker, *Love and the Quest for Identity in Henry James* (Princeton, 1980) pp. 131–2.
27. 'From *Study of Thomas Hardy*', *Selection*, p. 588.
28. June Singer, p. 318.
29. Mircea Eliade, *Mephistopheles and the Androgyne* (New York, 1965) p. 123.
30. Letter to Edward Garnett, 5 June 1914; in Coombes, p. 93.
31. T. S. Eliot, review of *Son of Woman*, *Criterion*, July 1931; in Coombes, pp. 245–6.
32. See Emile Delavenay, *D. H. Lawrence and Edward Carpenter: A Study in Edwardian Transition* (London, 1971) pp. 198–235.
33. O'Flaherty, p. 285.
34. Havelock Ellis, *Man and Woman* (London, 1894); quoted Pearsall, p. 594.
35. Mrs Havelock Ellis, *Three Modern Seers* (London, 1910); quoted Pearsall, p. 243.
36. Quoted Pearsall, p. 242.
37. Edward Carpenter, *Intermediate Types Among Primitive Folk* (London, 1914); quoted Pearsall, p. 598.
38. These examples from the works of Mann are discussed in detail in Philip Sicker's *Love and the Quest for Identity in Henry James*, p. 130.
39. *Collected Letters*, p. 456.
40. Ibid., p. 171.
41. Ibid., p. 484.
42. Quoted by George Ford, 'Dies Irae', *Twentieth Century Interpretations of Women in Love*, p. 33, for an extensive discussion of the implications of this.
43. Zolla, pp. 86–7.
44. Frank Kermode, *Lawrence* (Fontana Modern Masters, London, 1973) p. 74.
45. D. H. Lawrence, 'Pornography and Obscenity', *Selection from Phoenix*, p. 304.
46. Sigmund Freud, *Collected Papers*, p. 4, eds Riviere and Strachey (London, 1936) p. 215. These quotations are discussed by Norman O. Brown, *Life Against Death: The Psychoanalytical Meaning of History* (Connecticut, 1959) pp. 186–8.
47. Ibid., p. 215.
48. Sigmund Freud, *Civilisation and Its Discontents*, translated by J. Riviere (London, 1930) p. 78n.
49. Germaine Greer, *The Female Eunuch* (London, 1971) p. 256.
50. Ibid., p. 256.
51. June Singer, p. 315.
52. Ibid., p. 330.
53. O'Flaherty, p. 314.
54. Ibid., p. 319.

55. Ibid., p. 319.
56. Quoted by Ronald Pearsall, *The Worm in the Bud* (Harmondsworth, 1983) p. 591.
57. D. H. Lawrence, 'Love', *Selected Essays*, p. 27.
58. Letter to Carlo Linati, 22 January 1925; reprinted in Coombes, p. 159.
59. D. H. Lawrence, 'A Propos of *Lady Chatterley's Lover*', *Selection from Phoenix*, pp. 350–1.
60. T. E. Apter, 'Let's Hear What the Male Chauvinist is Saying: *The Plumed Serpent*', *Lawrence and Women*, p. 159.
61. D. H. Lawrence, 'From *Study of Thomas Hardy*', *Selection from Phoenix*, p. 230.
62. Ibid., p. 232.
63. Ibid., p. 561.
64. Ibid., p. 566.
65. Ibid., p. 583.
66. Quoted by A. J. L. Busst, 'The Image of the Androgyne in the Nineteenth Century', *Romantic Mythologies*, p. 38.
67. Quoted ibid., p. 78.

CHAPTER SEVEN

1. Quoted by F. R. Leavis, 'D. H. Lawrence and Professor Irving Babbitt', in *Penguin Critical Anthologies: D. H. Lawrence*, ed. H. Coombes (Harmondsworth, 1973) p. 275.
2. Dorothy Brett, *Lawrence and Brett* (Philadelphia, 1933) p. 81. Quoted by Richard Ellmann, *James Joyce* (London, 1966) p. 628.
3. D. H. Lawrence, *Phoenix*, ed. Edward McDonald (London, 1936) p. 517. Quoted by Ellmann, p. 628.
4. *Letters of James Joyce*, ed. Stuart Gilbert (London, 1957) p. 309; quoted by Ellmann, p. 628.
5. To Edward Garnett, in *Penguin Critical Anthologies: D. H. Lawrence*, p. 73.
6. D. H. Lawrence, *Selection from Phoenix*, ed. A. A. H. Inglis (Harmondsworth, 1971) p. 353.
7. Ibid., p. 357.
8. Frieda Lawrence, 'A Bit about Lawrence', in E. W. Tedlock (ed.), *Memoirs and Correspondence* (London, 1961) p. 132.
9. James Joyce, *A Portrait of the Artist as a Young Man* (Harmondsworth, 1960) p. 247.
10. Quoted by Ellmann, p. 177.
11. See Ellmann, p. 52, for references to pronouns and womanly man.
12. See Harold Bloom, *The Anxiety of Influence* (London, 1973) pp. 56–65 for the wider implications of this.
13. Mary Ellmann, *Thinking about Women* (London, 1979) p. 206.
14. Quoted R. Ellman, p. 175.
15. Elémire Zolla, *The Androgyne: Fusion of the Sexes* (London, 1981) p. 42.
16. Leslie Fiedler, *Freaks: Myths and Images of the Secret Self* (Harmondsworth, 1981) p. 25.

17. *Letters of James Joyce*, vol. 2, ed. R. Ellmann (London, 1966) p. 96.
18. Ibid., p. 53.
19. David Hayman, 'The Empirical Molly', *Approaches to Ulysses*, eds Thomas F. Staley and Bernard Benstock (Pittsburgh, 1970) pp. 108 ff.
20. Ronald Pearsall, *The Worm in the Bud: The World of Victorian Sexuality* (Harmondsworth, 1971) p. 81.
21. Ibid., p. 86.
22. Quentin Bell, *Virginia Woolf, 1882–1912* (London, 1976). See pp. 157–9 for the 'Dreadnought Hoax' in which she impersonated a visiting Abyssinian dignitary.
23. Frank Budgen, *James Joyce and the Making of Ulysses* (Oxford, 1972) pp. 111–13.
24. *Letters 2*, p. 243.
25. Colin MacCabe, *James Joyce and the Revolution of the Word* (London, 1978) p. 124.
26. Hugh Kenner, *Ulysses* (London, 1980) p. 92.
27. R. Ellmann, p. 303.
28. John Nicholson, *A Question of Sex: The Differences between Men and Women* (London, 1979) p. 156.
29. Ibid., p. 156.
30. Budgen. p. 354.
31. Stanislaus Joyce, *My Brother's Keeper*, ed. R. Ellmann (London 1958) pp. 158–9.
32. Frieda Lawrence, *Not I But the Wind* (London, 1935) pp. 52–3.
33. Pearsall, p. 263.
34. Nicholson, p. 78.
35. Ibid., p. 79.
36. MacCabe, p. 124.
37. Budgen, p. 286.
38. Zolla, p. 51.
39. A. Strindberg, Preface to *A Dream Play*, translated by M. Meyer (London, 1971).
40. D. H. Lawrence, 'From *Study of Thomas Hardy*', *Selection from Phoenix* (Harmondsworth, 1971) pp. 568–9.
41. Wendy Doninger O'Flaherty, *Women, Androgynes and Other Mythical Beasts* (Chicago, 1980) p. 308.
42 Fiedler, *Freaks*, p. 32.
43. Ibid., p. 32.
44. Ibid., p. 32.
45. Ibid., p. 339.
46. Ibid., p. 340
47. R. Ellmann, p. 381.
48. Matthew Hodgart, 'Aeolus', *James Joyce's Ulysses: Critical Essays*, eds Clive Hart and David Hayman (London, 1974) p. 133.
49. Budgen, p. 149.
50. June Singer, p. 34.
51. D. H. Lawrence, *Selection*, p. 578.
52. Budgen, p. 214.
53. June Singer, p. 33.

54. Hayman, 'The Empirical Molly', p. 120.
55. *Letters 2*, p. 249.
56. Quoted by Lionel Trilling, 'James Joyce in his Letters', *Joyce: A Collection of Critical Essays* (New Jersey, 1974) p. 165.
57. Zolla, p. 22.
58. Declan Kiberd, 'The Vulgarity of Heroics', *James Joyce; An International Perspective*, eds Bushrui and Benstock (Gerrards Cross, 1982) pp. 164–5.
59. Zolla, p. 25.
60. Ibid., pp. 68–9.
61. Otto Weininger, *Sex and Character* (London, 1906) p. 198.
62. Mary Ellmann, pp. 74–5.
63. *Letters 2*, p. 173.
64. C. G. Jung, 'Ulysses: A Monologue', *The Spirit in Man, Art and Literature*, trans. R. F. C. Hull (London, 1966) p. 134.
65. *Letters 2*, p. 106.
66. Weininger, p. 9.
67. Stanislaus Joyce, p. 164.

CHAPTER EIGHT

1. Simone de Beauvoir, *The Second Sex* (Harmondsworth, 1972) p. 740.
2. Quoted by Beatrice Faust, *Women, Sex and Pornography* (Harmondsworth, 1982) epigraph.
3. Quoted by Corinne Hutt, *Males and Females* (Harmondsworth, 1972) p. 46.
4. De Beauvoir, p. 280.
5. D. H. Lawrence, 'The Real Thing', *Selection from Phoenix* (Harmondsworth, 1979) p. 372.
6. Ibid., p. 375.
7. Ibid., p. 373.
8. Alison Lurie, *The Language of Clothes* (New York, 1981) p. 70.
9. Fraser Harrison, *The Dark Angel: Aspects of Victorian Sexuality* (London, 1979) p. 133.
10. Lurie, p. 178.
11. Kate Millett, *Sexual Politics* (London, 1977) p. 117.
12. Reay Tannahill, *Sex in History* (London, 1980) p. 383.
13. Ibid., pp. 422–3.
14. Lasch, p. 324.
15. Angela Carter, *The Sadeian Woman: An Exercise in Cultural History* (London, 1979) p. 15.
16. Faust, p. 16.
17. Mary Ellmann, *Thinking About Women* (London, 1979) p. 5.
18. Carter, p. 27.
19. Ibid.
20. Germaine Greer, *The Female Eunuch* (London, 1971) p. 42.
21. Christopher Lasch, *The Culture of Narcissism* (London, 1980) p. 349.
22. Quoted and discussed by Millett, pp. 94–5.
23. Quoted by Harrison, p. 34.

24. Thom Gunn, 'Carnal Knowledge', *Fighting Terms* (London, 1962) pp. 20–1.
25. Carter, p. 8.
26. Hutt, p. 51.
27. Ibid., p. 49.
28. Millett, p. 93.
29. Faust, p. 84.
30. Ibid., p. 84.
31. Ibid., p. 107.
32. On this see Herbert Marder, *Feminism and Art: A Study of Virginia Woolf* (Chicago, 1968) p. 35.
33. Hutt, p. 132.
34. Marder, p. 89.
35. V. Woolf, 'Dr Bentley', *The Common Reader* (London, 1925) p. 270.
36. W. B. Yeats, Introduction, *Oxford Book of Modern Verse* (London, 1936) p. xxxvii.
37. Lasch, p. 125.
38. Helene Deutsch, *Female Sexuality: The Psychology of Woman*, vol. 2 (New York, 1945) p. 103; quoted by Millett, p. 206.
39. C. S. Lewis, *The Four Loves* (London, 1963) p. 93.
40. Ibid., p. 92.
41. Lasch, p. 331.
42. Johan Huizinga, *Homo Ludens* (London, 1970).
43. Rubem Alves, *Tomorrow's Child: Imagination, Creativity and the Rebirth of Culture* (New York, 1972) p. 91.
44. Patrick Lee, *Sex Differences: Cultural and Developmental Dimensions*, eds Patrick C. Lee and Robert Sussman Stewart (New York, 1976) p. 14.
45. V. Woolf, *The Common Reader*, pp. 162–3.
46. D. H. Lawrence, 'From *Study of Thomas Hardy*', *Selection from Phoenix*, p. 253.
47. June Singer, *Androgyny: Towards a New Theory of Sexuality* (London, 1977) p. 120
48. Ibid., p. 269.
49. Quoted by Georgina Howell, *In Vogue: Sixty Years of Celebrities and Fashion from British Vogue* (Harmondsworth, 1978) p. 2.
50. Ibid., p.3.
51. Lurie, p. 74.
52. Quoted by Howell, p. 3.
53. Ibid., p. 82.
54. Quoted by Jeannette Kupfermann, *The Mistaken Body: A Fresh Perspective on the Women's Movement* (London, 1981) p .23.
55. Quoted by Howell, p. 62.
57. Erving Goffmann, *Gender Advertisements* (London, 1979) p. 51.
58. A. H. Maslow, *Maturation and Personality* (New York, 1954) pp. 245–6; quoted by Greer, p. 144.
59. Shere Hite, *The Hite Report on Male Sexuality* (London, 1981) pp. 545–7.
60. Greer, p. 44.
61. Ibid., p. 46.
62. John Berger, *Ways of Seeing* (Harmondsworth, 1972) p. 51 .
63. Ibid., p. 46.

64. Faust p. 49.
65. Lasch, p. 160.
66. J. S. Mill, 'The Subjection of Women', *Three Essays* (London, 1966) p. 522.
67. Kupfermann, pp. 25ff.
68. Ibid., p. 27.
69. Quoted by Kupfermann, p. 28.
70. D. H. Lawrence, 'From *Study of Thomas Hardy*', *Selection from Phoenix*, p. 566.
71. Hutt, p. 136.
72. Ibid.
73. Millett, p. 126.
74. For an extended discussion, see Ferdinand Mount, *The Subversive Family: An Alternative History of Love and Marriage* (London, 1982).
75. Quoted and discussed by Lasch, pp. 131–3.
76. See Lewis for a Christian version of this view, pp. 95–6.
77. June Singer, pp. 314–15.

Index

Adam, 1–2, 31
Addison, Joseph, 18
adolescence, 6, 137
Adonis, 5, 176
advertising, x, 100, 176, 222, 223–4, 227
Africa, 152, 155
aggression, 3, 9, 11, 14, 25, 37–8, 51, 56, 85, 99, 104, 109, 210–11, 214–15, 216, 219, 223
Allen, Woody, 209
Alves, Rubem, 218; *Tomorrow's Child*, 218
America, 111
Anglicanism, 98
anima, 2, 82, 83–4, 115–17, 127, 128–31, 133, 145, 210, 222, 223, 234, 236
animus, 127–8, 130, 236
'Annie Hall', 94
anthropology, 214
Apter, T. E., 166
Aristophanes, 2; his myth of androgyny, 2, 150
Arnold, Matthew, ix, 20, 25, 148; 'A Farewell', 25
asexuality, 18, 56, 58, 62, 90–1, 95, 141, 143, 223
Ashley, Laura, 169
Austen, Jane, 40; *Mansfield Park*, 48, 86–8

Balinese, 163
Balzac, Honoré de, 33
Barber, C. L., 9
Bardach, Emilie, 75, 80
bards, 3, 5, 119
Barnacle, Nora, 170–1, 176–7, 192, 197, 201
Baudelaire, Charles, 19
Beardsley, Aubrey, 125, 135
Beauvoir, Simone de, 204–7; *The Second Sex*, 205–7; *The Mandarins*, 205
Beckett, Samuel, 49, 82, 97
Benjamin, Walter, 72
Berger, John, 224

Bergman, Ingmar, 55; *Scenes from a Marriage*, 55
Bernhardt, Sarah, 175
Bethlehem, 134
Bible; *Genesis*, 1; *Deuteronomy*, 92
bisexuality, 190, 194–6
Blake, William, 14, 15, 107, 133
Bloomsbury, 18, 95, 175
Blutbruderschaft, 151, 154, 207–8
Blyton, Enid, 105
Boaistuau, Pierre, 174
Boehme, Jacob, 2
Bois, Jules, 167; *L'Eve Nouvelle*, 167
Bradbrook, Muriel, 81
Brandes, Georg, 64
Brontë, Charlotte, 19, 212
Brontë, Emily, 18–19; *Wuthering Heights*, 18–19
Brown, Norman O., 159
Bruno, Giordano, 199
Brustein, Robert, 57
Bryn Mawr, 111–12
Budgen, Frank, 168, 176, 180, 187, 194–5
buggery, 157, 193
Busst, A. J. L., 3, 26, 167
Butler, Samuel, 31
Byron, Gordon Lord George, 21, 32

Cabra, 171
capitalism, 218, 227
Carmen, 137, 171
Carney, James, 131
Caro, M. Elmer, 29; *Life of George Sand*, 29
Carpenter, Edward, ix, 153–4
Carter, Angela, 209–10, 213
Casanova, 166
Cassandra, 220
Catholicism, 133–5
character, 42–3, 45, 47–50, 88–9, 146–9, 164–5, 188–9, 193–4, 222
Chekhov, Anton, 77, 160
Chicago Catholic College, 122

244

childbirth, 175, 180, 188, 207, 226
childhood, 21–3, 36–8, 42, 58, 67–70, 78, 104, 123, 137, 142–3, 179–80, 222
'Cherry Tree Carol', 134
Chopin, 21
Christian Brothers, 134, 158
Christianity, 46, 80, 98, 101–2, 109, 133–5, 186, 199
Clare, St, 199
clothing, 31–2, 42, 48, 52–3, 54–5, 57, 69, 75–6, 89–90, 92–4, 188, 190–1, 208, 221–2, 223
contraception, 207
coprophilia, 159
copulation *a posteriori*, 157
Costelloe (Gaelic chieftain), 131
Courtivron, Isabelle de, 21
couvade, 180
Crews, Frederick, 23
'Croppy Boy', 179

Dalkey, 173
Darwin, Charles, 132; Darwinism, 40
Davie, Donald, 109
death, 23, 25–6, 154–5, 160–1, 162, 228
Defoe, Daniel, x, 15–16, 18, 85; *Moll Flanders*, 15–16, 18, 85–6; *Roxana*, 16, 18, 33, 86
Deuteronomy, 92
Dickens, Charles, 20; *David Copperfield*, 20, 47, 207
Dietrich, Marlene, 94, 222
Dionysian revels, 124
divorce, 51, 108–9
domesticity, 28, 51, 65–70, 75–80, 103–4, 107–8
Don Juan, 138, 166
Donne, John, 1–2, 14, 165; 'The Canonisation', 1–2, 14, 165
Dowden, Edward, 111
dreams, 81, 116–18, 188–93
droit de seigneur, 41
Dryden, John, 16
Dublin, 171
Dupee, F. W., 136
Dusinberre, Juliet, 7–8, 10, 11, 13–14

Eagleton, Terry, 16–17; *The Rape of Clarissa*, 16–17
Easter Rebellion, 118–20
education, 17, 30, 36, 59, 70–3, 106–7, 110–12, 135, 142–3, 215, 219, 227
Edwards, V. C. Wynne, 206
ego, 148–9

Eliade, Mircea, 26, 146–7
Eliot, George, 80–1, 110; *Middlemarch*, 48
Eliot, T. S., 7, 101, 123–4; *The Waste Land*, 101, 139, 149
Elizabethans, 6–14, 32
Ellis, Havelock, ix, 153, 183
Ellis, Mrs Havelock, 153, 162
Ellmann, Mary, 41; *Thinking about Women*, 41, 173, 205, 210
Ellmann, Richard, 180, 193, 197
Emerson, Ralph Waldo, 143
Empedocles, 188
Enfantin, 3, 26
Engels, Friedrich, 227
England, 156–7, 170, 199
Erikson, Marthe, 62
Essen, Siri von, 50, 59
excremental vision, 156–60

family, 21–3, 28, 35–40, 45, 62–84, 97–102, 104, 108, 173, 219–20, 226–7
Farr, Florence, 105–6
Faust, Beatrice, 214, 224; *Women, Sex and Pornography*, 214, 224
female impersonation, 15, 85–6, 130–3, 175, 190–1, 202
femininity, 6–14, 23, 26, 30, 33, 63, 89–91, 93, 116, 129, 145, 211–16, 221–2
femme fatale, 21, 27
fetishism, 181, 184–5, 195, 198, 199, 224
'Féuch féin, an obair-se, a Aoidh', 131
Fiedler, Leslie, 5–6, 191–3; *The Stranger in Shakespeare*, 5–6; *Freaks*, 191–3
Fielding, Henry, 15
Fitzgerald, F. Scott, 172; *The Great Gatsby*, 172
Flaubert, Gustave, 19; *Madame Bovary*, 19, 81
Foucault, Michel, 44–5; *History of Sexuality*, 44–5
France, 26
Francis, St, 199
freaks, 191–2
Freeman's Journal, 175
Freud, Sigmund, 2, 62, 99, 114, 159, 173, 202
Fuller, Louie, 105
Fuller, Margaret, 24

Gaelic lore, 113; bards, 3, 5, 130–1
Galahad, 104, 178
Galway, 171
Garbo, Greta, 94, 222–3
Garnett, Edward, 147

Gautier, Theophile, 21; *Mademoiselle de Maupin*, 21, 26
'Géisidh Cuan', 131
Genesis, 1
Gibraltar, 200
Gibson, Charles Dana, 20, 207
Gide, André, 76–7, 227; *Fruits of the Earth*, 76–7
God, 1, 2, 34, 126, 149, 158, 174, 203, 217, 228
Godwin, William, 219
Goethe, Johan Wolfgang von, 112
Goffmann, Erving, 222; *Gender Advertisements*, 222
Gogarty, Oliver St John, 171, 203
Gonne, Iseult, 118
Gonne, Maud, 104–6, 110, 113–20, 129–30
Gray, Ronald, 67, 70
Greek drama, 124
Greeks, 2, 174, 177–8
Greer, Germaine, x, 39–40, 159, 205, 210–11, 223–4; *The Female Eunuch*, x, 39–40, 159, 205, 210–11, 224
Grimstaad, 62
Gunn, Thom, 212; 'Carnal Knowledge', 212–13

'Hag of Beare', 131
Hardwick, Elizabeth, 68, 90–1
Hardy, Thomas, 205; *Jude the Obscure*, 85–102, 140, 150, 160, 205, 220, 223, 227; *Tess of the d'Urbervilles*, 90
Harrison, Fraser, 207–8
Hathaway, Ann, 176
Hawthorne, Nathaniel, x, 19–24; *Scarlet Letter*, 21–4, 45; *Blithedale Romance*, 24
Hayman, David, 196
Hecht, Ben, 221
Heilbrun, Carolyn, x–xi, 15, 18; *Toward Androgyny*, x–xi, 15, 18
Heilman, R. B., 136
Helen of Troy, 5, 106
hermaphrodite, 174
Hinton, James, 153–4
Hite Report on Male Sexuality, 204
Holmes, Oliver Wendall, 24
Holst, Rikke, 62
Homer, 154
homme fatale, 21
homosexuality, 2, 21, 26–32, 138, 149, 151, 156–7, 170, 177–8, 181, 190
Howe, Irving, 89, 100
Howth, 194, 196, 200

Huizinga, Johan, 217–18
Hutt, Corinne, 213–15, 226
Huxley, Aldous, 168
Hyde-Lees, Georgina, *see under* Yeats, Mrs George

Ibsen, Henrik, 33, 37, 50, 61–84, 205, 215, 227–8; *A Doll's House*, 37, 63–73, 169, 196; *Hedda Gabler*, 40, 73–4, 75, 78; *Ghosts*, 45; *Master Builder*, 63; 74–84, 117; 'Notes for a Modern Tragedy', 64; *Rosmersholm*, 73
I Ching, 199
impotence, 19, 193, 209
inauthenticity, 101–2
Incarnation, 125–6, 133–4, 158
industrialism, 15, 163
Ireland, 5, 29, 108, 133–4, 182
Irish Catholicism, 133–5
Irish Labour Party, 172
Irish language, 131
Irish nationalism, 29, 184
Irish Republican Army, 58
Irish Senate, 103, 108
Irish sexuality, 29, 184

James, Henry, 223; *Portrait of a Lady*, 223
Jennings, Blanche, 137
Jesus, 109, 122, 125, 126, 134–5, 154, 168, 199
Joan of Arc, 31, 92–4
John of the Cross, St, 199
Johnson, Lyndon Baines, 58
Jolas, Maria, 180
Joyce, James, xi, 6, 10, 33, 37, 63–4, 73, 81, 104, 106, 125, 135, 144, 148, 158, 168–203, 204–5, 210–11, 215, 217; *Dubliners*, 168, 170; *Portrait of the Artist as a Young Man*, 135, 164, 170–1; *Ulysses*, 137, 162, 168–203, 209, 220, 223–5, 227; *Finnegans Wake*, 189
Joyce, Stanislaus, 10, 176, 180–1, 201–3
Judaism, 162, 189, 194–5, 197
Juliana of Norwich, 4
Jung, Carl-Gustave, 2, 83–4, 115–17, 128, 130, 201, 227—8

Kaufmann, F. W., 76
Keats, John, 34–5, 163
Kenner, Hugh, 179
Kensington Register Office, 169
Kermode, Frank, 157
King, Walter, 9
Kinsey Report, 30–1

Kipling, Rudyard, 207
Klein, Melanie, 2
Kupfermann, Jeannette, 225

Lamb, Lady Caroline, 32
Lasch, Christopher, x, 44, 99, 101, 209,
    211, 216–17, 225; *Culture of Narcissism*,
    x, 44, 99, 101, 209, 211, 216–17, 225
Lawrence, D. H., x, 6, 22, 33, 35, 85, 93,
    136–67, 168–70, 181, 187, 189, 194–5,
    204–5, 207, 217, 220, 226–8; *Lady
    Chatterley's Lover*, 121, 139, 168–9, 207;
    'A Propos of *Lady Chatterley's Lover*',
    164; *Plumed Serpent*, 166; *Rainbow*, 140–
    2, 172; *Sisters*, 140; 'The Real Thing',
    207–8; *Study of Thomas Hardy*, 137, 145,
    166, 189, 194–5; *Women in Love*, 26,
    139–67, 168–9, 197, 206, 210, 223
Lawrence, Frieda, 168, 181
Lazarus, 186
Lee, Patrick, 219; *Sexual Differences*, 219
Lee, Vernon, 139
lesbianism, 2, 30, 50 96, 208
Lesbos, 155
Lewis, C. S., 216–17; *Four Loves*, 217
Linati, Carlo, 163
Linton, Lynn, 31
Lizst, 21
London, 62, 90, 96, 175
Lothario, 196
Lowell, James Russell, 24
Lowenthal, Leo, 77
Luna, 118
Lurie, Alison, 94
Luther, Martin, 34
Lynch, David, 107–8
Lysanger, 75

MacCabe, Colin, 184
'Macleod, Fiona', *see under* Sharp, William
Mailer, Norman, ix, 204–5; *Naked and the
    Dead*, 204; *Prisoner of Sex*, ix, 205
male chauvinism, 166–7, 182
male friendship, 169–70
male impersonation, 6–12, 15–16, 19, 26,
    31, 52–8, 85–102, 176, 207–8, 210
man-haters, 36, 41–3, 49–50, 52, 108, 207
Mann, Thomas, 45; *Magic Mountain*, 154;
    Tonio Kroger, 154
Mannin, Ethel, 127
Markievicz, Constance, 105, 120–1
marriage, 7, 10–11, 34–60, 62–84, 85, 91,
    98, 108–9, 114–18, 123, 130, 141, 149,
    162, 164, 174–5, 198, 228

Martineau, Harriet, 21
Marx, Karl, 9, 148
masculinity, 6–14, 19–20, 21, 26, 30, 33,
    36, 63, 85, 89–91, 93, 116, 129, 137,
    161–7, 173, 195–6, 206–7, 211–16,
    221–2
Maslow, A. H., 223
masochism, 21–2, 34–60, 176–200, 210
masturbation, 97, 177, 185–7, 197, 208–9,
    223–4, 225
Maurier, George du, 207; *Trilby*, 207–8
McMurrough, Dermot, 182
Mead, Margaret, 226
Meir, Golda, 58
Melville, Herman, 19–20; *Moby Dick*, 19–
    20, 31
menstruation, 182–3, 185, 189
Meredith, George, 8; *Essay on Comedy*, 8
Meyer, Michael, 62
Michelangelo, 136–7
Middle Ages, 114
militarism, 16, 39, 44–5, 61, 106–7, 154–
    5, 163
Mill, John Stuart, 74, 212, 225; *Subjection
    of Women*, 74
Millett, Kate, x, 138–9, 141–2, 146, 205,
    208–9, 214, 227; *Sexual Politics*, x, 138–
    9, 141–2, 146, 205, 208–9, 214, 227
Mills and Boon, 168, 185
Milton, John, 16
Minnesingers, 138
misogyny, 10, 34–60, 139–40, 187
Molière, 217
'Mona Lisa', 83
Monroe, Marilyn, 224–5
Moore, Tom, 175
More, Thomas, 16
Morris, William, 127
motherhood, 13, 70–2, 76, 108, 141–2,
    173, 179–80, 188, 226
multiple self, 45, 47–9, 75, 87–9, 133, 147–
    9, 188–9, 193–4, 222, 224
Murry, John Middleton, 141
Musil, Robert, 81
Musset, 21

Nabokov, Vladimir, 82
narcissism, x, 99, 100, 101, 176, 179, 183–
    4, 189, 196, 223, 225
Navajo Indians, 25, 153
Nelson, Admiral Horatio, 104
neurosis, 192
New England, 21–4
Newman, F. W., 21

Nietzsche, Friedrich, 57–8, 108, 172
Nijinsky, 124
Nineteenth Century, 31
Northam, John, 67, 70
Norwegian Society for Women's Rights, 64
Novalis, 117
Novy, Marianne, 12–13

O'Connell, Daniel, 103
Odysseus, 106, 178, 200
O'Flaherty, Wendy Doninger, 2, 25, 161, 191
Ó hUiginn, Tomas, 131
old age, 131–2, 219
oral sex, 190
orgasm, 100, 114, 165–6, 185, 190, 208, 211, 216, 224
Ó Ruairc (chieftain), 131
Oxford, 29

Pall Mall Gazette, 29
Pankhurst, Emily, 40
Paris, 48, 90
Paris (hero), 106, 175, 186, 192
Park, Clara Claiborne, 11
Parnell, Charles Stewart, 104
passivity, ix, 11, 17, 19, 24, 48, 62, 90, 104, 137–8, 162, 176–203, 210–23
paternity, 21–3, 36–40, 47, 70–1, 130, 171–3, 178, 179–80, 193
Paul, St, 199; *Epistle to Galatians*, 93
Pearse, Patrick, 184
Penelope, 106
personality, 45–6, 48, 87, 95–102, 133, 146–9, 164
phallic cult, 155–6, 207
phallocritics, 157–8
Plato, 135, 150
play, 44, 209, 216–18, 222
Pokot tribe (East Africa), 25
Pola, 176–7
pornography, 142–4, 156–7, 158–9, 164, 209–10
Praz, Mario, x
promiscuity (pansexuality), 6, 149, 218, 227
prostitution, 15–16, 85–6, 90, 181, 193

Qabbalah, 174

Radford, Dollie, 154
Raff, Helene, 76
rape, 125, 209

Raphael, 135
Ravenna, 174
Reich, Wilhelm, 114; *Function of the Orgasm*, 114
religion, 1, 2, 43, 98–102, 110, 149, 164
Renaissance, 137
Restoration comedy, 17, 32, 90
Richardson, Samuel, 15–16; *Clarissa*, 17; *Pamela*, 85–6; *Sir Charles Grandison*, 16–17
Rilke, Rainer Maria, 206
Rogers, Katherine, 17–18; *Feminism in Eighteenth Century England*, 17–18
Rome, 50
Rosenfeld, Paul, 138; *Men Seen*, 138
Rose of Lima, St, 135
Rossetti, Dante Gabriel, 127
Ruddock, Margot, 106
Russell, George (A. E.), 128

Sacher-Masoch, Leopold von, 178, 193; *Tales of the Ghetto*, 178; *Venus im Pelz*, 193
Sade, Marquis de, 227; *Philosophy in the Boudoir*, 227
Saint-Simonians, 3
Sand, George, 21
Sandymount, 177, 190
Sappho, 155
Sartre, Jean-Paul, 172; *Les Mots*, 172–3
Savage, Henry, 154
Scheherazade, 124
Scotland, 5
Scotus Eriugena, 199
sexism, 18, 28, 97, 109, 121, 187, 222
sexologists, 157
Shakespeare, Olivia, 105, 131–2
Shakespeare, William, ix, x, 4–20, 24–5, 32, 90, 172, 176–8, 193, 200, 217; sonnets, 4–6; *Two Gentlemen of Verona*, 7, 10; *As You Like It*, 6–7, 90, 221, 223; *Twelfth Night*, 8–10; *Midsummer Night's Dream*, 6; *Hamlet*, 10, 11–14, 17, 172, 175–6, 177; *King Lear*, 10–11, 14; *Macbeth*, 13–14, 17, 160; *Merchant of Venice*, 36; *Cymbeline*, 6
Sharp, William ('Fiona Macleod'), 127–8
Shaw, George Bernard, 61–2, 139, 195; *Arms and the Man*, 61; *Mrs Warren's Profession*, 62; *Quintessence of Ibsenism*, 61
Sheba, 113, 115, 118, 123
Sicker, Philip, 145
Sidney, Sir Philip, 127

Singer, June, x, 129, 130, 137, 146, 160–1, 194–5, 220, 228; *Androgyny: Towards a New Theory of Sexuality*, ibid.
single people, 220
Siva dance, 125, Siva character, 161
Sligo, 104
socialism, 98, 227–8
Sodom, 157
Sol, 118
Solomon, 113, 115–16, 118, 123
Southampton, Earl of, 5, 6
specialisation, x, 15, 28–9, 47–9, 65, 73, 74–84, 160, 163–4, 169, 171, 215
Stanford University, 183
Stein, Gertrude, 221
Steinach operation, 132
Stratford, 176–7
Strindberg, August, 33, 34–60, 73, 141, 147–8, 188–9, 205, 217, 227; *Father*, 35–40, 41; *Miss Julie*, 37, 40–50, 147, 184; *Comrades*, 50–7, 206; *Bond*, 59; *Dance of Death*, 59; *Dream Play*, 188–9; 'Stronger One', 52; 'An Attempt at Reform', 58
suffragettes, 137, 141–2
suicide, 46–7, 67, 73, 97
Susannah, 224
Swedenborg, 132, 228
Swift, Jonathan, 17–18, 158–9; *Gulliver's Travels*, 17
Swinburne, Algernon Charles, 127
Synge, John Millington, 163; *The Playboy of the Western World*, 111, 115, 121

Tannahill, Reay, 3, 20, 209; *Sex in History*, 3, 20, 209
Tantrism, 2, 138, 161
Taoism, 3, 4
tarantella, 69
Tennyson, Alfred Lord, ix, 20
theosophists, 57
Theresa, St, 199
Third Reich, 92
third sex, 56–7, 92–3, 138–67
Thomas Aquinas, St, 135
Thoresen, Susannah, 62
Tilley, Vesta, 175
Tintoretto, 224
Tone, Theobald Wolfe, 184
Trilling, Lionel, 87–8
Trinity College Dublin, 110
Truth, 62
Tynan, Katharine, 104, 110, 116

unisex, 32, 195

universities, 110, 215, 219

Vedic texts, 191
Venus, 216
Verlaine, Paul, 134
'Vernon, Diana', *see under* Olivia Shakespeare
Vice Versa (drama), 190
Victoria, Queen, 63
Victorians, 19, 27–33, 41, 58, 81–2, 94, 105, 187, 191–2, 195–6, 199, 209, 212, 222
Vienna, 75
Virgin Mary, 105, 126–7, 134, 135, 199
Vogue, 221
voyeurism, 193

war, 220–1, 222–3
Warner, Marina, 92–3, 126
Watt, Ian, 15
Waugh, Evelyn, 154; *Brideshead Revisited*, 154
Wayne, John, 17
Weininger, Otto, 162, 189, 201–2; *Sex and Character*, 162, 189, 201–2
Wellesley, Dorothy, 127–8, 132
West, Rebecca, 1
Whitton, Charlotte, 61
Wickes, Frances, 128–30
Wife of Bath, 4
Wilde, Oscar, xi, 20, 27–32, 172, 199; *Lady Windermere's Fan*, 27, 32; *Importance of Being Earnest*, 27–30, 32, 111–12; *Salome*, 27
will, 37, 42, 57, 79–80, 93, 139, 146–7, 223
Wollstonecraft, Mary, 219
Woolf, Virginia, 16, 32–3, 96, 211, 214–15, 219; *Orlando*, 223; *Room of One's Own*, 33; *Voyage Out*, 210

Yeats, Mrs George (*née* Georgina Hyde-Lees), 113–15
Yeats, Jack B., 111
Yeats, John Butler, 103–4, 111
Yeats, Mrs Susan, 104–5, 130
Yeats, William Butler, xi, 33, 58, 87, 103–35, 137, 144, 144–5, 157–8, 205, 211, 215, 223, 229; *On Baile's Strand*, 1, 106–8, 124; *Deirdre*, 113, *Essays and Introductions*, 124; *A Vision*, 184; 'Michael Robartes and the Dancer', 109–13, 124–5, 225; 'Adam's Curse', 112, 121, 124; 'Solomon and the Witch', 113, 116; 'Broken Dreams',

114; 'An Image from a Past Life', 116; 'Easter 1916', 118–19, 124; 'Wild Swans at Coole', 118–19; 'On a Political Prisoner', 120; 'Prayer for My Daughter', 120–1; 'Among Schoolchildren', 121–4; 'The Choice', 123; 'The Statues', 124; 'Lapis Lazuli', 124; 'Leda and the Swan', 125–7; 'Solomon and Sheba', 125; 'The Mother of God', 126; 'Crazy Jane', 127, 129, 130–4; 'Woman Young and Old', 127, 132–3; 'Magi', 134

yin and yang, 3, 4 195, 199

Zeus, 118, 127
Zolla, Elemire, x, 3, 14–15, 124–5, 188, 197; *The Androgyne:Fusion of the Sexes*, x, 3, 14–15, 124–5, 188, 197